TENTH EDITION

A Student's Guide to History

Jules R. Benjamin

Ithaca College

Bedford/St. Martin's

Boston ◆ New York

For Bedford/St. Martin's

Executive Editor for History: Mary Dougherty
Director of Development for History: Jane Knetzger
Developmental Editor: Katherine A. Retan
Production Editor: Annette Pagliaro
Production Supervisor: Jennifer Wetzel
Executive Marketing Manager: Jenna Bookin Barry
Production Assistant: Kristen Merrill
Copyeditor: Patricia Herbst
Indexer: Steve Csipke
Cover Design: Billy Boardman
Cover Art: Theatrum Orbis Terrarum: Map of the World by Abraham Ortelius. Image: © Archivo Iconografico, S. A./CORBIS
Composition: Laserwords Private Limited
Printing and Binding: Haddon Craftsmen, Inc., an R.R. Donnelley & Sons Company

President: Joan E. Feinberg
Editorial Director: Denise B. Wydra
Director of Marketing: Karen Melton Soeltz
Director of Editing, Design, and Production: Marcia Cohen
Managing Editor: Elizabeth M. Schaaf

Library of Congress Control Number: 2006933433

1   0   9   8   7
f   e   d   c   b

For information, write: Bedford/St. Martin's, 75 Arlington Street, Boston, MA 02116 (617-399-4000)

ISBN–10: 0–312–44674–8
ISBN–13: 978–0–312–44674–1

Acknowledgments

Figure 1.3: From *Libraries through the Ages* by Fred Lerner. Copyright © 1999, Continuum International Publishing Group. Reprinted with permission of the publisher, The Continum International Publishing Group.

Figure 2.1: From *World Civilizations*, Ninth Edition, Volume I by eds. Philip Ralph, Robert E. Lerner et al. Copyright © 1997, 1991, 1986, 1974, 1969, 1964, 1958, 1955 by W. W. Norton & Company, IncPL. Used by permission of W. W. Norton & Company, Inc.

Pages 22–23: From *Rise to Globalism* by Stephen E. Ambrose, copyright 1971, 1976, 1980, 1983, 1985, 1988, 1991, 1993 by Stephen E. Ambrose. © by Stephen E. Ambrose & Douglas Brinkley. Used by permission of Viking Penguin, a division of Penguin Putnam Inc.

Acknowledgments and copyrights are continued at the back of the book on page 256, which constitutes an extension of the copyright page. It is a violation of the law to reproduce these selections by any means whatsoever without the written permission of the copyright holder.

To Elaine, Aaron, and Adam

Preface

I was originally motivated to write *A Student's Guide to History* in response to a barrier I noticed between my students and the historical material I was teaching. Although this barrier differed somewhat from one student to the next, the need to learn basic study, research, and writing skills was consistently the core issue. If my students could not take concise notes, tackle common assignments, write clearly, or understand what an exam question required of them, then my efforts to explain the meaning of the past ran up against their inability to respond. Today, my students still need practical help with basic skills, and in addition they need advice on how to make use of the new and constantly evolving technology that is available to those engaged in the study of history.

In my ongoing efforts to improve and update *A Student's Guide to History*, I have turned to my students and to students across the country, asking them what they need to know to demonstrate their understanding of historical material. Since publication of the earliest editions, some needs have changed, particularly as new technologies have arisen to facilitate teaching and learning. For today's students, taking effective classroom notes requires an ability to analyze multimedia presentations, and writing requires skills not only with language but with word-processing. Conducting research requires a knowledge of how to enter the Web through a reliable portal such as the online library catalog and how to evaluate the wide variety of material available on the Internet. This tenth edition of *A Student's Guide to History* offers expanded and updated coverage of skills appropriate to the digital age.

My goal has been to equip students with all the skills they need to succeed in a history course by providing concrete advice and annotated examples that teach students to read critically, discern key concepts, and synthesize information into coherent notes and written assignments. *A Student's Guide to History* discusses the discipline of history; reviews basic study, research, and writing skills; explains how to approach common assignments; offers test-taking strategies; and includes extensive coverage of the Web as a research tool.

Chapter 1 discusses why people study history, how historians go about their investigations, and how to distinguish between primary and secondary sources, as well as how the study of history can prepare students for a variety of careers. It also examines differing interpretations of history and the directions of historical research. Chapter 2 teaches fundamental skills that students need to read a variety of history assignments, take notes in class, and study for exams. This chapter includes annotated examples guiding students to the main ideas of a text; a section on reading maps, charts, graphs, illustrations, and artifacts and other nonwritten materials; and information about collaborative work and communicating online. Chapter 3 focuses on writing skills and uses examples to demonstrate clear and connected writing. It takes the reader through the steps of building and revising an essay, provides guidance on matters of style and mechanics, and offers examples of writing appropriate to a variety of history assignments, including a sample book review.

Chapters 4 and 5 and the appendixes address the more complex tasks of preparing and writing a research paper. Chapter 4 helps students choose a research topic, narrow it to a practical theme, and craft a workable thesis; use library resources to gather information; and evaluate print and electronic sources and mine information from them. It also warns of the dangers of plagiarism and helps students understand how to avoid them. Chapter 5 stresses the importance of good writing skills, using quotations, and documenting sources with over one hundred models that illustrate proper footnote/endnote and bibliography style. The complete, annotated sample research paper that concludes the chapter illustrates how to pull together research findings, how to incorporate visual materials, and how to document sources, providing a model for students as they tackle this complex assignment. Appendix A points students toward places to start their research, highlighting the most helpful indexes, references, collections, and periodicals and hundreds of print and electronic resources. Appendix B includes sections on local and family history. The glossary includes all of the key terms that appear in boldface throughout this book. In addition, guidelines boxes throughout the book serve as checklists for students, succinctly summarizing the most helpful tips.

New to This Edition

Important new coverage in this tenth edition of *A Student's Guide to History* reflects the changing needs of history students:

- A more spacious page design with more prominent guidelines boxes and section headings makes the book easier to use.
- Expanded coverage of the research process includes new sections on using print and electronic databases as well as sections on how to enter the Web through a reliable portal such as the online library catalog and how to navigate a large Web site to locate useful sources.
- A new section on "Evaluating Sources" provides expanded advice on working with primary and secondary sources—including non-written and Web-based sources.

- Expanded coverage of "Interpreting Sources and Taking Notes," now in a separate section, offers additional help with using research sources to support a thesis. The section also includes advice on how to use computerized note-taking programs, with samples of digital source folders and digital note cards.
- New coverage of crafting a strong argument shows students how to use evidence to support a thesis and how to anticipate and address counterarguments.
- New sections on "Taking Notes in a 'Wired' Classroom" and "Giving a PowerPoint Presentation" provide more help for students in today's multimedia classrooms.
- New boxed guidelines provide tips on such topics as finding an article in a periodical database, conducting Internet searches, evaluating Web-based sources, incorporating visuals in a paper, and revising and rewriting a research paper.
- Appendix A, "Resources for History Research," which guides students to some of the best tools available for the most common research areas, has been thoroughly revised and updated. Digital resources have been integrated throughout the appendix to reflect the fact that many print resources are now available online. The number of digital resources included in the appendix has doubled from the previous edition, and annotations help point students to the most useful Web resources for their topic.
- The book's Web site, *A Student's Online Guide to History Reference Sources* at **bedfordstmartins.com/benjamin**, provides an easy-to-navigate hypertext version of Appendix A that includes additional digital resources as well as complete contact information for state, local, and professional history organizations.

Acknowledgments

Each edition has benefited from comments and suggestions made by some of the hundreds of instructors who have assigned *A Student's Guide to History* and by some of the third of a million students who have read it over the years. I particularly wish to thank the many people who reviewed the manuscript in preparation for this edition. Laurie Bernstein, Rutgers University–Camden; Carol M. Bresnahan, University of Toledo; Roger Bromert, Southwestern Oklahoma State University; Rainer F. Buschmann, California State University Channel Islands; Dianne Glave, Tulane University; Anne Hardgrove, University of Texas at San Antonio; James Stephen Krysiek, Mount St. Mary's University; Kathryn Lynass, Arizona State University; C. Wade Meade, Louisiana Tech University; Karen Pastorello, Tompkins Cortland Community College; Susan D. Siemens, Ozarks Technical Community College; Kenneth Wilburn, East Carolina University; and thirteen student reviewers.

I want to express my great respect for those at Bedford/St. Martin's who have contributed to this edition of *A Student's Guide to History:* Mary V. Dougherty, Jane Knetzger, Annette Pagliaro, Patricia Herbst, and Marissa Zanetti. I would also like to thank Kathy Retan, whose editing sharpened my prose and whose many suggestions helped me to better organize this book. Finally, I thank my wife, Elaine, who spent almost as many hours on this book as I did. I am indebted to her for that; and for much, much more.

Jules R. Benjamin
Ithaca College

Brief Contents

Contents

Appendix A   Resources for History Research   *185*

A Note to Students

Since I wrote the first edition of this book in 1975, more than a third of a million students have used it in their history classes. Each year, students have written to tell me how the book helped them to master parts of their work, as well as how I might make improvements, and I have incorporated many of their ideas into the text you are about to read.

I have tried to make this book useful regardless of whether you are taking world history, Western civilization, ancient history, modern history, social history, economic history, or the history of a particular region or nation. This book presents all the tools you need to succeed in any history course as well as the skills that will open the past to you.

Each section discusses how to tackle a specific kind of assignment. Clear guidelines, practical examples, and concise explanations guide you through reading, studying, researching, and writing tasks. Care has been taken to make it easy for you to find answers to your questions about history assignments and about the Web as a resource tool. The appendixes highlight the most helpful print and electronic resources for starting your research. *A Student's Online Guide to History Reference Sources,* an easy-to-navigate hypertext version of the digital resources in Appendix A, can be found at the book's Web site, **bedfordstmartins.com/benjamin**, along with complete contact information for state, local, and professional history organizations.

I have also written this book to introduce you to the enormous world that is the heritage of people everywhere. This world is as fascinating as the world of today or as any vision of the future. I hope to convince you that the study of history is not a journey into a dead past but instead offers a way to understand and live in the present. You can use the tools of historical research to succeed not only in history courses but in your future career. And you can use them to answer important questions about your own life and your relationship to the rest of the world. This broader purpose is what makes the study of history so valuable.

Jules R. Benjamin
Ithaca College

CHAPTER

1

The Subject of History and How to Use It

WHAT HISTORY CAN TELL YOU

The interstate highway system connects all of the major cities of the United States. The speed limits are high, and cross traffic is carried over or under the interstate. Where the interstates connect, the spaghetti-like on and off ramps form a pattern that seems to express what is most new about our society. Traveling at seventy miles per hour, you may not realize that these highways have a history—that construction of the interstate system began in the 1950s.

The car that carries you comfortably and swiftly along the highway and the music that plays on the car radio have a history even older than the highway's. Your car has the same basic components—engine, rubber tires, steering wheel, axles—as the boxy "touring" cars of the 1920s, whose design was based on the design of horse-drawn carriages. The rock or rap music playing on your car radio is a descendant of country music, folk music, and jazz with roots extending into the distant past. American folk music traces its roots to the British Isles, from which it was brought to the Appalachian Mountains of the eastern United States in the eighteenth and nineteenth centuries. Jazz traces its roots to the music of enslaved Africans brought to the American South and the Caribbean in the seventeenth and eighteenth centuries.

Looking for the marks of history in the world around us is something like the task of the geologist or archaeologist. However, instead of digging into the earth to uncover the past, the historical researcher digs into the visible, everyday elements of society to find the historical roots from which they sprang. The interstate highway system, parts of which are still being built today, is in the uppermost layer of history. If a study of the newest superhighways can

1

take us back fifty years, what about the historical roots of older highways or country roads? How far into the past can we travel on them?

Turn off the eight-lane interstate, past the gleaming gas station, past the drive-up window of the nearest fast-food restaurant, past the bright signs before the multistory motel, and onto U.S. Route 51 or 66 — older highways built in the 1940s and 1950s. Being from an earlier period, perhaps they can tell us something about life in mid-twentieth-century America.

When you leave the interstate system for this older road network, you first notice that the speed limit is lower and many of the buildings are old. As you ride along at the slower pace, there are no signs saying "Downtown Freeway ½ mile" or "Indiana Turnpike — Exit 26N." They say "Lubbock 38 miles" or "Cedar Rapids 14 miles." As you approach Lubbock or Cedar Rapids, you will see small, single-story motels. They may be wooden cottages with fading paint and perhaps a sign that says "Star Motor Court" or "Stark's Tourist Cabins." Instead of fast-food restaurants, you pass "Betty's Restaurant" or "Little River Diner." If you pay close attention to these buildings, you can take a trip into history even as you ride along. All of the older restaurants, stores, and gas stations that you see were built before the large shopping centers where people usually shop today, and they provide clues to the history of the road on which you are riding. Places like the Star Motor Court and the Little River Diner probably were built when the road was new. Unless they have been modernized, they are relics of a previous historical period — when Franklin Roosevelt and Harry Truman were president and when the cars had rounded hoods, trunks, and fenders. The diner isn't air-conditioned, and the sign over the tourist cabins proudly proclaims that they are "heated." This is the world of the 1930s and 1940s.

Now turn off at State Route 104 where the sign says "Russell Springs 3 miles" or "Hughesville 6 miles." Again the speed limit drops. You are on a road built in the 1920s and 1930s or earlier (some country roads are a hundred or more years old). Time has claimed many of the buildings that once stood along this road, but if you look closely, the past is there ready to speak to you. The gas station has only one pump, and the station owner sells bread, eggs, and kerosene. Faded advertisements on the wall describe products that you may have never heard of — NeHi Orange and Red Man Chewing Tobacco. If you see a restaurant or motel, it may be boarded up because the people who used to stop in on their way to Russell Springs or Hughesville now go another way or have moved to a nearby city. However, many homes are still standing along Route 104. They were built when only farmland straddled the road, and they may date back to a time when horses pulled traffic past the front door. Relics of early technology such as wringer-washing machines and iceboxes may stand on the tilting wooden porches, and a close look behind the tall weeds beside the dirt driveway may reveal the remains of a 1936 La Salle automobile. As you stop before one of the old farmhouses, the past is all around you. With a little imagination you can reconstruct what life was like here on the day in 1933 when

President Roosevelt closed all the banks or the day in 1918 when the Great War in Europe ended.

The line linking past to present never breaks, and the house itself has a history, as do the people who once lived in it. In this sense, every house is haunted with its own past, and a keen eye can see the signs. If you enter the house, you can see the stairway that was rebuilt in 1894 and, in the main bedroom upstairs, the fireplace that was put in about 1878, the year the house was built. Perhaps the old Bible on the table near the bed notes the year the family came to the United States and the dates in the early nineteenth century when the parents of the immigrants who built the house were born.

The story could extend far back into the past, although the evidence would become slimmer and slimmer. From county records you could find out who owned the land before the house was built, going back perhaps to the time when the people who lived on the land were Native Americans. In distance you may have traveled only ten or twenty miles from the interstate highway, and the trip may have taken you less than an hour; but while looking in the present for signs of the past, you traveled more than a hundred years into history.

If you think about and study the passage of time between the old farmhouse on the country road and the gleaming service station by the interstate, you may come to understand some of the social, political, and economic forces that moved events away from the old wooden porch and sent them speeding down the superhighway. The more you know about this process, the more you will learn about the time when the farmhouse was new and the more you will understand how the interstate highway came about, what you are doing riding on it, and into what kind of a future you may be heading.

WHAT HISTORIANS ARE TRYING TO DO

Since the invention of writing, people have left records of their understanding of the world and of the events in their lives and how they felt about them. By studying the records left by previous generations, we can find out about the lives they led and how they faced their problems. We can use what we learn about the experiences of people who lived before us to help solve the problems we face. Though the modern world is quite different from the societies in which our ancestors lived, the story of their accomplishments and failures is the only yardstick by which we can measure the quality of our own lives and the success of our social arrangements.

All of us look into the past from time to time. We read historical novels or books about historical events. We gaze at old photographs or listen to the stories our grandparents tell. **Historians**[1] attempt to make a systematic

---

[1]Terms in **boldface** are defined in the Glossary at the back of the book.

study of the past and to use the knowledge they gain to help explain human nature and contemporary affairs. Professional historians spend their lives pursuing the meaning of the past for the present. Students too make journeys into the past that may contribute to the store of human knowledge and can greatly influence their own lives. Your study and research as a student is similar to that of the professional historian. Your examination of the past is part of the same search for knowledge carried on generation after generation.

History and the Everyday World

Most of us are curious. Children are always asking their parents the "why" of things. When we grow up, we continue to ask questions because we retain our fascination with the mysteriousness and complexity of the world. Because everything has a history, most questions can be answered, at least in part, by historical investigation.

What are some of the things about which you are curious? Have you ever wondered why women's skirts in old movies are so long, or why French men often embrace one another but English men almost never do? Perhaps you have wondered how the Kennedy or Rockefeller families came to be rich, or why the Japanese attacked Pearl Harbor. Have you thought about why most of the people of southern Europe are Catholic and most northern Europeans are not? Many Asian peoples bow when they greet one another; many Americans shake hands. The questions could go on forever; the answers are somewhere in the record of the past.

This record is not only contained in musty volumes on library shelves; it is all around us in museums, historical preservations, and the antique furnishings and utensils present in almost every household. Our minds are living museums because the ideas we hold (for example, democracy, freedom, equality, competitiveness) have come down to us by way of a long historical journey. Though we are usually unaware of the past, it is always with us.

HOW HISTORIANS WORK

Like you, historians are challenged by the complexity of the world, and many want to use their studies of the past to help solve the problems of the present or future. The questions that can come to mind are numberless, and serious historical investigators must choose wisely among them. They do not want to spend a lot of effort pursuing the kind of question to which history has no answer (for example, "What is the purpose of the Universe?" or "Who is the smartest person in the world?"). Nor do they want to struggle to achieve the solution to a problem that is not of real importance. (Historical investigation can probably tell you who wore the first pair of pants with a zipper, but that piece of information might not be worth knowing.)

The main difficulty facing historians is not eliminating unanswerable or unimportant questions but choosing among the important ones.

A historian's choice among important questions is determined by personal values, by the concerns of those who support the historian's work, by the nature of the time in which the historian lives, or by a combination of all of these. The ways in which these influences operate are complex, and historians themselves often are unaware of them.

When the historian has chosen his or her subject, many questions still remain. For example, does historical evidence dealing with the subject exist, and if so, where can it be found? If someone wanted to study gypsy music from medieval Europe, and that music was never written down or mentioned in historical accounts of the Middle Ages, then little or nothing could be found about this subject through historical research. Even if records exist on a particular subject, the historian may be unaware of them or unable to locate them. Perhaps the records are in an unfamiliar language or are in the possession of individuals or governments that deny access to them. Sometimes locating historical evidence can be a problem.

Having determined that records *do* exist and that they can be located and used, the historian faces a more important problem: How complete is the evidence? Are there significant gaps in it? What is the credibility or reliability of the evidence? Is it genuine? How accurate are the records, and what biases were held by those who wrote them? If sources of information are in conflict, which source is correct? Or is it possible that most of the sources are in error? Historians must pick and choose among the sources they uncover, and that is not always easy to do. The historian's own **biases** also cloud the picture, making impartial judgment extremely difficult.

Philosophies of History

Historical investigation can lead to very different results depending on the aspect of human nature or society emphasized and the kind of information obtained. Even greater differences can result from historical investigations that employ different *philosophies* of history. A philosophy of history is an explanation not only of the most important causes of specific events but of the broadest developments in human affairs. It explains the *forces* of history, what moves them, and in what direction they are headed. The dominant philosophy of history of a particular age is the philosophy that most closely reflects the beliefs and values of that age. Most of the historians writing at that time write from the perspective of that philosophy.

Perhaps the oldest philosophy of history is the **cyclical school.** According to this view, events recur periodically — history repeats itself. The essential forces of nature and of human nature are changeless, causing past patterns of events to repeat themselves endlessly. As the saying goes, "There is nothing new under the sun." This view of history was dominant from ancient times until the rise of Christianity. The Aztecs conceived of history this way, as did the Chinese.

A central message of early Christianity was the uniqueness of the life, death, and resurrection of Jesus Christ. In societies influenced by the Christian Church — especially in Europe in the Middle Ages — the new concept of divine intervention to overthrow the past weakened the cyclical view.[2] The resulting philosophy of history, the **providential school,** held that the course of history is determined by God, and that the ebb and flow of historical events represents struggles between forces of good and evil. These struggles are protracted, but the eventual victory of good is foreseen.

That particular idea of the providential school — that history is characterized not by ceaseless repetition but by direction and purpose — became an element in the thinking of the more secular age beginning with the eighteenth century. In this new age of scientific inquiry and material advancement, there arose the **progressive school,** whose central belief was that human history illustrates neither endless cycles nor divine intervention but continual progress. According to this school, the situation of humanity is constantly improving, and this improvement results not from divine providence but from the efforts of human beings themselves. Each generation builds on the learning and improvements of prior generations and, in doing so, reaches a higher stage of civilization. The idea of history as continual progress remains powerful. Currently, many variations of the progressive philosophy share the field of historical investigation.

The newest school of history is **postmodernism.** It has not replaced the progressive school but has raised significant questions about the inherent nature of human progress. Postmodernism has influenced many academic disciplines. In history it raises the fascinating question of whether the past can truly be understood from the perspective of the present. Evidence from the past, say the postmodernists, takes on new meanings because the present is so different from the past that they cannot directly communicate with one another. According to postmodernists, when historians search the records of the past, the understanding of the past that they bring back is heavily influenced by the methods they use or the questions they ask. They do not "find" history or discover how things really were; rather, they "create" history in the process of looking for it. Few historians wholly accept this new postmodernist view, but it has affected and weakened the older idea of objectivity — the idea that, with time and effort, the historian could avoid bias and uncover the "truth" about history.

Historiography

Another approach to the study of history is through **historiography,** the study of changes in the methods, interpretations, and conclusions of historians over time. As historians examine a subject, they become aware that earlier studies of the subject they are pursuing often came to surprising conclusions. For example, between 1920 and 1939, most of the major

---

[2]An earlier development of this view is found in the Old Testament.

histories of World War I placed principal blame for the war on Germany. The prevailing view was that Germany's aggression against its neighbors caused the war. At the end of the war, the Treaty of Versailles required Germany to disarm, to accept blame, and to pay "reparations" to the countries it fought against for the great damage the war had caused — even though Germany too had suffered greatly. Despite this general agreement on the cause of World War I, the experience of World War II, lasting from 1939 to 1945, led many scholars to rethink the origins of World War I. Historians began to ask how the Nazi movement in Germany, which directed unprecedented brutality against civilians both before and during World War II, had been able to rise to power through elections. Why were so many Germans willing to follow Hitler?

Before coming to power, the Nazi Party repeatedly charged that Germany had to avenge itself for the war guilt placed on the German nation by the Treaty of Versailles. Slowly, historians of World War I realized that the idea that Germany alone was responsible for that conflict had helped the Nazi Party to exploit the patriotism of the German people. Historians looked more closely at the world of 1914 and concluded that there were *many* reasons for the erupting of World War I. Germany was no longer considered to be the sole culprit. Economic and strategic competition among the major powers (Germany, England, France, Russia, and the United States) was seen as an important factor. Intensified nationalism in all these nations — not just in Germany — had increased tensions. Also, it was realized that a series of interlocking alliances among the great powers — which turned a minor conflict in the Balkans into an all-European war — was another source of the explosion. The simplistic verdict of German guilt gave way to a complex explanation of the aims and security concerns of many nations. In this case, an attempt to understand Germany's role in World War II led to a new understanding of the German role in World War I. This kind of reinterpretation or "revision" is not uncommon in history.

Historians' views of Reconstruction, the period in U.S. history after the Civil War when the defeated South was under the military and political control of the victorious North, also changed. During Reconstruction, for the first time in U.S. history, black people, many of them former slaves, were allowed to be elected to and hold political office. Prior to the 1930s, almost all the books written on this subject (whether by northern or southern historians) concluded that southern politics was corrupted and made ineffective during the Reconstruction period by selfish northerners and ignorant black southerners. Since the 1950s, however, scholars have reached very different conclusions. Most now believe that southern blacks' participation in state and local government was a healthy development and that the standard of politics in the South was generally equal to that of other regions of the nation at that time.

One reason for this new interpretation was the later historians' more effective use of basic sources describing the work of the Reconstruction governments of the southern states. Also, historians compared southern

Reconstruction politics with politics in northern and western states of the period (an example of comparative history). And after looking back over the older literature and placing it in the historical **context** of race relations existing at that particular time, most scholars now conclude that an understanding of racist attitudes toward African Americans does much to explain the negative conclusions of earlier historians. Historiography lets historians use the tools of historical research to study themselves.

Historiography also can show how historians are influenced in their interpretation of the past by the ideas and events current in their own day. Recent decades have seen the breakup of the Soviet Union, the emergence of AIDS, and the globalization of economic change. These events may spur historians to take up questions about the past that may shed light on these recent developments. The breakup of the Soviet Union, for example, might lead to deeper study of the forces that created the Russian Empire. The AIDS crisis might lead to deeper study of the origin and transmission of earlier epidemics that spread across a wide area. Globalization might lead to deeper study of the rise of international trade in the late nineteenth century or its decline in the 1930s.

Changing Directions of Historical Research

When historians investigate the questions that interest them most, they are influenced in their approach by their own values and experiences, their academic training, and their beliefs about which aspects of human nature, human institutions, and the human environment are most important in understanding those questions. As a result, historians might look at a historical question from a wide range of perspectives, including social, cultural, intellectual, political, diplomatic, economic, and scientific.

Social historians often focus their research on the development of human communities and their interaction with the larger society. They might study the changing role of French peasants during the 1800s or the history of fraternal organizations over a broad region or a broad span of time. Cultural historians focus on group attitudes and behaviors and how they change over time; they might research the treatment of beggars in eighteenth-century London. Intellectual historians examine powerful ideas and how they influence beliefs and actions, such as Charles Darwin's early ideas on evolution. Political historians look at relations of power and how they operate in institutions such as governments, political parties, and interest groups. They might research the role of the colonial governor in Portuguese Angola. Diplomatic historians usually deal with relations between nations and how they change over time; they might examine the treaty system and the outbreak of World War I. Economic historians study developments in technology, production, transportation, consumption, and patterns of wealth and poverty; they emphasize the use of statistical data. An appropriate topic for an economic historian might be centers of Italian trade in the Renaissance. Historians of science examine the evolution of scientific knowledge, how changes in such knowledge arise, and how its application influences society; they might examine the failure of German scientists to develop an atomic bomb.

Demonstrating how current issues influence the direction and subject matter of history, several new approaches have become important in recent decades. Environmental historians, who examine the interaction between human communities and their habitat and the attitudes of these communities toward nature, might examine what nineteenth-century Mediterranean tidal data say about global warming. Historians of sport, media, and other aspects of popular culture might examine radio detective shows. Historians of the family and private life have taken up the examination of the structural and emotional development of small, intimate groups and the interaction of these groups with powerful social forces such as wars, depressions, class and ethnic conflict, and technological change; they might examine children's role in the French rural family during the eighteenth century. In contrast, the field of world history takes in centuries of change across large areas of the globe, and comparative historians seek to understand the significance of an institution, political system, people, or nation by comparing its history with that of others. Such historians can learn much about Vietnam, for example, by studying the ways in which its culture resembled or diverged from that of China.

Two of the most rapidly expanding areas of research in recent decades have been women's history and gender studies, enormous topics largely neglected by earlier generations of historians. Women's historians might study women in the workforce during World War II — who stayed home and who did not. Historians of gender study the ways in which ideas of masculinity and femininity have influenced history; they might study the portrayal of male and female characters in fairy tales.

Two older areas of historical research are reviving. Genealogy and local history are regaining prominence as people in countries or regions undergoing rapid change become concerned with holding on to or rediscovering their past. Genealogy traces the history of a particular family; local history examines the evolution of a town, community, or neighborhood. For more on family and local history, see "How to Research Your Family History" in Appendix B (pp. 245–49).

Methods of Historical Research

Certain kinds of historical research have been influenced by other disciplines: family history by psychology, **demography** by sociology, **ethnohistory** by anthropology, political history by political science, and economic history by economics. While still adhering to the special focus of history — examining and explaining the past — historians welcome ideas and methods of analyzing evidence from other fields. For instance, **quantitative history** (called *cliometrics*) uses quantitative data, such as election returns, price levels, and population figures of earlier periods, to re-create a picture of earlier times. Because quantitative data are uniform, they measure the same things — votes, prices, numbers of inhabitants — over time. Thus, comparisons can be made among **statistics** from different periods. The electoral support of a political party, the price of wheat, or the size of a town can be examined to see if it is rising or falling and at what rate.

If the uniformity of the data can be established (that is, if the numbers really *do* measure the same thing in each period), then the data can be subjected to mathematical analysis. Percentages, ratios, averages, the mean, median, and mode can be obtained. If the dataset is large, the historian may subject it to complex analyses that explore patterns within the numbers and among subgroups of them: the frequency distribution, the standard deviation, and the coefficient of variation. Elaborate statistical analyses not only can determine how fast prices are rising or where the majority of a party's voters reside but also can compare different kinds of changes — party registration with price levels, population decline with employment levels — in an attempt to describe the conditions under which certain changes occur. By noting those categories of numbers (variables) that move together, the historian can begin to explore the causes of the changes under examination. Computers make this task more manageable, allowing historians to work with very large datasets and to analyze them in new ways.

Primary and Secondary Sources of Evidence

Two basic forms of historical **evidence** help historians answer these different questions: primary and secondary. **Primary sources** (see Figure 1.1 on p. 11 and Figure 1.2 on p. 12) record the actual words of someone who participated in or witnessed the events described or of someone who got his or her information directly from participants. Primary sources can be newspaper accounts, diaries, notebooks, letters, minutes, interviews, and any works written by persons who claim firsthand knowledge of an event. Another primary source is official statements by established organizations or significant personages — royal decrees, church edicts, political party platforms, laws, and speeches. Primary sources also include any official records and statistics, such as those concerning births, marriages, deaths, taxes, deeds, and court trials. Recent history has been recorded by photographs, films, and audio- and videotapes. These recordings of events as they actually happened are also primary sources of evidence. **Artifacts** are another primary source. These are things made by people in the past: houses, public buildings, tools, clothing, and much more. For more information on primary evidence, see "How to 'Read' Nonwritten Materials" in Chapter 2 (pp. 25–36) and "Evaluating Primary Sources" in Chapter 4 (pp. 102–05).

Secondary sources record the findings of writers who were not participants in a historical episode but investigated primary evidence of it, as historians do when they conduct their research. When historians publish the results of their research, they create secondary sources, which are read by other scholars and by students. Most history books and articles are

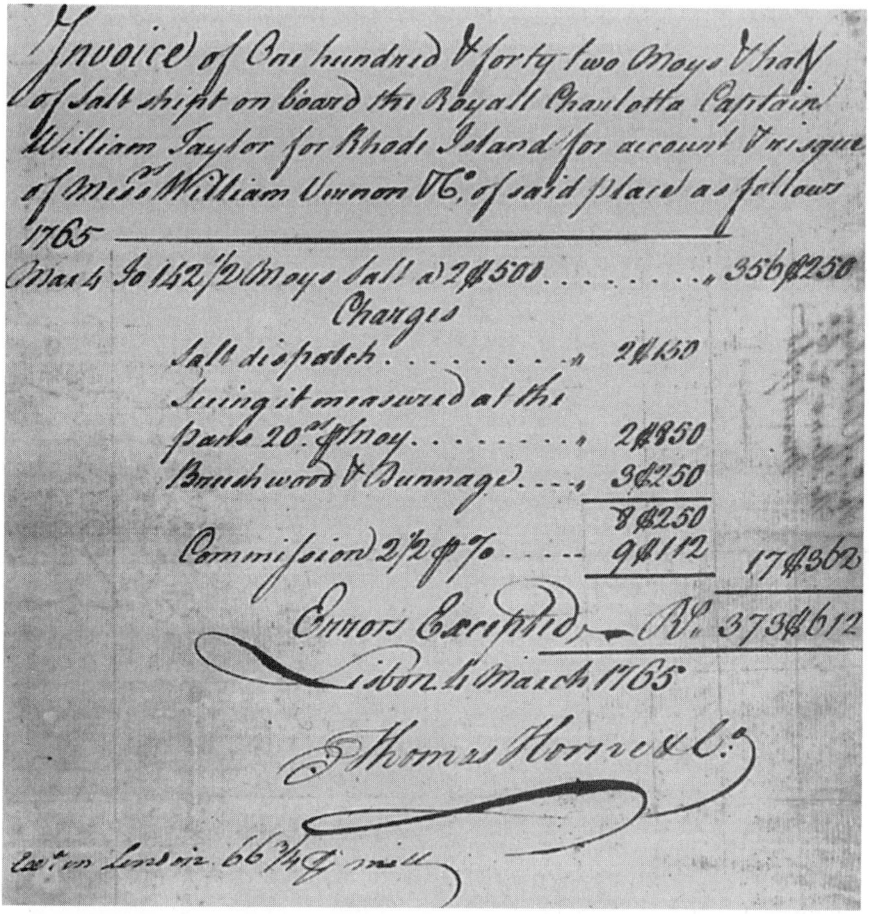

Invoice of One hundred & forty two Moys & half of Salt shipt on board the Royall Charlotta Captain William Taylor for Rhode Island for account & risque of Messrs William Vernon & Co of said place as follows

1765

Mar 4 To 142 1/2 Moys Salt a 2$500 .... 356$250

Charges

Salt dispatch .... 2$150

Seeing it measured at the parts 20rs p Moy .... 2$850

Brushwood & Dunnage .... 3$250

8$250

Commission 2 1/2 p % .... 9$112 17$362

Errors Excepted — Rs 373$612

Lisbon 4 March 1765

Thomas Horne & Co

Exc on London 66 3/4 d p mill

FIGURE 1.1 Example of Primary Evidence (1765).
Primary documents are often handwritten rather than printed and reflect the vocabulary and writing style of the period in which they were created. This invoice describes a shipment of salt carried from Lisbon, Portugal, to Providence, Rhode Island, in March 1765 "on Board the Royall Charlotta Captain William Taylor for Rhode Island for account & risque of Mr. William Vernon. . . ." The value of the cargo is written in Portuguese escudos. The document was handwritten and signed by Thomas Horne just after the salt was loaded onto the ship. It brings us as close as we can come to the actual scene on the docks at Lisbon over two hundred years ago.

secondary sources, and their **footnotes** and **bibliography** identify the primary sources that the historians examined. If your own work is based on primary sources, your research paper will become a secondary source for others to read. For an example of a secondary source, see Figure 1.3 on (p. 13).

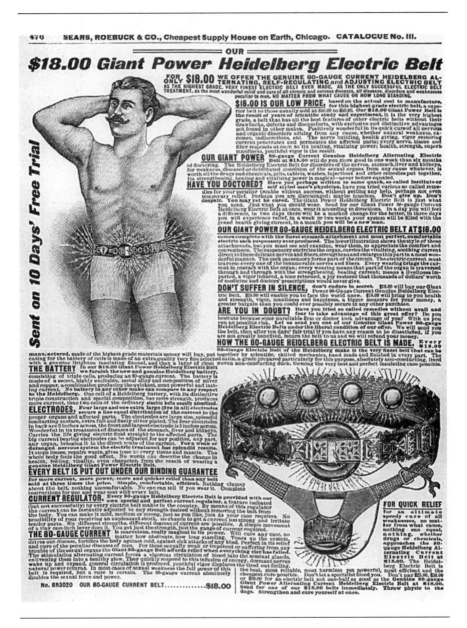

FIGURE 1.2   Example of Primary Evidence (1902).
This printed advertisement for a Heidelberg Electric Belt appeared in the 1902
Sears, Roebuck and Company catalog. If you are doing research on some of the
strange medical cures sold at that time, the claims made in this advertisement
would be an important piece of primary evidence. What kind of "illness" do you
think this belt was supposed to cure?

In continental Europe, the establishment of public libraries lagged behind developments in the English-speaking countries. The European education system emphasized the preparation of young men for their life's work rather than the production of an informed citizenry. And readers were accustomed to owning books rather than borrowing them, a practice encouraged by the comparatively low price of books on the continent.

In many countries of the nineteenth-century Europe, illiteracy was high and education opportunities limited. Even in the more literate countries of western Europe, public libraries served only a small number of people. Municipal libraries were concerned with preserving the nation's literary heritage, not with accommodating the needs of the reading public. Even in those libraries founded specifically for the use of the common people, the book collections reflected the literary standards of intellectuals and cultural bureaucrats rather than the tastes of ordinary readers. Books were chosen more for the conformity to approved political or religious doctrine than for their popular appeal. Serious literature rather than entertaining fiction was the rule. Even as late as 1952 an American visitor observed that "one simply does not find mystery stories and the like in the Parisian public libraries."[47] Subscription fees were often charged, which discouraged poor families from using the public libraries.

[47]Leon Carnovsky. "The Public Libraries of Paris," *Library Quarterly* 22 (3): 194–99 (July 1952), 196.

FIGURE 1.3   Example of Secondary Evidence.
This example comes from Fred Lerner, *Libraries through the Ages* (Continuum, 1999), 103–04. Lerner gathered his evidence from a few primary but mostly secondary sources. He points the reader toward these sources by including a footnote.

When a Secondary Source Becomes a Primary One.   It is important to understand the basic differences between primary and secondary sources, for there are certain situations in which a secondary source becomes a primary one. Here are two examples:

1. A contemporary historian is writing a book that discusses the views of early-twentieth-century historians on the reasons for the decline of the Roman Empire. The works from the early twentieth century that the historian uses as his sources would generally be considered to be secondary works, because they were written more than fifteen hundred years after the end of the Roman Empire. However, they are primary sources for the contemporary historian's study because they provide *direct* evidence of what early-twentieth-century historians thought about the decline of the Roman Empire.

2. In 1990 a U.S. senator writes an article about the background of the men in his state who signed the Declaration of Independence. The senator's article is a secondary source because it is based on primary sources from the time of the Revolution rather than on his direct experience. However, if a later historian writes a biography of the senator that includes an analysis of the senator's views about the period of the Revolution, then the senator's article becomes a primary document because it represents *direct* evidence about the senator's views.

The Reliability of Primary and Secondary Evidence. The problem of determining the reliability of primary evidence is a serious one. Primary sources can be fraudulent, inaccurate, or biased. Eyewitness accounts may be purposely distorted in order to avert blame or to bestow praise on a particular individual or group. Without intending to misinform, even on-the-scene judgments can be incorrect. Sometimes, the closer you are to an event, the more emotionally involved you are, and this involvement distorts your understanding of it. We can all recall events in which we completely misunderstood the feelings, actions, and words of another person. Historians have to weigh evidence carefully to see whether those who participated in an event understood it well enough to accurately describe it, and whether later authors understood the meaning of the primary sources they used. Official statements present another problem — that of propaganda or concealment. A government, group, or institution may make statements that it wishes others to believe but that are not true. What a group says may not be what it does. This is especially true in politics.

To check the reliability of evidence, historians use the tests of consistency and corroboration: Does the evidence contradict itself, and does it disagree with evidence from other sources? Historical research always involves checking one source against another. For example, Figure 1.4 (p. 15) presents two primary documents that report the fighting at Lexington and Concord, Massachusetts, in 1775 — battles that began the Revolutionary War. In what important ways do the two accounts differ? How do you think the conflicting goals of the colonists and the English soldiers biased each report of the battle? What phrases could you pull out of each document to highlight the bias? Note that the American version talks of "some inhabitants of the colony" who while "travelling peaceably" were "seized and greatly abused" by the English soldiers. The English officer, in contrast, says that the Americans were "drawn up in military order, with arms" and that his troops were "without any intention of injuring them." You should be able to find other important differences in the two reports of the fighting. Also, as you read the documents, consider what additional sources would help you decide which report is more accurate. The two accounts agree on some facts but disagree on the responsibility for the fighting. Eyewitness accounts from other English soldiers and from American colonials who were there will help in determining which description is more accurate. It might turn out, for example, that parts of *each* account are correct and other parts are distorted in some way. Sometimes there is no *one* true source for the history of an event. Still, the more primary sources you read, the closer you will come to knowing the event in all its details and meanings.

The **bias** of a source also presents difficulties. People's attitudes toward the world influence the way they interpret events. For example, you and your parents may have different attitudes toward music, sex, religion, or politics. These differences can cause you to disagree with them about the value of a rock concert, a Sunday sermon, or the president. Historians

AMERICAN ACCOUNT OF THE BATTLE OF LEXINGTON:

Account by the Provincial Congress at Watertown, Massachusetts,
April 26, 1775

By the clearest depositions relative to this transaction, it will appear that on the night preceding the nineteenth of April instant, a body of the king's troops, under the command of colonel Smith, were secretly landed at Cambridge, with an apparent design to take or destroy the military and other stores, provided for the defence of this colony, and deposited at Concord — that some inhabitants of the colony, on the night aforesaid, whilst travelling peaceably on the road, between Boston and Concord, were seized and greatly abused by armed men, who appeared to be officers of general Gage's army; that the town of Lexington, by these means, was alarmed, and a company of the inhabitants mustered on the occasion — that the regular troops on their way to Concord, marched into the said town of Lexington, and the said company, on their approach, began to disperse — that, notwithstanding this, the regulars rushed on with great violence and first began hostilities, by firing on said Lexington company, whereby they killed eight, and wounded several others — that the regulars continued their fire, until those of said company, who were neither killed nor wounded, had made their escape — that colonel Smith, with the detachment then marched to Concord, where a number of provincials were again fired on by the troops, two of them killed and several wounded, before the provincials fired on them, and provincials were again fired on by the troops, produced an engagement that lasted through the day, in which many of the provincials and more of the regular troops were killed and wounded. . . .

By order,
Joseph Warren, President.

ENGLISH ACCOUNT OF THE BATTLE OF LEXINGTON:
Report of Lieutenant-Colonel Smith to Governor Gage, April 22, 1775

I think it proper to observe, that when I had got some miles on the march from Boston, I detached six light infantry companies to march with all expedition to seize the two bridges on different roads beyond Concord. On these companies' arrival at Lexington, I understand, from the report of Major Pitcairn, who was with them, and from many officers, that they found on a green close to the road a body of the country people drawn up in military order, with arms and accoutrements, and, as appeared after, loaded; and that they had posted some men in a dwelling and Meeting-house. Our troops advanced towards them, without any intention of injuring them, further than to inquire the reason of their being thus assembled, and, if not satisfactory, to have secured their arms; but they in confusion went off, principally to the left, only one of them fired before he went off, and three or four more jumped over a wall and fired from behind it among the soldiers; on which the troops returned it, and killed several of them. They likewise fired on the soldiers from the Meeting and dwelling-houses. . . . While at Concord we saw vast numbers assembling in many parts; at one of the bridges they marched down, with a very considerable body, on the light infantry posted there. On their coming pretty near, one of our men fired on them, which they returned; on which an action ensued, and some few were killed and wounded. . . . On our leaving Concord to return to Boston, they began to fire on us from behind the walls, ditches, trees, &c., which, as we marched, increased to a very great degree, and continued without intermission of five minutes altogether, for, I believe, upwards of eighteen miles. . .

I have the honor, &c.,
F. Smith, Lieutenant-Colonel 10th Foot.

FIGURE 1.4   **Two Conflicting Primary Documents.**

have their own attitudes toward the subjects they are investigating, and these cause them to draw different conclusions about the character and importance of religious, political, intellectual, and other movements. Later historians must take these biases into account when weighing the reliability of the primary and secondary evidence. (See also "Evaluating Sources" in Chapter 4, pp. 100–06.)

Interpreting and Organizing Evidence

When analyzing primary and secondary evidence, historians must find some way of *organizing* it so that they can make clear its meaning. A mass of facts and opinions concerning a subject is not a historical study. The task of the historian is to arrange the material so that it supports a particular conclusion. This conclusion may have been partly formed in the historian's mind at the outset, or it might be the result of investigation. If the evidence does not appear to support the conclusion, however, then the historian must either change that conclusion or seek other evidence to support it.

Once a historian is satisfied that research has uncovered sufficient evidence to support a particular conclusion, then he or she works to display the evidence in a manner that will clearly show that the conclusion drawn is a proper one. If any evidence that leads to other conclusions is uncovered, the historian has a responsibility to include it. In doing so, he or she must show how the supporting evidence is stronger than the nonsupporting evidence. There are many ways of organizing evidence in support of a conclusion. The historian's **arguments** in favor of a particular conclusion must be strong and convincing, and the logic of these arguments must not be faulty.

You will confront these issues faced by all historians when you conduct your own historical research, an assignment that is part of all advanced (and some beginning) history courses. (See Chapters 4 and 5 for advice on researching and writing such an assignment.)

The Computer and Historical Research

Historians use computers not only to analyze quantitative data but also to gain access to sources of historical information. Unpublished information residing in **archives** around the world can be made available online to historians and students with access to the **World Wide Web.** Primary sources that have been placed on **Web sites** can be read (and even printed out) by researchers anywhere. Secondary sources that are available only in special libraries can be read in this way also if they have been put into computer-readable form. History **databases** containing millions of individual historical statistics and documents are available in many college libraries. The texts of documents, articles, and, in some cases, whole books can be brought to your computer screen. With Web **plug-ins,** researchers can gain access to art, maps, photographs, recordings, and even films that once resided only in faraway archives. (For more information on using computers in your own research, see pp. 84–100.)

HOW YOU CAN USE HISTORY

Experience is said to be the best teacher. Still, our learning would be very narrow if we profited only from our own experiences. Through the study of history, we make other people's experiences our own. In this way, we touch other times and places and add to our lifetime's knowledge the knowledge gained by others.

If history is the greatest teacher, what can we do with the knowledge we draw from it? In what practical ways does knowledge of the past help us to accomplish the work we do today or will do tomorrow? History is not merely a course you take in college; it is a way of thinking about the present, one that attempts to make sense of the complexity of contemporary events by examining what lies behind them. Such an examination is intellectual (its goal is to broaden understanding in general), but it can be practical as well.

There are any number of careers in which the tools of the historian are directly employed. You yourself could teach history at the secondary or college level. You could work in the archives of a library, museum, historical site, or large corporation with a record-keeping department. Labor unions have staffs of historians that research the history of important unions. The field of public history is a very large one, and you could be hired to the research staff of the U.S. government's National Archives and Records Administration, the Library of Congress, or any of the Cabinet departments or U.S. intelligence agencies. There are even more opportunities at the state, county, and local levels. For example, you could work for a local or county historical society. You might do archaeological research at the site of an ancient Indian village or a Civil War battlefield, or you might organize the nineteenth-century records of a great natural disaster or of a major exhibition of farm or industrial machinery. You could be hired to construct a family history from the photographs, diaries, and letters of one of the founding families of a town. Every step back in time calls on the skills of a historian.

When you learn how to read history, how to research the past, and how to write a summary of your findings, you are mastering career skills as surely as if you were taking a course in real-estate law or restaurant management. The ability to see the present in relationship to the past is a skill needed not only by academic, private, and public historians, archivists, historical novelists, and documentary producers; it is an essential preparation for almost any career. Understanding the past can be its own reward, but it pays off in other ways as well. In fact, people who think that history is irrelevant run the risk of history making that judgment of them.

2

How to Read a History Assignment, Take Notes in Class, and Prepare for and Take Exams

HOW TO READ A HISTORY ASSIGNMENT

Reading history can be a satisfying experience, but to enjoy the landscape you must first know where you are: you must have a general sense of the subject and of the manner in which it is being presented. If you begin reading before you get your bearings, you may become lost in a forest of unfamiliar facts and interpretations. Before beginning any reading assignment, look it over carefully. If you are reading a book, read the preface or introduction. This should tell you something about the author and his or her purpose in writing the work. Then read the table of contents to get a sense of the way in which the author organized the subject. Next, skim the chapters themselves, reading subheadings and glancing at illustrations and graphed material. If you have the time, preread sections of the book (especially the introductory and concluding chapters) rapidly before reading the full work.

After scouting the ground, you will be ready to read. By this time, you should be familiar with the **topic** of the book (what aspects of history it covers), the background of the author (politician, journalist, historian, eyewitness, novelist, etc.), when the book was written (a hundred-year-old classic, the most recent book on the subject, etc.), how it is organized (chronologically, topically, etc.), and, most important of all, its **thesis** and conclusions. The thesis is the principal point that an author wishes to make on a subject: that the geography of Spain was a significant factor in that nation's failure to industrialize in the eighteenth and nineteenth centuries; that disagreement on moral issues between J. Robert Oppenheimer and Edward Teller delayed development of the hydrogen bomb. Most authors set out their thesis in a preface or introduction. If you understand the principal point the author is trying to make, then the organization and conclusions of the work will become clear to you. The author will be organizing **evidence** and drawing conclusions to support the thesis. The ability to recognize and describe a weak thesis or unsupportive evidence is part of learning history too. (For a discussion of the difference between a **theme** and a thesis, see Chapter 4, pp. 78–83.)

Reading a Textbook

The most common history assignment is the reading of a textbook. Many students hope to get by with their lecture notes, and they put off reading the textbook until right before an exam. Reading the textbook week by week will give you the background knowledge necessary to understand the lectures and supplementary readings. In most courses the lectures embellish portions of the textbook, and lecturers assume that students are familiar with the textbook coverage. Sitting through a lecture on the economic aspects of the American Revolution may be confusing if you have not read the textbook discussion of the mercantilist theories behind many of the colonists' grievances.

Read textbook chapters in close conjunction with the lectures to which they are related. If particular passages are unclear, you might benefit from rereading the material. Underline or highlight the most prominent factual information. Also underline important generalizations, interpretations, and conclusions. In addition to underlining, look for passages emphasized by the author or passages that you feel reflect the author's viewpoint or with which you disagree, and write your reaction or a summary of these passages in the margin. All of this will come in handy when you prepare to take a test: you will be able to reread the underlined material and your comments and obtain a quick review of the chapter's contents. Before the exam, however, you may want to reread the textbook itself. Figure 2.1 (p. 21) shows an example of a textbook page with underlining and marginal annotations by a student.

Reading a Monograph

Another typical reading assignment is a **monograph**—a specialized history work on a particular subject. In addition to the procedures used in reading a textbook, you will want to pay special attention to the theme and point of view of monographs because your instructor may expect you to learn not only about the subject they deal with but also about the emphasis and methods of the work. Therefore, you will need to determine the author's assumptions and values, and to understand the book's theme and conclusions. Read this kind of work not only to absorb the facts but also to analyze, question, and criticize. If you own the book, you can again do your questioning and criticizing in the margins. If the book is not yours, or if

Civilizations in Sub-Saharan Africa

Leader of empire of Mali—Mansa Musa (1312–1337)

Under, Mansa Musa (1312–1337) Mali's authority reached into the middle Niger city-states of Timbuktu, Djenné, and Gao. He put Mali on the European world maps by performing a stunning gold-laden pilgrimage to Mecca, Islam's spiritual capital in the Middle East. Upon returning, Mansa Musa fostered the growth of Islam by constructing magnificent mosques in the major urban centers. With his seemingly inexhaustible supply of gold he com-

Growing influence of Islam

missioned Spanish and Middle Eastern scholars and architects to transform Malian cities into great seats of Islamic learning. Leading intellectuals were sent to Morocco and Egypt for higher studies, and at Timbuktu foundations were laid for a university at the famous Sankoré mosque. For decades after Musa, Mali enjoyed a reputation in the Muslim world for high standards of public morality and scholarship as well as for law, order, and security. People and goods flowed freely, enabling the cosmopolitan cities of Timbuktu, Djenné, and Gao to flower into major market centers. Through the leadership of Sungata and Mansa Musa Islam became more deeply implanted among the elite and spread widely in the important towns.

While Mansa Musa made great advances in establishing an efficient administrative bureaucracy, he neglected to develop a formula for succession. Court intrigue and factional disputes fol-

Leader of empire of Songhay—Sunni Ali (1464–1492)

lowed the death of each Mansa. Inevitably, central authority weakened. Gao seceded in 1375 and under Sunni Ali (1464–1492) it blossomed into an expansive territorial empire called Songhay.

As in Muslim India, it was not uncommon for slaves in Africa to assume considerable administrative and military reponsibilities

Important point

and on occasion usurp authority. This happened in Songhay in 1493 when a high-ranking Muslim slave, named Muhammad Touré, staged a brilliant palace coup. Lacking traditional legitimacy rooted in a pagan past, he promoted Islamic practices and found Islam an invaluable instrument for political and cultural control. Using the praise title of "Askia," Muhammad Touré (1493–1528) extended Songhay's frontiers deep into the strategic Saharan oases, across the Middle Niger to include Mali, and east-

Expansion of Songhay under "Askia" Muhammad Touré (1493–1528)

ward to the emporiums of Hausaland. He then created a labyrinthine bureaucracy of ministries for the army, navy, fisheries, forests, and taxation. Songhay itself was decentralized into provinces, each ruled by a governor chosen from among the Askia's family or royal followers.

FIGURE 2.1 Example of an Underlined and Annotated Textbook Page.

SOURCE: *Philip Ralph, Robert E. Lerner, et al., World Civilizations, 9th ed. Volume 1. (New York: W. W. Norton & Company, Inc.,1997), 605–06.*

you wish to have an organized set of notes about it, summarize the contents and the author's theme on index cards or on a computer file. You can then review your underlinings or index cards before the exam. (For more on taking notes, see pp. 37–43.)

Reading an Anthology

Some courses also include an anthology—a book of readings, usually short excerpts from larger works or from **primary documents** that deal with a single subject. All of the suggestions concerning the reading of textbooks and monographs apply here as well, but this type of assignment often calls for a particular kind of reading. Each selection usually discusses a different aspect or interpretation of the subject, and some pieces are likely to be in serious disagreement. Instructors expect students to be able to assess the arguments of the various authors and on occasion to take a position in the debate. Therefore, you should read this particular kind of book with an eye to analyzing the arguments of the different authors or to comparing their different approaches to the subject. A good way to do this is to summarize briefly the argument or approach of each selection.

Reading a Historical Novel

A **historical novel** is a work of fiction based on actual occurrences and people. It is often more dramatic and more personal than a textbook or monograph and describes the feelings of those caught up in important historical events. Reading a historical novel gives you a feel for the times in which it is set and for the historical material it contains, but be cautious not to treat the text as historical truth. Nevertheless, a novelist who knows a historical period or event well can bring it to life in ways that scholarly works cannot.

Examples of Reading Assignments

To help you appreciate the differences among the four types of reading assignments, here are passages from each type. The subject is the policy of the United States toward the Greek civil war of the late 1940s. As you read these passages, note the different manner in which each deals with this subject.

> **TEXTBOOK** The day before, 6 March, Truman had begun to prepare the ground. In a speech at Baylor University in Texas he explained that freedom was more important than peace and that freedom of worship and speech were dependent on freedom of enterprise. . . .
>
> The State Department, meanwhile, was preparing a message for Truman to deliver to the full Congress. He was unhappy with the early drafts, for "I wanted no hedging in this speech. This was America's answer to the surge of expansion of Communist tyranny. It had to be clear and free of hesitation or double talk."

Truman told Acheson to have the speech toughened, simplified, and expanded to cover more than just Greece and Turkey. He then made further revisions in the draft. . . .

At 1 P.M. on 12 March 1947, Truman stepped to the rostrum in the hall of the House of Representatives to address the joint session of the Congress. The speech was also carried on nationwide radio. He asked for immediate aid for Greece and Turkey, then explained the reasoning. "I believe that it must be the policy of the United States to support free peoples who are resisting attempted subjugation by armed minorities or by outside pressures."

The statement was all-encompassing. In a single sentence, Truman had defined American policy for the next twenty years. Whenever and wherever an anti-Communist government was threatened, by indigenous insurgents, foreign invasion, or even diplomatic pressure (as with Turkey), the United States would supply political, economic, and most of all, military aid. The Truman Doctrine came close to shutting the door against any revolution, since the terms "free peoples" and "anti-Communist" were assumed to be synonymous. All the Greek government, or any dictatorship, had to do to get American aid was to claim that its opponents were Communists. And the aid would be unilateral, as Truman never mentioned the United Nations, whose commission to investigate what was actually happening in Greece had not completed its study or made a report.

—From Stephen E. Ambrose, *Rise to Globalism: American Foreign Policy, 1938–1976,* (New York, Penguin, 1976), 148, 150.

MONOGRAPH   What was really on the mind of the president and his advisers was stated less in the Truman Doctrine speech than in private memos and in Truman's March 6 address at Baylor University. Dealing with the world economic structure, the president attacked state-regulated trade, tariffs, and exchange controls—". . . the direction in which much of the world is headed at the present time." "If this trend is not reversed," he warned, ". . . the United States will be under pressure, sooner or later, to use these same devices in the fight for markets and for raw materials. . . . It is not the American way. It is not the way to peace."[16] . . .

The question of how best to sell the new crusade perplexed the administration, not the least because Greece was a paltry excuse for a vast undertaking of which it "was only a beginning," and in the end it formulated diverse reasons as the need required.[18] The many drafts that were drawn up before the final Truman Doctrine speech was delivered to Congress on March 12 are interesting in that they reveal more accurately than the speech itself the true concerns of Washington. Members of the cabinet and other top officials who considered the matter before the twelfth understood very clearly that the United States was now defining a strategy and budget appropriate to its new global commitments — interests that the collapse of British power had made even more exclusively American — and that far greater involvement in other countries was now pending, at least on the economic level.

Quite apart from the belligerent tone of the drafts were the references to ". . . a world-wide trend away from the system of free enterprise toward state-controlled

[16] DSB, March 16, 1947, 484. See also Acheson, *Present at the Creation,* 219; Jones, *Fifteen Weeks,* 139–42. . . .

[18] Acheson, *Present at the Creation,* 221.

economies," which the State Department's speech writers thought "gravely threatened" American interests. No less significant was the mention of the "great natural resources" of the Middle East at stake.

—From Joyce and Gabriel Kolko, *The Limits of Power: The World and United States Foreign Policy, 1945–1954* (New York: Harper & Row, 1972), 341.

ANTHOLOGY (EXCERPT FROM A SPEECH)   The United States has received from the Greek government an urgent appeal for financial and economic assistance. Preliminary reports from the American Economic Mission now in Greece and reports from the American Ambassador in Greece corroborate the statement of the Greek Government that assistance is imperative if Greece is to survive as a free nation. . . .

At the present moment in world history nearly every nation must choose between alternative ways of life. The choice is too often not a free one.

One way of life is based upon the will of the majority, and is distinguished by free institutions, representative government, free elections, guarantees of individual liberty, freedom of speech and religion, and freedom from political oppression.

The second way of life is based upon the will of a minority forcibly imposed upon the majority. It relies upon terror and oppression, a controlled press and radio, fixed elections, and the suppression of personal freedoms.

I believe that it must be the policy of the United States to support free peoples who are resisting attempted subjugation by armed minorities or by outside pressures. . . .

It is necessary only to glance at a map to realize that the survival and integrity of the Greek nation are of grave importance in a much wider situation. If Greece should fall under the control of an armed minority, the effect upon its neighbor, Turkey, would be immediate and serious. Confusion and disorder might well spread throughout the entire Middle East.

Moreover, the disappearance of Greece as an independent state would have a profound effect upon those countries in Europe whose peoples are struggling against great difficulties to maintain their freedoms and their independence while they repair the damages of war. . . .

The free peoples of the world look to us for support in maintaining their freedoms.

If we falter in our leadership, we may endanger the peace of the world — and we shall surely endanger the welfare of this Nation.

Great responsibilities have been placed upon us by the swift movement of events.

I am confident that the Congress will face these responsibilities squarely.

— From an address delivered by President Harry Truman before a joint session of Congress on March 12, 1947.

HISTORICAL NOVEL   Tzelekis was right: now it was 1949, and war was beautifully organized — things were done in an orderly fashion. Various specialists had come in, trained in "wars of movement": The British, the Americans, with a good deal of experience in such matters. They put things in their places, taught enemies and friends to recognize each other — you over here, them over there. Work with a system, no fooling around! Back in '46, you see, everything was topsy-turvy. The army was an indiscriminate herd, no organization whatever; everyone did as he pleased, everything pell-mell, all mixed up together slaughtering: EAM-ites, EDES-ites, X-ites — you didn't know who was your enemy and who your friend. At night they sent out patrols — in the morning they came back in company with the others and cut up their captains. Other times when they fought at night with knives and bayonets it was like mother losing child and child losing mother: same clothes (all the rags of the world resemble each other), same appearance — you came face to face with the enemy, you went at him with a dagger to rip out his guts, and you saw — if you had time — that he was one of your own men, so you let him go and went for the one beside him. And don't forget, what mixed things up even worse was the language; since they were all spouting Greek, who could tell them apart? . . .

Later when foreign aid began to arrive, the army got new uniforms, munitions, wireless transmitters, codes of recognition. Things were put in order, names were given to the enemy, and the radio blared them out every day, they were written on the walls and in the newspapers; and finally, for the first time in their history, the Greeks began to kill each other systematically. The solution was a very simple one; and a considerable number of people couldn't understand why they had not thought of it before.

—From Aris Fakinos, *The Marked Men* (New York: Liveright, 1971), 92–93.

Note that the textbook is general in its coverage. It does not use **footnotes**. It tries to summarize the content and meaning of the event without too much detail and without extensive proof for its conclusions. The monograph, in contrast, covers a small portion of the topic, gives more detail, quotes from primary materials, and uses footnotes to record its sources of information. The selection from the anthology is a **primary source** — the Truman speech itself. The section from the historical novel is very different from the first three passages. The author gives us the imaginary thoughts of some of the soldiers who fought in the Greek civil war, far away from the formulation of foreign policy in Washington.

No matter what kind of reading assignment you may be given, the goal is to understand the author's meaning and to relate that understanding to the content of the course.

HOW TO "READ" NONWRITTEN MATERIALS

Many textbooks now come with CD-ROMs or with special-access Web sites. These discs and sites usually emphasize nonwritten sources. Depending on an assignment, you may need to interpret maps, videos, sound recordings, artwork, photographs, statistical data, and so forth. Some of these resources will be interactive so that you can pose or answer questions, organize evidence, and interpret sources, among other tasks. To use these kinds of resources effectively, you will need to learn how to understand the historical significance of a wide variety of nonwritten materials.

Interpreting Maps

Important aspects of the historical record can be displayed in maps. The landscape is one of history's fundamental settings. The rise and fall of empires, the course of wars, the growth of cities, the development of trade routes, and much more can be traced on maps of large areas. Figure 2.2 indicates the years in which parts of Africa came under European colonial rule. This map tells you which European countries controlled which parts

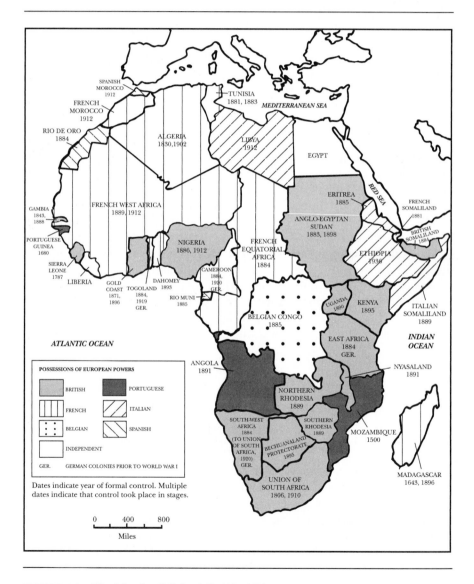

FIGURE 2.2   The March of Colonialism in Africa

of Africa and when this control was established. Analyzing the map, you can see that Britain and France had the largest colonial empires in Africa and that most of Africa was free of colonial rule before the 1880s. Figure 2.3 indicates the dates on which the nations of Africa became independent. By comparing this map with Figure 2.2, you can determine which countries changed their names upon achieving independence. Comparing the dates on the two maps, you can figure out how long colonial rule lasted in different countries. Note also that the first wave of independence

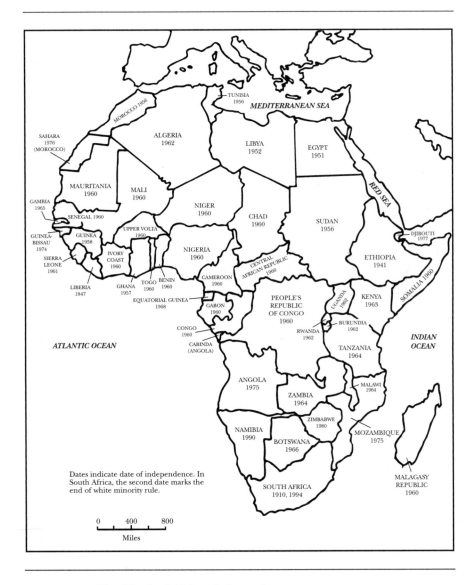

FIGURE 2.3 The March of African Independence

came in the 1960s and that the date for Namibian independence is 1990 — less than two decades ago.

Small area maps can show the layout of villages, the outcome of battles, or the location of mines, canals, and railroads. To read a map, you must understand the *key*, which translates the symbols used on the map. A line on a map may be a road, a river, or a gas pipeline. The key tells you which it is. The *scale* of a map tells you the actual size of the area the map represents. Maps are an important aid in understanding history because they display the physical relationship between places. Never ignore maps in a textbook or other reading. It is also wise to put a good map of the area you are studying near your desk so that you can see the location of places mentioned in lectures and readings.

Old maps are primary documents. The way that old maps describe the territories they cover can give you clues as to what was going on in the mind of the mapmaker when the map was created.

Analyzing Statistical Data

In addition to maps, history resources often include statistical data arranged in **charts, graphs,** or **tables.** These data describe the amounts of something (such as warships, marriages, schools, bridges, or deaths from smallpox) at a specific time in the past, and usually they compare these amounts (such as the number of marriages in relation to the number of schools) or trace changes in amounts over time (such as the number of warships in 1820, 1830, and 1840). Figure 2.4 shows a tabular arrangement of statistical data with an explanation of how to read them. The table organizes population **statistics** from different regions of the earth and across more than three hundred years. Reading across the rows allows you to trace the changes in population of a particular region (Europe, Africa, Asia) over time. By doing so, you can follow the population of each region at hundred-year intervals

	1650	1750	1850	1900	1950	1980	1996
Europe	100	140	265	400	570	730	800
United States and Canada	2	2	25	80	165	252	295
Latin America	12	10	35	65	165	362	489
Africa	100	95	95	120	220	470	732
Asia	330	480	750	940	1370	2600	3430

FIGURE 2.4   Estimated World Population
Numbers represent millions of persons. These are rough estimates only. The figures for 1650 and 1750 in particular come from a time before it was common to conduct a periodic count (*census*) of populations. There is great debate about the size of the native populations of the Western Hemisphere before 1850.
SOURCE: *Adapted from L. S. Stavrianos, The World since 1500: A Global History, 4th ed. (Upper Saddle River, N.J.: Prentice-Hall, Inc., 1982), 181.*

(the population of Latin America in 1650, 1750, 1850, and 1950). You can note the change for each region and the rate of change. For example, the population of the United States and Canada did not increase in the hundred years between 1650 and 1750, but it more than doubled in the fifty years between 1900 and 1950. Reading down the columns, you can examine the population of each region during the same period. This allows you to compare the populations of the different regions. In 1650 the populations of Europe and Africa were the same, but in 1950 the European population was more than two-and-one-half times that of Africa.

More complex comparisons can be made from Figure 2.4 by combining the differences between regions (reading down) and their rates of growth over time (reading across). For example, you can discover that whereas the population of Asia grew more than that of any other region in absolute terms, its *rate* of growth from 1850 to 1980 (750 million to 2600 million, or about 350 percent) was much less than that of Latin America (35 million to 362 million, or around 1,000 percent).

Even the cold statistics of a table can provide images of the great drama of history. The decrease in African population between 1650 and 1850 may tell us something of the impact of the slave trade, and the decrease in population in Latin America between 1650 and 1750 hints at the toll taken among Native Americans by the introduction of European diseases. The large increase in the U.S. population between 1850 and 1900 tells us something about the history of European emigration.

The information in the table can be presented differently in order to highlight different aspects of the data. In Figure 2.5, the numbers for each region are represented as percentages of the total world population. By changing the numbers from absolute amounts to percentages, the new table facilitates the comparing of populations and population growth.

Another way of presenting these population data is in the form of a graph. Note that Figure 2.6 makes more obvious the differences between numbers and thus makes comparisons easier. However, ease of comparison is traded for a loss in precision; the graph gives less specific numbers

	1650	1750	1850	1900	1950	1980	1996
Europe	18.4	19.3	22.8	25.0	23.2	16.5	13.9
United States and Canada	0.2	0.1	2.3	5.1	6.7	5.7	5.1
Latin America	2.2	1.5	2.8	3.9	6.3	8.2	8.5
Africa	18.4	13.2	8.1	7.4	8.8	10.6	12.7
Asia	60.8	65.9	64.0	58.6	55.0	58.9	59.7

FIGURE 2.5 Estimated World Population

Numbers represent percentages of the total world population.

SOURCE: *Adapted from L. S. Stavrianos, The World since 1500: A Global History, 4th ed. (Upper Saddle River, N.J.: Prentice-Hall, Inc., 1982), 181.*

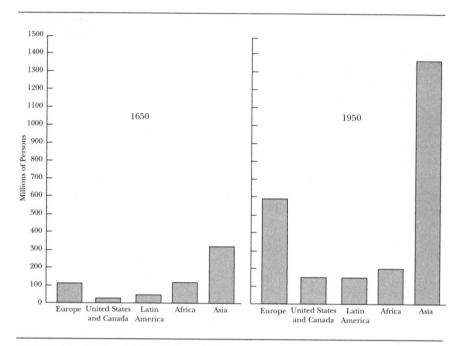

FIGURE 2.6   Estimated World Population

(reading along the vertical axis) than the table. A graph also often requires more space than a table to convey the same information. If Figure 2.6 included all of the time periods of the table, it would be very large.

The more detailed the data and their arrangement are, the more historical information that can be displayed and the more intricate the comparisons that can be made. Figure 2.7 (p. 31) presents a table that lists the percentage of the total vote and the number of deputies elected to the German parliament (the Reichstag) by each of the major political parties in each election from 1919 to 1933. (Note that in a parliamentary system, elections do not come at regular intervals.)

This table allows you to follow the changing fortunes of each political party. A wealth of information on German political history is contained in these figures. Between the lines one can also find pieces of the social and economic history of Germany. For example, the strength of the Communist and Social Democratic (Socialist) parties attests to the deep dissatisfaction of many German workers with the state of the economy during the period known as the Weimar Republic. Even more striking is the tremendous growth of the National Socialist (Nazi) Party after 1930. This development brought Adolf Hitler to power in 1933, and the results of that event would eventually reverberate around the world. As you can see, a table is more than just numbers.

Party	1919	1920	1924	1928	1930	1932	1933
Communist							
# of deputies	0	4	45	54	77	89	81
% of total votes		2.1	9.0	10.6	13.1	14.6	12.3
Social Democratic							
# of deputies	165	102	131	153	143	133	120
% of total votes	37.9	21.6	26.0	29.8	24.5	21.6	18.3
Democratic							
# of deputies	75	39	32	25	20	4	5
% of total votes	18.6	8.3	6.3	4.9	3.8	1.0	.8
Centrum							
# of deputies	91	64	69	62	68	75	74
% of total votes	19.7	13.6	13.6	12.1	11.8	12.5	11.7
Bavarian People's							
# of deputies	0	21	19	16	19	22	18
% of total votes		4.4	3.7	3.0	3.0	3.2	2.7
German People's							
# of deputies	19	65	51	45	30	7	2
% of total votes	4.4	13.9	10.1	8.7	4.5	1.2	1.1
National People's							
# of deputies	44	71	103	73	41	37	52
% of total votes	10.3	14.9	20.5	14.2	7.0	5.9	8.0
National Socialist							
# of deputies	0	0	14	12	107	230	288
% of total votes			3.0	2.6	18.3	37.4	43.9

FIGURE 2.7 Reichstag Elections, 1919–1933
Under the electoral system provided for in the Weimar Constitution, each party received approximately one representative for every sixty thousand popular votes cast for its candidates. Various small parties, not listed here, were underrepresented in the Reichstag.
SOURCE: L. S. Stavrianos, *The World since 1500: A Global History*, 4th ed. (Upper Saddle River, N.J.: Prentice-Hall, Inc., 1982), 419.

Interpreting Illustrations, Photographs, and Other Visual Material

Visual material also can present historical information. Gathering information from old paintings, drawings, photographs, and films, however, can be surprisingly difficult. First, you need to recognize the actual information that they present—what Columbus's ships looked like, how Hiroshima appeared after the explosion of the atomic bomb, and so on. Then you need to interpret them. Interpreting requires an effort to understand what the artist or photographer was "saying" in the work. When an artist draws something and when a photographer takes a picture, he or she is not simply recording a visual image but is sending a message to everyone who looks at the work. In this way, artists and photographers are like writers whose written work needs to be interpreted.

Figures 2.8 and 2.9 present two illustrations of the Spanish conquest of Mexico. Look at them and see whether you can detect what they are saying.

Figure 2.8 is by a European artist and shows Hernán Cortés, who conquered Mexico for Spain, being offered young Indian women by a coastal tribe. The Indians seem happy to greet the Spaniards. Figure 2.9 was drawn by an Aztec Indian and shows Cortés's soldiers (having fought their way from the coast to the Aztec capital) massacring Indians in their main temple. Not all drawings have such obvious (and opposite) messages: the Spanish as friends of the Indians and the Spanish as murderers of the Indians. The interpretation of some visual material requires knowledge about the subject matter, the artist, the style, and the context in which the work appeared. Like written descriptions of past events, art does not simply "speak for itself."

Now look at Figure 2.10, a photograph of a clash in 1968 between Chicago police and demonstrators opposing the war in Vietnam. Like the illustrations in Figures 2.8 and 2.9, it too contains information. Even a casual glance shows confusion and violence. Examining it closely, you can see the kinds of weapons used by the police and the facial expressions of some of the demonstrators. The more difficult part, again, is interpreting

FIGURE 2.8   Indian Offerings to Cortés

SOURCE: *Courtesy of the Bancroft Library, University of California, Berkeley.*

FIGURE 2.9   Massacre of the Aztec Indians

SOURCE: The Broken Spears by Miguel Leon-Portilla. Copyright © 1962, 1990 by Miguel Leon-Portilla. Expanded and Updated Edition © 1992 by Miguel Leon-Portilla. Reprinted by permission of Beacon Press, Boston.

FIGURE 2.10   Antiwar Demonstration at the 1968 Democratic National Convention in Chicago
SOURCE: *Copyright © Bettmann/Corbis.*

the photograph. Is this a scene of provocation by lawless demonstrators or an attack by the police? A careful look at the picture may help you answer this question. In any case, you need more evidence. While an unaltered photograph does show something that actually happened, another photograph — even one of the same event — might show something very different. In most cases, the person taking the photograph has made an effort to say something, and you need to take this motive into account, as well.

Not all pictures have controversial interpretations. Figure 2.11 (p. 35) is a photograph of a city street in Ithaca, New York, in the 1890s. There is a wealth of information here about nineteenth-century town life. Note that at this early date the town already had electric trolleys. Note also that the horses are pulling not wagons or carriages ("buggies," as they were called) but sleighs ("cutters"). This simple fact opens up a window to farm life in winter. When roads were covered with snow and ice, the flat, smooth wheels of wagons could not navigate, but the sharp runners of the cutter dug into the ice and gave it stability.

Interpreting Artifacts

An **artifact** is a physical object from the past: a radio from the 1920s; a rifle from the U.S. Civil War; the ruins of a fourteenth-century church in Paris; a

FIGURE 2.11   Town Life in Ithaca, New York, during the 1890s

SOURCE: Courtesy of the History Center of Tompkins County, Ithaca, New York, General Photo Collection.

10,000-year-old arrowhead. If you have the opportunity to examine an artifact in a museum or in an attic or under the foundations of an old building, do so carefully. Try to figure out how old it is and how it might have been used. (In a museum this is done for you.) Suppose you find a heavy metal object half buried in the floor of an old wooden building. First, look around the building for clues to the age and purpose of the object. If you are lucky, you may find broken bricks on the floor. If you dig down, you may find a layer of ash. Where the old wooden walls are still intact, you may find bent or broken horseshoes nailed into the beams. A few more clues, such as hammers and other tools and a stone hitching post outside the door (for tying up horses securely), may lead you to guess that you are in the ruins of a blacksmith's shop. The heavy metal object you found is an anvil.

A blacksmith was someone who heated bars of iron and hammered them into horseshoes and other useful objects. A blacksmith used many tools to flatten, round off, bend, or work the hot metal, but his principal tool was the anvil — a block of iron or steel on which he shaped the metal. Figure 2.12 shows a nineteenth-century anvil. On the flat surface the black-smith thinned out the heated bar of metal by pounding it with special hammers. The tapered, rounded end on the right was used to bend the thinned metal to the desired shape.

After you identify the object you found, the next step is to place it in its proper historical context — in this case, a nineteenth-century blacksmith's shop. If you wish to delve deeper, you can read about the work of black-smiths, the many kinds of objects they made, and how their work with metal contributed to the village economy.

Visual materials are as vital to historians and history students as are writ-ten records. As our methods of creating and preserving visual images in-crease, more and more of our historical records take the form of pictures. Students need to learn to interpret these new kinds of evidence. (See also "Locating Primary Sources," pp. 92–95, and "Evaluating Primary Sources," pp. 102–05, in Chapter 4.)

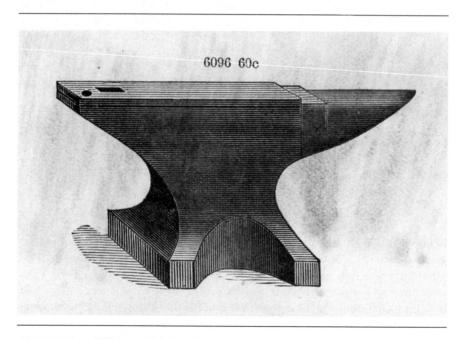

FIGURE 2.12   A Blacksmith's Anvil
SOURCE: Copyright © Bettmann/Corbis.

HOW TO TAKE NOTES IN CLASS

Your time in class is vital to your learning. True, you can learn on your own outside of class, but the interaction with your instructor and other students is most intense during class time. Learning to record that interaction in your notes is an important skill.

From Class Lectures

The first rule of note taking is simple: pay attention. Learn to concentrate on what is being said. Read assigned texts before going to class so you won't end up taking notes on the material in the book. If everything the instructor says is new to you, you will spend so much time writing that you may not be able to grasp the theme of the lecture. If you have obtained some basic information from outside readings, however, you will be able to concentrate on noting points in the lecture that are new or different.

An instructor is most likely to prepare exam questions from the material that he or she considers most important. It is therefore essential in preparing notes to determine which points in the lecture are given most prominent attention. Some instructors are very open about their preferences and clearly emphasize certain points, often writing them on the blackboard. Never fail to note something that the instructor indicates is important. Other instructors are less explicit about their biases and values, and you will have to try to figure them out. Listen closely, and make note of interpretations and generalizations that seem to be stressed, especially when they differ from the approach in the textbook. You should not feel obliged to parrot your instructor's interpretations in an exam, but ignorance of them could work against you.

Your notes should be written legibly and begin with the date and subject of the lecture. They should reflect a general outline of the material covered, with emphasis on major interpretations and important facts not covered in the textbook. It is often best to write on every other line or to leave a large margin on at least one side of the page. This will allow you to add material later and to underline your notes and write additional comments without cluttering the page.

If possible, reread your notes later in the day on which they were written. If your handwriting is poor or your notes are disorganized, it is best to rewrite them. Check the spelling and definitions of any unfamiliar words, and be sure that your notes are coherent. Remember, your notes are an important source of information in your studies.

Guidelines for Taking Lecture Notes

- Prepare for a lecture by reading all related course materials ahead of time.
- Write the course information, lecture subject, and date at the top of each page of notes.
- Be selective — don't try to write everything a lecturer says.
- Be sure to write anything that the instructor (a) puts on the board; (b) says is important; (c) emphasizes as he or she speaks.
- Leave room in your notes to add material later if necessary.
- Reread your notes later in the day on which they were written.
- Underline especially important points.
- Look up the meaning of any unfamiliar words.
- Rewrite any parts of your notes that are poorly organized.
- If something important in your notes is unclear to you, ask your instructor about it.

Examples of Note Taking

To illustrate some of the essentials of good note taking, here are portions of two sets of class notes taken from the same lecture. The first example illustrates many of the common errors of note takers; the second example is a well-written set of notes. The subject of the lecture was early European contact with Africa.

POOR NOTE TAKING   Colonization of Africa — People were afraid to sail out. Afraid of sea monsters. But they liked the stories about gold in Africa. The Portuguese King Henry sailed south to find the gold mines and built a fort at Elmina.

England and France want to trade with Africa. They begin trading. Competing with Portugal. These countries got into wars. They wanted to control Africa.

China had spices. They traded with Cairo and Venice. The Asians wanted gold, but the Islams stopped all trade. They fought wars about religion for hundreds of years. Fought over Jerusalem. The Pope called for a crusade. This was in the Middle Ages.

Spices came from Asia. In Europe they were valuable because the kings used them to become rich. They also ate them.

The Portuguese wanted to explore Africa and make a way to India. Their boats couldn't get around until Bartholomew Diaz discovered the Cape of Good Hope in 1487.

Most of all, the Portuguese wanted slaves. They shipped them back from Africa. Columbus took them after he discovered America (1492). The Pope made a line in the Atlantic Ocean so the Catholics wouldn't fight. The colonies needed slaves. They sent 15 million from 1502 to the 19th century. Slaves did the hard work. They got free later after the Civil War.

Immigrants go to Africa from Europe but they don't like the hot weather and they catch diseases. The Dutch set up their own country at the Cape. Then the English conquer them.

GOOD NOTE TAKING

Early European Contact with Africa   History 200
Why Did Europeans Come to Africa?   10/23/06

1. Desire for gold
   —Medieval legends about gold in Africa.
   —Prince Henry (Portuguese navigator) sent men down coast of Africa to find source of gold. (Also to gain direct access to gold trade controlled by Muslims.)
   —Portuguese built forts along the coast. Their ships carried gold and ivory back to Portugal (16th century).
   —Then the other European states came (England, Holland, France, Spain) to set up their own trading posts.
   —Competed with each other for African trade. (Will talk about rivalry next week.)
2. Wanted to trade with Asia and weaken the Muslims
   (The Muslims had created a large empire based on the religion of Islam.)
   —Religious conflict between Christianity and Islam. Fought a religious war in the 11th–12th centuries — the Crusades.
   —The Muslims had expanded their empire when Europe was weak. In 15th century they controlled North Africa and they dominated trade in the Mediterranean. They controlled the spices coming from Asia, which were in great demand in Europe. In Europe they were used to preserve meat. So valuable, sometimes used as money.
   —Portugal and Spain were ruled by Catholic monarchs. Very religious. The Catholic monarchs wanted to force the Muslims out of Europe. (They still held part of Spain.) Wanted to convert them to Christianity.
[IMPORTANT]—The Muslims controlled North Africa and Mediterranean trade. If the Portuguese and Spanish could sail to the Indian Ocean directly, they could get goods from China and the Muslims couldn't stop them. The way to Asia was the sea route around Africa.
3. The Europeans wanted slaves
   —When the Portuguese explored West Africa (15th century), they sent back the first slaves (around 1440).
   —The Spanish conquered the New World (Mexico, Peru, etc.). (Columbus had made several trips for Queen Isabella I of Spain.)
   —In America (the name for the New World), they needed slaves. Most slaves were sent to America.
   —Native Americans died from diseases of white men. They were also killed in the wars. There was nobody to work the mines (gold and silver).
[IMPORTANT]—Sugar plantations of the Caribbean (and Brazil) needed labor. Cotton and rice plantations in the south of U.S. also. It was hard work and nobody wanted to do it.
   —15 million slaves were brought to work the plantations starting in 1502 until mid-19th century.

Colonization of Africa
1. Immigration (why white people didn't come)
   —They couldn't take the climate.
   —There were a lot of tropical diseases.
   —The Europeans didn't want to live in Africa, only run it.
   —Only the Dutch settlers came. They set up the Boer states in South Africa. After them came British settlers.
   —Some French settled in Algeria.
   —Some English also moved to Rhodesia.
2. Dividing Africa
   —Whites began exploring the interior. (Will discuss exploration next week.)

Taking notes during a lecture is difficult, and even a good set of notes can be greatly improved by being rewritten. Here is a rewriting of these notes. Note how much clearer everything becomes.

REWRITTEN GOOD NOTES

Early European Contact with Africa   History 200
What Drew Europeans to Africa?   10/23/06
   Gold

There were medieval legends that there was a lot of gold in West Africa. Access to the gold was controlled by non-Christian powers (Muslims — believers in Islamic religion). Tales of gold lured the Portuguese (led by Prince Henry) to explore the coast of West Africa in the late 15th century. By the 16th century, the Portuguese had built several trading posts and forts along the West African coast and were bringing back gold, ivory, and pepper.

By the 17th century, English, Dutch, French, and Spanish ships challenged the Portuguese trading monopoly and set up their own trading posts. This was the beginning of rivalry between European countries over the wealth of Africa.

Desire to weaken the power of the Islamic Empire (Muslims) and expand trade with Asia

Conflict between Christianity and Islam was an old religious conflict (the Crusades as an example in 11th and 12th centuries). The Muslims controlled North Africa and the Mediterranean. They also controlled the spice trade from Asia. Spices were important in Europe because they were the only known way to preserve meat.

The Catholic states of Portugal and Spain wanted to fight with the Muslims. They wanted to drive them out of Spain and challenge the large Muslim empire in Africa, the Middle East, and Asia. They hoped to convert them to Christianity. *The Muslims were strong in North Africa, but if European powers could discover a way around Africa into the Indian Ocean, they could outflank the Muslims and obtain direct access to the trade with India and Asia.*

Slaves

Portuguese trading posts in Africa had sent a small number of slaves to Europe starting in the late 15th century. With the discovery and conquest of America at the turn of the 16th century, a new and larger slave trade began to European colonies in the New World (America).

The Native Americans died (they were killed in war and by European diseases in great numbers). There was a shortage of labor. In the 17th and 18th centuries, large sugar plantations were set up in the Caribbean and Brazil and rice and cotton plantations in the southern United States. *The need for laborers to do the hard agricultural work led to the importing of millions of slaves from Africa.* Approximately 15 million Africans were sent to America as slaves between 1502 and the mid-19th century. This slave trade made Africa valuable to the European powers.

The Colonization of Africa
　Immigration
　　　Because of the unsatisfactory climate and tropical diseases, there was no major European immigration to Africa. The only significant white colony was set up in South Africa by the Boers (Dutch) and later the English. There were smaller European settlements in Rhodesia (English) and Algeria (French).
　Dividing up the continent
　Exploration

If you reread the poor notes now, you can easily see how little of the lecture material is recorded in them and how confusing and even erroneous a picture you get from them. What is there about the poor notes that makes them inferior? First, they are not well organized. They do not even record the title of the lecture, the course number, or the date — omissions that could be problematic if the notes get out of order. They are little more than a series of sentences about gold, trade, spices, Portugal, and slaves. The sentences are not in any particular order and do not say much of anything important. Even the factual information does not cover the major points of the lecture. By paying too much attention to trivial points about sea monsters, China, Jerusalem, Bartholomew Diaz, and Columbus, the note taker missed or did not have time to record the principal theme of the lecture — the relationship between European-Asian trade and the religious struggle between Islam and Christianity. The note taker also missed another major point — the connection between the enslavement of Africans and the need for plantation labor in the New World. Without these two points, this student cannot write a good exam essay on this subject.

The good notes, in contrast, follow the organization of the lecture and touch on the major points made in class. The notes make sense and can serve as the basis for reviewing the content of the lecture when the note taker studies for exams. These notes have a wide margin for extra comments and the marking of important passages. Notice the sections marked "important." The instructor had emphasized these points in class, and by specifically identifying them, the student will be sure to master them.

The rewritten version, which eliminates unimportant or repetitious phrases and smoothes the language into connected sentences, is even better as a study guide. The greatest value of rewriting, however, is that re-creating the lecture material in essay form helps it to become part of the note taker's own thinking. The mental effort that goes into revising lecture notes serves to impress the material and its meaning upon the mind. This makes it much easier to review the material at exam time.

From Slides and Films

Some instructors present slide lectures or show videotapes. Note taking in these instances presents special problems. If a lecture is accompanied by slides, you will need to include in your notes information about what the slides illustrated (for example, the Pyramid of Cheops, the novels of Willa Cather, the assassination of John F. Kennedy, the dances of Martha Graham) and anything of importance your instructor said about the slides.

Taking notes on films or videotapes also presents the unusual problem of dim lighting. The greatest problem, however, may be the film itself. In our culture, films are a medium of entertainment rather than education. Your natural response may be to sit back and relax your mind, but you will need to fight this response and learn to probe a film as you would a lecture. If a film is essentially factual (*Walled Cities of the Middle Ages*), note the major facts and interpretations as you would in a lecture. If a film is dramatic rather than documentary (*Hotel Rwanda, Citizen Kane,* or *Schindler's List*), examine the emotional message and artistic content as well as any historical facts it describes (or claims to describe). Ask yourself, What is the movie director trying to say, and what dramatic and technical devices does he or she use to say it? Your notes should record important narration and dialogue that illustrate the theme of the film. Finally, you will need to take note of cinematic elements (camera angles, sets, lighting, gestures and movements, facial expressions) because the impact of a dramatic film is essentially visual. Taking notes on slides and films takes practice, but the effort is worthwhile because photographs, films, videotapes, and DVDs are used increasingly in history courses.

Taking Notes in a "Wired" Classroom

A newer form of class presentation is the multimedia lecture, which usually combines traditional lecturing and questions with material in video or audio form from CD-ROMs or the **World Wide Web.** The use of nonprint material requires a looser form of note taking, one that will help you to recall a mixed-media presentation.

In this kind of class, your instructor's comments will be complemented by various visual and aural materials, such as outlines, charts, artwork, photographs, video recordings, and audio recordings. The key to note taking here is to follow carefully the ways in which the use of new media complements the instructor's lecture. In general, the purpose of incorporating new media is to present you with a richer and more dramatic exposure to a wide variety of historical sources. This material helps to get across the main points that the instructor is covering. Ask yourself, How do the photographs, or timelines, or audio tapes complement the theme of the lecture? Be sure to take notes not only on the media themselves but also on their relation to the topic under discussion. Perhaps your instructor will use media to reinforce a fact—how something looked or sounded. Most likely he or she will also explain the "meaning" of an image or recording: the way it represents nineteenth-century European romanticism, or the popular culture of a large city in the twentieth century, or the connection between rice paddies and villages in twelfth-century China. Don't fill your notes with long descriptions of images or sounds. Instead, focus on the aspects of the topic that the new media bring to life. If the media are part of a CD-ROM that comes with the textbook, be sure to understand the organization of the disc so that you can carry out assignments and research effectively.

CLASSROOM PARTICIPATION

The modern classroom is a place where students are expected to actively participate in their own learning. This section discusses some ways of doing so.

Classroom Discussions

Many instructors encourage class participation. Some base a portion of the final grade on it. Come to class prepared to answer (and to ask) questions. Follow the discussion as it develops. If you are called on, contribute what you know. If some part of an instructor's presentation or a classmate's comments is unclear to you, don't hesitate to ask a question. If class ends and something remains unclear, raise your question with your instructor after class or during your instructor's office hours.

Guidelines for Speaking in Class

- Be familiar with the subject under discussion.
- If you are unclear about something the instructor or another student has said, compose and ask your question.
- If you disagree with something said, make your point clearly and constructively.
- If you don't have a chance to raise a question in class, ask your instructor after class.

Giving an Oral Presentation

Some instructors require students to give an oral presentation in class. Eloquence and effectiveness in public speaking cannot be mastered in a week or two, but you can make a start by taking such an assignment seriously and adequately preparing yourself for it. If you are allowed the option, reading from a prepared text is often the safest procedure. However, this type of delivery can lead to a dull presentation. It is usually better to speak from notes: your presentation will be livelier and more enjoyable for the class. To do a good job, you need to be fully familiar with your subject and pay close attention to getting your points across. Prepare your presentation outline as you would that of a short paper (see "Writing Short Essays" in Chapter 3, pp. 73–74). Be sure to cover all the important points and to present them in a logical manner.

Use short phrases rather than sentences in your presentation notes. Suppose you intend to tell the class the following: "Before 1848, most of the large landowners in California were Mexicans. In the decades after the United States annexed California, these Californios, as they were called, lost most of their lands to migrants from the eastern states." Your notes need only say: "(a) Until 1848 big landowners Californios. (b) Cal. annexed in 1848. (c) Lost land to easterners." Once you are fully prepared, do a dry run of your presentation before a relative, friend, or roommate (or even in front of a mirror). Be sure that you exhibit knowledge of your subject because this is most likely to determine your grade. Effective public speaking is one of the most important tools for success in many fields of work, and giving a talk in class is a good opportunity to develop your skills in this area.

Guidelines for Giving an Oral Presentation

- Use 3-by-5 note cards, each with one or (at most) two major points on it.
- Write neatly and use phrases, not whole sentences.
- Put a number in the corner of each note card so that the cards will not get out of order.
- If you have a time limit, rehearse your talk beforehand so that you won't need to rush. Pare down your notes to fit the time needed to present the material clearly.
- Visual aids (such as overhead projections, slides, or videos) can make your presentation much more interesting. Make sure, however, that you have the resources you need beforehand and that you know how to integrate them easily and smoothly into your verbal remarks.
- Relax! Speak slowly and clearly, and make eye contact with your audience every few sentences.

Giving a PowerPoint Presentation

PowerPoint, as you probably know, is a software program that enables you to make a presentation to the class in the form of a digital "slide show." You can use several toolbars to create screens that will appear as a series of "slides." These slides allow you to make a series of points about your assigned (or chosen) topic. Screens can contain text in various fonts and colors, data organized into tables and graphs, artwork from a variety of sources, and much more. You also can animate and sequence your screens.

Don't underuse or overuse PowerPoint. If screen after screen is merely a series of bulleted lines, you might as well write them on the blackboard. At the other extreme, don't turn your presentation into a Hollywood-style extravaganza — even if you know the program well enough to do so. Know what points you want to get across; then create just enough screens with just enough visual elements to do so clearly and effectively.

Be sure to **proofread** your screens to keep errors out of your presentation. Preview the screens for both content and sequence. Rehearse the presentation to make sure it fits into the time allotted. Make sure that the classroom has the necessary hardware for you to run your PowerPoint presentation.

Don't expect the screens to do all of the work for you. Assist the class with each screen by explaining how the text, data, and images illustrate and advance your main points.

Group Work

Your instructor may ask you to be part of a small group and carry out an assignment working with members of that group. Instead of an individual oral presentation, your group may be asked to make a presentation to the class. Conducting research and preparing a group presentation can be tricky but also rewarding. The key to success is to clarify who in the group is to do what part of the assignment and to be sure that each member is prepared when the time comes.

Another kind of group work takes place outside the classroom. Known as **peer reviewing** or peer editing, this type of work requires you to evaluate the work of a classmate. For example, you may be asked to read and comment on a student's **rough draft** of an assignment. Your peer review may take the form of an informal one-on-one review in which you go through the paper with the author point by point. Some instructors may ask you to write your evaluation; others may want your review in the form of a class presentation. No matter what the format is, remember to provide *constructive* criticism that will help your classmates develop their papers. Be sure to point out a paper's strengths in addition to any weaknesses.

If you are asked to peer-edit the work of a classmate, remember also to pay particular attention to the theme and thesis of the paper. Ask yourself whether the theme and thesis are stated clearly and whether there is sufficient evidence to support them. Additionally, you should consider whether the information has been presented in an organized manner, such that your classmate's conclusions are justified.

Guidelines for Peer Reviewing

- Don't be overly critical. Your goal is to assist your classmate in seeing the strengths and weaknesses in her or his draft. Your ability to do this comes from your outsider status: you have not been submerged in the research and are able to take a fresh look at the essay.
- Pay special attention to the thesis of the essay. Is it stated in clear terms?
- Does the body of the paper provide important evidence to support the thesis?
- Are the points made in support of the thesis well organized, and are they clear to you as a reader?
- Are the paper's conclusions justified by its arguments and documentation?
- Whether your comments to your classmate are written or oral, be supportive. Give the writer the kind of help you hope to get from your own peer reviewer.

You also can share your comments with classmates either through e-mail or through a course Web page. You can send drafts of your work to other students or exchange peer-review drafts directly online. Computer technology also allows you to extend your learning beyond the classroom. You can talk to students at other schools in chat rooms or e-mail questions to authors of course materials. Learning to work collaboratively will be of use when you leave school and enter a working environment in which these kinds of personal and digital interactions are common.

COMMUNICATING ONLINE

Your professor may post the course syllabus and assignments online. Some professors and students also use the Web as a means of expanding their academic experience. There are several ways of communicating online that you can use as educational tools. Online tools help you to gain control of course material, avoid dangerous pitfalls, make connections to relevant material, and understand the larger framework of your course. They allow you to communicate with scholars, archivists, and Web masters in your field, find important and underexploited resources for your research, and broaden your knowledge of the theories surrounding a particular period or aspect of history. You will likely find e-mail, **listservs**, **chat rooms**, e-conferences, and e-seminars especially useful.

E-mail, Listservs, and Chat Rooms

The speed of e-mail interaction varies according to how quickly the participants initiate and respond to messages. Listservs (list servers) are a way of managing e-mail lists of people interested in a particular topic. Instead of allowing one-to-one or one-to-many communication — as with e-mail — listservs send out everyone's messages to everyone else on the list. Listservs are especially valuable in settings that emphasize group-oriented work. Chat rooms allow users to communicate with others who are in a specific "room." Your Internet service provider (ISP) may give you access to chat rooms. You may also find chat rooms by surfing for them on the Web. Chat-room communication may be either one-to-one or one-to-many; however, unless you are in a "private" chat room—just you and the recipient— your messages can be read by others. Chat rooms provide users with immediate communication, but unlike e-mail or listservs they do not provide users with any tangible record of the dialogue.

For educational purposes, you can use these tools to varying degrees. You may decide to pose a question to a classmate by e-mail or in a chat room: "What was Professor Smith's advice about reading this document?" You can work out difficult concepts in a chat room. Perhaps you are dealing with a complex topic. You know you need to understand the material because it forms the basis for future lessons. By communicating with others, you can work through that material and master it in much the same way as you would in a study group.

If you subscribe to a listserv for your class, you might post the following message:

> I understand Prof. Smith's discussion of the factors that led to an anticommunist belief/paranoia in the U.S. during the late 1940s and early 1950s. However, I'm confused about which groups expressed these fears. From the readings it appears that only the Republicans did; however, Prof. Smith's lecture leads me to believe that both Republicans and Democrats did. Can anyone help me with this point?

By posting this message, you are assessing what you know and what you don't know and trying to deepen your understanding. Your message may stimulate another student's thinking. A classmate might offer the following reply:

> I think that is exactly Prof. Smith's intention. As I understand it, both Republicans and Democrats expressed these fears; however, they employed different means to achieve the same ends. Because the Democrats' activities were less dramatic, the Republicans charged them with being "soft" on communism.

Responding gives the student an opportunity to think about the material, understand the connections, and see how the material works.

Despite the advantages of e-mail, listservs, and chat rooms, there are dangers as well. Most of this kind of communication is unmediated or unedited. This means that anyone can say anything at any time. Perhaps someone with whom you are communicating tells you that the Holocaust was a Hollywood creation. Although it is important to give credit to new theories, it is equally important to read electronic communication with a skeptical eye. If someone says something with which you are unfamiliar, it is perfectly acceptable to ask for references where you could find more information on that topic. The best advice is to know the individuals with whom you communicate, read messages critically, and don't be afraid to challenge someone if you have reason to believe that he or she is wrong.

The cooperative learning fostered through communicating over the Web is of great value. Too often at the undergraduate level students look at learning from a competitive rather than a cooperative viewpoint. Some students never study or work with others. They believe that if they do so they will lose their "edge." Historians, however, do not work in a vacuum; historical research relies on access to the discoveries, interpretations, and analyses of others. Seminar-type classes often rely on cooperative learning, but you can have a similar experience in any class by communicating with classmates and others by means of the Web. By sharing information, you are not losing any competitive advantage; you are increasing and solidifying your knowledge, pointing out errors, and sharing important findings.

E-conferences and E-seminars

E-conferences and e-seminars are becoming important interactive means of scholarly discussion. Both make possible the online presentation, discussion, and criticism of scholarly papers; however, e-conferences present several papers and e-seminars deal with only one. You may find it difficult to locate these forums on the Web. Most are either sponsored by or affiliated with universities. If you do find one, check the participation requirements. Some are open only to scholars; others allow both students and scholars to participate.

There are important things to keep in mind when joining and participating in these online scholarly activities. Both assume a high level of knowledge and waste little time with introductions and background material. They assume that participants are thoroughly familiar with the topic of the conference or seminar and are able to read and write on a sophisticated level.

Web Communication and Advanced Research

Web communication can help students doing advanced course work to locate important resources. If you decide to tackle an obscure topic, you can use the Web to contact scholars who have done research in that area. If possible, contact more than one scholar so that you have more than one interpretation of the topic. The scholars, archivists, and Web masters with whom you would communicate are busy individuals. When contacting them, introduce yourself, describe your research, and outline your reason for contacting them. Be sure that you are knowledgeable about your topic, that your contact can actually help you, and that you ask specific questions.

In communicating online, you are "talking" with others who can increase your understanding and whom you may be able to help as well. You will improve your grasp of the material about which you have questions. You will see the pitfalls to avoid by pointing out errors in other people's interpretations. This experience will give you insight into an important principle of the humanistic disciplines: your best work results from dialogue with other researchers. (For information about conducting research on the Web, see Chapter 4, pp. 95–100.)

HOW TO STUDY FOR AND TAKE EXAMS

When a test is announced, try to find out what kind of exam it will be: essay, short answer, multiple choice, or a combination of those formats. Determine what topics will be covered and what portions of the reading material and lectures deal with those topics. If you have not done all of the necessary reading, do so immediately and record the important facts and interpretations as indicated in the "How to Read a History Assignment" section of this chapter (pp. 19–25). If you missed any lectures, try to obtain lecture notes from someone who knows the rules of good note taking. Then gather together all the materials to be covered in the exam. Reread the parts of the texts that you underlined (or otherwise marked) as being important. Reread all of the relevant lecture notes, paying special attention to any points emphasized by the instructor. Sometimes it helps to do your rereading aloud. If an exam will cover visual materials — slides, films, maps — be sure to go over this information, even if you have to watch a video a second time.

If the test is to be an **essay exam,** compose sample questions based on the important topics and themes in the readings and lectures. Many textbooks contain sample exam questions or topics for discussion at the end of each chapter. If you do not know how to answer any portion of the sample question, go over your study materials again and look for the information needed. If you are preparing for an **objective exam** — that is, one requiring short factual answers — pay special attention to the important facts (persons, places, events, changes) and key terms in your study materials. You must be precise in order to get credit for your answer. Make a list of outstanding people, events, and historical developments, and be sure that you can adequately identify them and explain their importance. Again, your textbook may help you by providing sample short-answer questions.

Take the time you need to prepare adequately. If tests make you nervous, keep on studying until you master your sample questions and until the material to be covered makes sense to you.

Objective and Short-Answer Exams

Objective exams call for short, factual answers. The three most common objective exams are (1) **short answer,** (2) **identification,** and (3) **multiple choice** or true/false. Read each question carefully, and don't jump to conclusions. Answer short-answer and identification questions briefly (there is usually a time and space limit) and directly. Don't put anything in your answer that wastes space or time. If you are asked to identify John F. Kennedy, don't mention how he was killed (unless that is part of the question); instead talk about some aspect of his presidency that was stressed in class or in course readings. When you have so little room to show what you know, answers that stray from the core of the subject are as bad as wrong answers.

Example of a Short-Answer Question

QUESTION   Describe one of the motives that caused the European powers to explore Africa beginning in the late fifteenth century.

INCORRECT ANSWER   They wanted to dominate Africa and get all the gold for themselves. Columbus wanted to take slaves from Africa, but the Pope said it would start a war. But the war didn't start and the Europeans dominated Africa anyway because they were stronger.

CORRECT ANSWER   The wars between Christianity and Islam were an important factor. The Christian states wanted to weaken the hold of the Muslim religion on Africa and to convert the natives. They also hoped to break Muslim control of trade with Asia by finding a sea route around Africa.

(Check these two answers against the example of good note taking on pp. 39–40. The notes presented there make clear why the second answer is satisfactory and the first one is not.)

Example of an Identification Question

QUESTION   Identify the "progressive" philosophy of historical interpretation.

INCORRECT ANSWER   Historians who believed that our country was always making progress because Americans were very hardworking people.

CORRECT ANSWER   The interpretation of history that holds that human beings and their condition are continually improving as each generation builds on the foundation laid by previous ones.

(See the "Philosophies of History" section in Chapter 1 on pp. 5–6 to find the basis for the correct answer.)

Example of a Multiple-Choice Question

The British monarch at the time of the American Revolution was:

   a. George II
   b. Charles I
   c. James II
   d. George III
   e. Henry I

If you look up the reign dates of these monarchs, you will discover that George III (who was king from 1760 to 1820) was the ruler of England at the time of the American Revolution.

Preparing for In-Class Essay Exams — Composing Sample Questions

Of course, the best preparation for an essay exam is to be given the question in advance. Some instructors do this (usually in the form of a **take-home essay exam**), but many give in-class essay exams and hand out in advance a number of possible topics or questions from which they will choose when making up the exam. (For more on take-home exams, see pp. 53–56.) If you face an essay exam without *any* questions presented in advance, the key to successful preparation is to come up with potential questions on your own.

As your instructor probably will tell you, the essay questions will deal with the major topics covered in the course so far. Using your textbooks, lecture notes, and other course materials, determine what these topics are. Then compose your own questions.

For example, if the material to be covered in the exam is reasons for the decline of the Roman Empire, list the major reasons mentioned in the course work. Among them may be civil war, military insubordination, the cost of defending distant frontiers, declining agricultural output, "barbarian" invasion, heavy tax burdens on the peasantry, the growth of central bureaucracy, the decline of the Senate, the cult of the Emperor, the rise of Christianity, and the rise of Islam. The exam question is likely to focus on one or more of these explanations. Be prepared to write about *each* of these factors and how they relate to one another.

If the course has covered the rise of industrialization in New England, study carefully the major social and technological changes and how people responded to them. Think about the aspects of industrialization that you might be asked about. One question might ask you to describe the ways in which factory production was different from the 1workshop production that it displaced. Other questions might be "How did industrialization affect family life?" "What were the major technological innovations behind early industrialization?" "How did the rise of the textile industry affect the lives of young women?"

Don't prepare for an essay exam by composing questions that are too broad. If the class spent six weeks examining the decline of the Roman Empire, don't expect a broad question such as "Discuss the decline of the Roman Empire." Don't prepare questions that are too narrow either. For example, "Who owned the biggest textile mill in New England in the 1830s?" is a question for a short-answer or an identification exam.

Writing a Good In-Class Essay Exam

Even if you have prepared properly for an essay exam, you must stay calm enough to remember what you studied, you must understand the questions, you must answer them directly and fully, and you must not run out of time. None of this is easy, but here are a few pointers to follow until you gain the experience to overcome these problems.

Read over the exam slowly. Given the length and complexity of the questions asked, allot the proper amount of time to answer each question. Think about the central points you wish to make in your answer, and create a brief outline of these points in the margin of the exam booklet. Directly address the questions asked. If the questions are very specific, for example, respond to them with the amount of detail required. Support the points you make with facts, but avoid composing an answer that is

---

Guidelines for Writing In-Class Essay Exams

- When you are given the exam, don't panic. Read the entire exam slowly, including all of the instructions. Gauge the amount of time you will need to answer each question. Then choose the question you know most about to answer first.
- Don't write the first thing that comes to mind. Read the question slowly, and be sure you understand it.
- Determine how you will answer the question and the central points you wish to make.
- Write these central points or even a full outline in the margin of the exam booklet. As you compose each sentence of your answer, make sure that it relates to one of these points.
- Model your answer on the question. Be as specific or general, as concrete or reflective, as the question suggests. Never allow your answer to wander away from the focus of the question. If the question asks you to "describe" or "trace" or "compare" or "explain," be sure that that is what you do.
- Don't repeat yourself. Each sentence should add new material or advance a line of argument.
- Where necessary, refer to the facts that support the points you are making. But the mere relation of a series of facts is not enough. You must also give evidence that you have thought about the question in broad terms.
- Toward the end of your answer, you may wish to include your own opinion. This is fine, even desirable, but be sure that your answer as a whole supports this opinion.
- If there is time, reread and correct an answer after it is finished. The pressure of an exam can often cause you to write sentences that are not clear.

merely a series of facts. Think about the questions asked in broad terms, and pursue your central points. As you write, refer back to your outline and be careful not to repeat yourself. Each sentence should add new material to your answer or advance its line of argument. Finally, try to leave a few minutes to proofread your answers.

Writing Take-Home Essay Exams

When you are writing take-home essay exam answers, all of the points made earlier in this chapter about clarity and continuity apply. A take-home essay exam question requires you to write an original essay of usually two to five pages. **Documentation** (footnotes and a **bibliography**) is not usually required. Of course, if your instructor asks for a specific length, topic, approach, or format, you need to follow those requirements even when they differ from the information provided here.

First, note the length requirements of the exam and the due date. Obviously, you will need more time to prepare a six-page essay answer than a three-page one. If your instructor allows you access to sources (which is common), you will need to review all course material that relates to the exam question. If you have not yet outlined or taken notes on this material, do so now. Focusing on the portion of the course material that relates to the question, make a list of the most important points. Try to find from two to six main points for each essay, depending on the length of the essay. Compose your answer by introducing and then supporting these points in logical order. Like all essays, your answer should have a clear, central **theme**. In this case, your theme is determined by the exam question. Be sure that your essay directly addresses the question. (See the section on writing in-class essay exams on pp. 52–53.)

The goal of any essay exam is to demonstrate (1) adequate knowledge of the subject, (2) clear thinking about the points covered, (3) clear and connected writing, and (4) clear understanding of the question. Read the following two answers to an exam question on Chinese history. Do they meet those four requirements?

QUESTION   Explain the origins of the Chinese civil war of 1945–1949. How did the differing political programs of the two contenders affect the outcome of that conflict?

POOR ANSWER   The Guo Mindang (Kuomintang) had a stronger army than the Communists, but the Communists won the civil war and took over the country. Their political program, communism, was liked by the peasants because they didn't own any land and paid high taxes.

China was based on the Confucian system, which was very rigid and led to the Manchu dynasty being overthrown. The Chinese didn't like being dominated by foreigners, and Sun Zhongshan (Sun Yat-sen) founded the Guo Mindang to unite China. He believed in the Three People's Principles. At first he cooperated with the Chinese Communists, but later Jiang Jieshi (Chiang Kai-shek) tried to destroy communism because he was against it. Communism was not in favor of the wealthy people.

The Communists wanted a revolution of the peasants and gave them land. They also killed the landlords. Jiang Jieshi worried more about the Communists than about the Japanese invasion. The Japanese looked to conquer China and make it a part of their empire. Jiang Jieshi wanted to fight the Communists first.

After World War II the Chinese Communists attacked Manchuria and took over a lot of weapons. They fought the Guo Mindang army. The Guo Mindang army lost the battles, and Jiang Jieshi was chased to Taiwan, where he made a new government. The Communists set up their own country, and their capital was Beijing (Peking). That way the Communists won the Chinese civil war.

GOOD ANSWER   The origins of the 1945–1949 civil war can be traced back to the rise of Chinese nationalism in the late nineteenth century. Out of the confusion of the Warlord period that followed the overthrow of the Manchu dynasty in 1911, two powerful nationalist movements arose — one reformist and the other revolutionary. The reformist movement was the Guo Mindang (Kuomintang), founded by Sun Zhongshan (Sun Yat-sen). It was based on a mixture of republican, Christian, and moderate socialist ideals and inspired by opposition to foreign domination. The revolutionary movement was that of the Chinese Communist Party (CCP), founded in 1921, whose goal was a communist society but whose immediate program was to organize the working class to protect its interests and to work for the removal of foreign "imperialist" control.

Although these two movements shared certain immediate goals (suppression of the Warlords and resistance to foreign influence), they eventually fell out over such questions as land reform, relations with the Soviet Union, the role of the working class, and the internal structure of the Guo Mindang. (The CCP operated within the framework of the more powerful Guo Mindang during the 1920s.)

By the 1930s, when Jiang Jieshi (Chiang Kai-shek) succeeded Sun, the CCP was forced out of the Guo Mindang. By that time the CCP had turned to a program of peasant revolution inspired by Mao Zedong (Mao Tse-tung). A four-year military struggle (1930–1934) between the two movements for control of the peasantry of Jiangxi (Kiangsi) Province ended in the defeat but not destruction of the CCP.

The Japanese invasion of Manchuria (1931) and central China (1936–1938) helped salvage the fortunes of the CCP. By carrying out an active guerrilla resistance against the Japanese, in contrast to the more passive role of the Guo Mindang, which was saving its army for a future battle with the Communists, the CCP gained the leading position in the nationalist cause.

In the post–World War II period, the CCP's land reform program won strong peasant support, whereas the landlord-backed Guo Mindang was faced with runaway corruption and inflation, which eroded its middle-class following. The military struggle between 1945 and 1949 led to the defeat of the demoralized Guo Mindang army and the coming to power of the CCP.

Let's compare how well the two essays meet the requirements for a well-written answer.

1. *Adequate knowledge of the subject.* The writer of the poor answer fails to indicate adequate knowledge in several ways. The answer omits many important facts. It describes the political programs of the two contending parties in vague terms. It refers to the CCP only as the Chinese Communists, leaving the impression that they were a loose grouping of like-minded individuals rather than a strong, well-disciplined political organization. It does not even mention the name of the most famous leader of the CCP — Mao Zedong. Jiang Jieshi, the leader of the Guo Mindang, is mentioned, but there is no discussion of his political program or beliefs, other than that he was opposed to communism. Another serious defect is chronological confusion. The answer jumps back and forth between earlier and later periods, and no dates are given for major events.

The well-written answer illustrates good knowledge of the subject matter. The origins, philosophies, leaders, and relationship of the two contending parties are clearly described. This answer brings in related issues such as nationalism, Warlords, guerrilla warfare against Japan, corruption, and inflation, thus indicating knowledge of the historical **context** in which the Chinese civil war developed. The chronology is clear: events are mentioned in proper time sequence, and the dates of all major events are given.

2. *Clear thinking about the points covered.* The poor answer is not well organized. The paragraphs do not make separate points, and each succeeding paragraph does not further develop the theme of the essay. The first paragraph is a conclusion rather than an introduction. The second paragraph goes back to the founding of the Guo Mindang but, instead of discussing the origins of the hostility between it and the CCP, merely states that hostility came into existence. Paragraph three begins by introducing the CCP (though not by name). However, it does not expand on the CCP's programs and points of conflict with the Guo Mindang. Instead, it abruptly changes the focus of events and the time frame by introducing the Japanese invasion of China, which the last sentence of the paragraph only vaguely relates to the question. Instead of drawing conclusions about the causes of the Communist victory in the civil war, the last paragraph merely states that it occurred.

The well-written answer uses each paragraph to make a separate important point, and each succeeding paragraph further develops the theme of the essay. The first paragraph sets out the political programs of the two groups and the historical context in which the movements originated. The second paragraph explains the beginning of the conflict in the 1920s. Paragraph three discusses that conflict in relation to the Chinese peasantry during the early 1930s. The fourth paragraph relates the development of the conflict to the Japanese invasion of the late 1930s. The final paragraph summarizes the effects of the conflicts and of postwar developments on the outcome of the civil war.

3. *Clear and connected writing.* Many sentences in the poor answer are badly constructed: they are awkward, or what they say adds nothing to the answer. Some of the awkward phrases are "the Communists won the civil war and *took over* the country"; "communism was *liked by* the peasants"; "China was *based on* the Confucian system"; "communism was not *in favor* of the wealthy people"; "the Japanese *looked* to conquer China"; "the Communists *set up their own country*." These phrases cause the sentences to be unclear, and they keep the student from getting his or her point across. The other major defect in sentence structure is repetitious or irrelevant sentences and phrases. These are "Jiang Jieshi (Chiang Kai-shek) tried to destroy communism *because he was against it*"; "they *fought the Guo Mindang army*"; "that way *the Communists won the Chinese civil war*." The sentences of the well-written answer are clear, and each adds new material to the essay.

4. *Clear understanding of the question.* The poor answer does not deal with the central issue of the question — the political programs of the Guo Mindang and the CCP. It notes that the Guo Mindang was founded on the Three People's Principles, but it does not explain what these were. Of the CCP, it says that there was a belief in communism (which is obvious) and peasant revolution (which is vague). These are the only references to political programs in the entire answer! It is obvious that the writer of this answer failed to understand that the central focus of the question was on political philosophy.

The well-written answer is directed to the central issue of political programs and begins on that very point. The remainder of the answer makes clear the relationship of political programs to the origins and course of the Chinese civil war as called for in the first sentence of the question.

The Dangers of Plagiarism.   A problem that sometimes arises with take-home exams is plagiarism. Your instructor may allow you to paraphrase the sources you use in preparing your essay. Be sure, however, that you write these paraphrases totally in your own words. If you use sentences or even phrases from another source, you are plagiarizing whether you realize it or not. Most schools require instructors to penalize students severely for plagiarizing. This is a very serious matter. If you still have questions, turn now to the longer discussion of plagiarism and paraphrasing in Chapter 4 (pp. 115–18).

Studying history provides you with a variety of skills. Reading effectively, taking class notes, and understanding what you need to know for an exam are three primary skills. These prepare the way for more advanced goals: clear writing, adequate research, and the presentation of a well-prepared thesis. The next chapters turn your attention to these additional skills.

3

How to Write History Assignments: The Importance of Writing Skills

WHY CLEAR WRITING IS IMPORTANT

The most important tasks in a history course often are the written assignments. You may be asked to write a short book review or a lengthy research paper. Whatever the writing assignment, you must take the time and care to make it your best work. Every instructor has had the experience of reading a poorly written paper from a student who did not take the trouble to do his or her best. If you hand in sloppy or thoughtless work, you will earn a poor grade and indicate that you are not aware of the importance of good writing. Writing is a task of great significance. You will be judged not only by your history instructor but also by everyone else who reads your words. Your writing skills tell the reader a lot about your ability to think clearly, whether you are writing a student paper or a proposal to your boss. As this chapter emphasizes, clear thinking is the source of clear writing. Two years after graduating, you may no longer remember the causes of World War I, but if you sharpened your writing skills in history assignments, you will have acquired a skill and an asset that will last a lifetime.

Clear writing accomplishes two important goals. First, it demonstrates that your thinking about a subject is logical. You cannot write clearly about something that you do not understand clearly. Second, it enables you to convey to your readers in a convincing way exactly what you want them to understand. Clear writing is persuasive.

THE COMPONENTS OF CLEAR WRITING

Think of your readers when you write. Tell your readers what you want them to know. Tell them this clearly, briefly, yet adequately.

Write Clear Sentences

Clear writing begins with clear sentences. A clear sentence leaves no doubt about the *subject* of the sentence. Consider the following examples. What are the subjects of these sentences?

> **EXAMPLES**   On September 1, 1939, Germany was strong and Poland was weak, and so it attacked.
> When Lindbergh landed his plane in Paris, everybody was very excited to see the first person to fly across the Atlantic Ocean by himself.

The subject of the first sentence, describing the outbreak of World War II, is unclear. The reader cannot tell if the subject is *Germany* or *Poland* and therefore cannot tell who attacked whom. In the second example, the subject, *Charles Lindbergh,* is removed from *fly,* the verb that describes his great feat; the reader must slog through an unclear and confusing sentence.

Now look at these revised sentences:

> **REVISED EXAMPLES**   On September 1, 1939, Germany attacked Poland.
> Charles Lindbergh made the first solo flight across the Atlantic Ocean.

The reader will know who (or what) the subject of the sentence is if that subject is placed as close as possible to the verb that describes what the subject is doing.

Do Not Clutter Sentences with Unnecessary Phrases

A phrase can add information. But phrases that are used indiscriminately can obscure a sentence's meaning.

> **EXAMPLE**   Lindbergh took thirty-three hours to make the first solo flight across the Atlantic Ocean.

In that example, the phrase added to the original clear sentence tells the reader how long the flight took. This added information does not affect the clarity of the sentence. But look what happens when several phrases are added.

> **EXAMPLE**   Although his plane was loaded down with extra fuel, Lindbergh was still able to get off the muddy runway in New Jersey despite very bad weather that rainy morning in 1927 and the fact that several other people had been

killed trying to become the first person to stay awake for the thirty-three hours it took to fly solo across the Atlantic Ocean.

In that sentence, Lindbergh's flight is surrounded by so many phrases that the main point of the sentence is lost. You should not attempt to pack into one sentence every fact you have learned. If some facts are not necessary, leave them out. If they are necessary, make room for them by creating additional sentences. For example, if the weight of the fuel and the muddy runway are important but the weather conditions and the failed attempts by others are not, writing two sentences instead of one makes the additional points and makes them clearly.

> **REVISED EXAMPLE**   Lindbergh's plane was so heavily loaded with fuel that it almost failed to get off the muddy runway in New Jersey. Once in the air, however, Lindbergh was able to stay awake for the thirty-three hours it took to fly across the Atlantic.

Avoid Using the Passive Voice

The subject and verb are the core of any sentence. In the passive voice, the verb indicates that the subject is *receiving* rather than *performing* the action described by the verb.

> **EXAMPLE**   A vaccination against smallpox was introduced by Edward Jenner in 1796.

A clear sentence usually uses the *active voice,* which shows the subject *initiating* rather than *receiving* an action (or thought).

> **REVISED EXAMPLE**   In 1796, Edward Jenner introduced a vaccination against smallpox.

At times, however, the passive voice is acceptable, such as when you desire to emphasize the *receiver* of an action or thought. So although it is preferable to avoid the passive voice, you may find occasions in your writing to use it.

Use the Past Tense

When writing about historical events, use the past tense. The only exception occurs when you are referring to a specific written document or to an object (such as an old building or a work of art) that still exists. Use the present tense to describe them.

> **EXAMPLE**   Thomas Jefferson *wrote* the draft of the Declaration of Independence.

Jefferson's action took place in the past, so it is correct to use the past tense when writing about the event. Because the Declaration of Independence is a written document that still exists, you should use the present tense to describe its content:

> **EXAMPLE** The Declaration of Independence *says* that "all men are created equal."

The effort to write clear sentences forces you to think about what your subject is doing and how many points about the subject's actions (or thoughts or feelings) you need to include. The result of this effort is a series of sentences that give the reader a clear understanding of what you have written.

Link Your Sentences

Another element of good writing is **continuity** — the *relationship* between words, sentences, and paragraphs as a writer moves from one point to the next. Every sentence and every paragraph should say something *new* and *significant* about the **theme** of the paper. And each sentence (or paragraph) should be connected to the sentences (or paragraphs) around it.

Sometimes a single sentence (or paragraph) cannot do both. Only a skilled writer can craft a sentence that advances the theme while also connecting with the surrounding sentences. Writers often separate these two tasks by means of a **linking sentence.** Such a sentence does not have to introduce new evidence about the theme. Its job is to tell the reader that the writer is shifting gears, moving from one point to a different but related one.

The middle sentence in the following example is a linking sentence.

> **EXAMPLE** Therefore, changes in printing technology made newspapers cheaper and more available. *But new technology alone does not explain rising readership.* As immigrants poured into the country from Europe, it was the new look of the newspaper, especially the use of large illustrations and photographs, that attracted these new "readers."

The linking sentence tells the reader that the paragraph (dealing with technological change) is to be followed by the introduction of a new point about the theme: how changes in the look of newspapers attracted new readers.

Linking sentences usually appear toward the end of a paragraph. Sometimes it is necessary to write an entire **linking paragraph** if the shift in focus is a major one or if you are moving from one section of a long essay to another (see pp. 61–62).

Write Clear and Coherent Paragraphs

A paragraph is a series of sentences about the same point. Each sentence in a paragraph needs to be clear, and each, as noted above, needs to add something to the theme or provide a link between sentences or paragraphs. Each paragraph also needs to be coherent — that is, to hold together. In a coherent paragraph, each sentence expands on the point being made. Look for places in your writing where you repeat yourself. When a sentence does not add anything significant to what you already said, leave it out. Also look for places where you begin to talk about a new and different point. It is there that you will need to begin a new paragraph.

Consider again the following sentences about Lindbergh's historic flight:

> **EXAMPLE**   Lindbergh's plane was so heavily loaded with fuel that it almost failed to get off the muddy runway in New Jersey. Once in the air, however, Lindbergh was able to stay awake for the thirty-three hours it took to fly across the Atlantic.

Both sentences describe the famous flight. That is why they belong in the same paragraph. But suppose you are finished writing about the flight and want to talk about the wild celebration in Paris after Lindbergh's landing. That information probably belongs in a new paragraph.

> **EXAMPLE**   Once Lindbergh was on the ground, his plane was mobbed by excited Parisians who lifted him onto their shoulders.

In the new paragraph you would describe the reception Lindbergh received in Paris, until you decided to make a new point about him. If you wanted to describe the celebration when Lindbergh returned to New York, you would not add that account to your paragraph about the events in Paris; you would start another new paragraph.

Of course, a paragraph can be short — three or four sentences — or long — seven or eight sentences. There is no rule about the correct number of sentences in a paragraph. The key to knowing when a paragraph is complete is to ask yourself: Am I moving on to a point different from the one I am making in this paragraph? If the answer is "yes," begin a new paragraph.

Link Your Paragraphs

Since each paragraph says something new, you must help the reader to see the *connection* between paragraphs. Disconnected paragraphs (like disconnected sentences) can leave the reader confused about what is coming next and why.

> **EXAMPLE**   Once in the air, however, he was able to stay awake for the thirty-three hours it took to fly across the Atlantic.
>
> In 1926, Lindbergh flew mail from Chicago to St. Louis.

Note the disconnect between the end of the paragraph about the flight and the sentence that begins the new paragraph. Unless you say something in the new paragraph to explain why you are going back to the period before the famous flight, the reader will be confused and may think that you are too. If you have a good reason for going back in time in the new paragraph, make sure that the reader understands your reason.

REVISED EXAMPLE

Once in the air, however, he was able to stay awake for the thirty-three hours it took to fly across the Atlantic.

No one had expected the twenty-five-year-old Lindbergh to make it. Less than a year before the famous flight, he had been an inconspicuous pilot flying mail between Chicago and St. Louis.

By connecting your paragraphs, you let the reader understand why you are bringing up Lindbergh's earlier career. The addition of a linking sentence shows the reader why a new paragraph is necessary and what direction the writer is taking.

Guidelines for Clear Writing

- Be sure that each sentence clearly names its subject.
- Be sure that each sentence is clear about what the subject is doing (or saying, or feeling, etc.).
- If you have several points to make about the subject, split them up into separate sentences.
- Be sure that each sentence adds something to the thesis of the essay.
- Be sure that each sentence is connected logically to the sentences around it.
- Avoid the passive voice.
- Use the past tense when writing about past historical events. Use the present tense only when writing about documents or objects (buildings, artwork, etc.) that still exist.
- Be sure that each paragraph is clear about the point it is making.
- When you get to a new point, start a new paragraph.
- Prepare your reader for the transition from one paragraph to another with a phrase or sentence linking the two paragraphs. (The link can be placed at the end of one paragraph or at the beginning of the next.)
- Be sure that each paragraph is connected logically to the paragraphs around it.

BUILDING AN ESSAY

Clear and coherent paragraphs, held together by linking phrases or sentences, are the building blocks of essay writing. But clear and coherent paragraphs are just the foundation. To unify your points in an essay, your paper needs to have a beginning, a middle, and an end.

The Need for a Clear Beginning

The very first paragraph of an essay has a special task. In it, you should state briefly and clearly what you are going to write about. State your **theme** clearly, and tell the reader briefly what central point or points you intend to make about it. This central point is your **thesis.** Conclude your opening paragraph with a statement about why your thesis is important. Generally you can accomplish all of this in one paragraph. However, if your paper is long or if your thesis is complex, you might need more than one opening paragraph.

Here is an example of a single, well-constructed opening paragraph.

EXAMPLE OF GOOD OPENING PARAGRAPH

This paper will explore the early history of the native peoples of New Mexico. It will describe their way of life before the arrival of European explorers in the sixteenth century. The paper will focus in particular on the evidence that over a thousand years ago many tribes living in this area had developed complex communities. Although European conquest destroyed most of these communities, there are still more than a dozen of them in New Mexico today.

The theme of this paper is "the early history of the native peoples of New Mexico." The thesis is that for a very long time these people have had complex communities. The opening paragraph accomplishes several important tasks:

- The first sentence announces the theme.
- The second and third sentences tell the reader the thesis that the paper will focus on.
- The final sentence prepares the reader for the **conclusion** of the paper and makes clear why the theme is worthy of study.

Now read another opening paragraph to the same paper and see if you can spot the problems in it.

EXAMPLE OF POOR OPENING PARAGRAPH

European conquerors took away the native peoples' way of life in New Mexico. Some of their villages were caves cut into hillsides; others were made of hardened clay with many rooms. They were happy for one thousand years, but all this came to an end. This paper will show you how they lived.

Instead of announcing the theme, the first sentence of this paragraph starts with the paper's conclusion. The reader does not know that the paper is about the way of life of the native peoples of New Mexico. The writer then jumps ahead and includes specific points about the kinds of houses in which they lived. The reader is left to guess that these dwellings are evidence of a complex civilization. All the reader is told about the ancient, native way of life is that the native peoples were "happy." The reader is given no idea of why the theme is important or how it will be presented. The writer's only way of telling the reader what the core of the paper will be about is vague: it will "show you how they lived." The writer should have included in the opening paragraph a thesis statement — in this instance saying that the native peoples of New Mexico had an ancient and complex way of life. The poor organization of the introductory paragraph leaves the reader uncertain of both the theme and the thesis.

Remember, your opening paragraph summarizes your thesis. If you change the organization or conclusions of your paper in an important way, be sure to rewrite the opening paragraph to reflect that change.

Creating a Writing Outline

Before you begin the actual writing of your paper, make a **writing outline** of the points that you intend to discuss. Your instructor may provide this outline, or you may have to create it yourself. This outline should reflect your research for the essay. You may have read one article or five articles, one book or five books. You may also have watched videos or researched on the **World Wide Web.** The information in those materials will provide the main points of your outline. Tailor your outline not only to your theme and thesis but also to the assigned length of your paper. If you include too many points in your outline, you will never fit them all in your paper. If you include too few, your paper will be short and probably weak.

Be aware that you may need to revise your outline during the research process. You may discover the need to add new points to your outline or to discard old ones. (For more on research and the outlining of papers, see Chapters 4 and 5.)

SAMPLE WRITING OUTLINE FOR A SHORT PAPER

Pueblo Culture:
The Ancient Roots of Modern New Mexico
1. The arrival of ancient peoples
2. Their way of life
   a. Architecture
   b. Agriculture
   c. Art
3. The Spanish conquest
4. Becoming part of Mexico
5. Becoming part of the United States
6. Pueblo villages today

(For examples of longer outlines, see pp. 120–24 and 162–63.)

The Importance of Continuity

Just as important as clarity is **continuity.** Each paragraph should be connected to the paragraphs before and after it by **linking sentences.** Pay attention to the continuity of your essay. As you write each paragraph, ask yourself: "Does this paragraph follow from the preceding one?" "Does it add something significant to the theme of the paper?" "Do it and the following paragraphs move toward the thesis I announced in my opening paragraph?" Every time you begin a new paragraph, ask those questions. If you cannot see how the new paragraph connects with the one before it or if the content of the paragraph doesn't add anything to the theme, rewrite the paragraph so that it accomplishes these goals.

Writing a Conclusion

How do you know when to end your paper? If your instructor gives you a specific length, obviously you need to wrap up the paper once it reaches the limit allowed. But how do you know when you have written enough? You are ready to conclude your paper when you have covered all of the points in your *revised* writing outline.

How much space should you give to your conclusion? The overall length of your paper influences the length of your conclusion. For a short essay of five to seven pages, one or two concluding paragraphs are usually sufficient. A long essay of ten to twenty pages probably will require a concluding page. Some very long papers may need a concluding section of several pages.

What should your conclusion say? Your conclusion should summarize the main points of your essay. Take another look at your opening paragraphs. What did you tell the reader you intended to do? By the time you reach the concluding part of your paper, this job should have been accomplished. (If your paper has not yet accomplished this, you must ensure that your revision does.) Your conclusion is also a place to remind the reader of the significance of what he or she has read. Finally, the conclusion is the place where you can state your own opinion (unless your instructor has told you to be as objective as possible). As with your opening paragraph, it is often necessary to rewrite your conclusion after any significant revision of the body of your paper.

Revising Your Paper

The Rough Draft. Even a skilled writer cannot produce a finished product from scratch. Good writing, in addition to following the guidelines in this chapter, is the product of revision. Think of writing as a multistage process. Whether you are sitting down to write a sentence, a paragraph, or an entire essay, what you are really doing is writing a **rough draft.** The goal of this rough draft is to present the most important information you have gathered (or been given) on the subject. Don't worry about writing style too much at this stage.

Organize your rough draft according to your writing outline. Keep in mind, though, that the writing process is not a rigid process. If your thoughts on your theme have changed, you may need to revise your writing outline before starting to write.

The Revised Draft.   Next comes the crucial task of refining your thoughts and words to produce the revised draft. Remember, the longer the paper is, the more important the jobs of organization and revision are. To **revise** your paper, go over each page carefully, paragraph by paragraph, making sure that each conforms to the writing guidelines in this chapter. As you read each sentence and paragraph, ask yourself the following questions:

Is this sentence (paragraph) clear?
Have I put too many phrases in my sentences?
Have I made more than one main point in my paragraphs?
Does each of my sentences and paragraphs add something significant to my theme?
Is each sentence (and paragraph) connected to the sentences (and paragraphs) around it?
Do I need a linking sentence to make a transition clear?
Will my intended audience be able to follow what I am saying?

Rework each sentence and paragraph until it meets each of those tests. Then step away from your paper for a time (an hour, a day, or several days) to give yourself a fresh view of it when you return. For this final revision, pay special attention to organization on a broad scale. Ask yourself the following questions:

Does the introductory paragraph give an overall sense of the paper?
Does the introductory paragraph state my thesis clearly?
Do the paragraphs include all of the important information?
Does each paragraph make its contribution to advancing the topic and supporting the thesis?
Does the conclusion effectively summarize the main points I have made about my thesis?

If your revised draft meets those requirements, you are done writing. If there are still problems with clarity or continuity, go through your paper again carefully to find out what your paper lacks and to revise the weak sections. (For instructions on writing and revising long research papers, see Chapter 5.)

Proofreading Your Paper

The last step in preparing a writing assignment is **proofreading** the complete paper. Read your paper carefully, looking for misspellings, missing punctuation marks, typos, and layout issues (that is, how the text looks on the page). Read slowly to catch as many small errors as you can. It may be helpful to read the paper out loud. If you can, have a friend read the paper also. Your reader may spot something you missed. Even more important, your peer reviewer can tell you if something in your paper is confusing or not easily understood (for more on peer reviewing, see pp. 45–46).

Spell-checkers are a terrific help in avoiding typos and incorrect spellings, and you should always make use of them before turning in a paper. However, don't expect the spell-checker to catch every misspelled word. The spell-checker flags any word that it does not recognize, including correctly spelled words not in its electronic dictionary. It also will not catch misspelled words that it reads as other words. For example, if you write "him" when you mean to write "his," or "no" for "know," the spell-checker will not read it as a mistake. You must catch these kinds of errors yourself when you proofread your paper.

Grammar-checkers are even less reliable. When you use a grammar-checker, consider its advice as a suggestion for revision. If the grammar-checker questions the way you have said something, consider the advice given before deciding to make any changes to your original sentence, phrase, or word. Keep in mind that you, and not your computer, are the author of your paper.

You are done! It may have taken you a lot longer than you had expected. Some of the work may have been difficult and some tedious. For your effort, you should feel good about yourself even before you learn your grade. You have produced your best work. And with each paper to come, your "best" will get even better.

PREPARING SPECIFIC WRITING ASSIGNMENTS

Instructors give many kinds of writing assignments: among them are book reviews, papers that analyze historical arguments, and research papers. These papers range in length from a few pages to ten or twenty. This section helps you prepare some of the different kinds of writing assignments that you are likely to encounter in your history courses.

Writing Book Reviews

A **book review** is not usually a summary. Unless your instructor asks you to summarize a book's contents, devote most of your review to *analyzing* its contents. Determine its theme; then describe how the theme is presented and how well it is defended. Were you persuaded by the author's arguments? If doing so is part of the assignment, compare the book to other course materials. Be sure that your review makes it clear that you read and understood the book — or article, document, excerpt, or essay — and always provide the kind of analysis asked of you.

The following is an example of a book review of *Libraries through the Ages* by Fred Lerner (Continuum, 1999).

Sample Book Review

Jane Q. Student

History 100

February 14, 2006

Book Review of

Fred Lerner, *Libraries through the Ages* (Continuum, 1999)

The thesis of this history of libraries around the world over the last 2,000 years is that libraries now have a greater impact on society than ever before and that the advent of the computer age is not likely to reverse that development. In the view of the author, libraries' current roles of preserving and dispensing information and of guiding users to what they need will sustain the modern public library in the information age. To support his thesis, Lerner examines the long evolution of libraries from places that trained a governing elite to places that serve the needs of a wide range of patrons. The author holds degrees in history and in library science and is also the author of *The Story of Libraries*.

Lerner gives a clear and concise history of the collecting and use of books that followed the invention of writing by the Sumerians some 5,000 years ago. He begins with the earliest writing—characters that were pressed into clay tablets that later hardened. He then describes Egyptian papyrus rolls (rolls of paper made from the stems of papyrus plants) that were stored in jars and Jewish holy books that were written on animal skins.

The first true library was in the Greek colony of Alexandria (in Egypt). Here, possibly for the first time, the effort was made to bring together large numbers of manuscripts, organize them by subject, and make them available to scholars. Service to an elite of rulers, administrators, and scholars remained the role of the library until the nineteenth century.

Lerner then looks at libraries in the Roman Empire and in the early Christian Church, when books were no longer rolls but individual, bound pages placed between hard covers. In medieval Europe, monasteries played a vital role in the preservation and duplication of manuscripts (handwritten books). This was the era of the private library owned by kings, aristocrats, bishops, and scholars.

Lerner turns next to an examination of the history of books and libraries in ancient China and India. In China, writing goes back more than 3,000 years (p. 40), and books were under the control of the state. The Chinese invented the modern form of paper, and Chinese scholars wrote down and then copied the classic works that sustained the role of the emperor. In the tenth century, the Chinese developed woodblock printing, making copying much easier. In India, Buddhist monasteries collected manuscripts that were usually written on palm leaves. Indian books were very unusual; according to Lerner, "The pages were pierced in the center and held together with string, then covered with wooden boards, which were often lacquered and brightly painted" (pp. 47–48).

A very important center of learning and writing, libraries developed in the Islamic world after the seventh century. By the year A.D. 1000, Muslim libraries had spread all the way from Spain to India. Many books were religious texts; others dealt with medicine, astronomy, geometry, and philosophy. Islamic emphasis on the words of God (in the Koran) led to rising literacy, and bookshops arose in nearly every major Arab city. Great Islamic libraries were erected. The largest, at the University of Córdoba in Spain, had 400,000 volumes (p. 60). Between the twelfth and fifteenth centuries, however, various invaders destroyed the great Islamic libraries.

In Europe, the copying of books was tremendously accelerated when, in the 1450s, Johannes Gutenberg used a printing press to mass-produce them. A printed book was not only easier to make than a manuscript but also more portable and affordable, and its contents were uniform, enabling scholars to compare and discuss texts.

At the Vatican, the Catholic Church built a very large library that still exists. Elsewhere in Europe, university libraries were established—although in this period, they served only professors and not students (p. 72).

In the early nineteenth century, a library was built in Washington, D.C., for the members of Congress. This is now the enormous Library of Congress. Large libraries were established in major U.S. cities and universities in the nineteenth century, and they were open many days a week and had large reading rooms for the public.

As literacy spread in the United States and Europe, public libraries were erected in cities and towns. At first, the libraries' stacks of books were closed, and patrons had to ask a librarian to get a specific book. By the mid-twentieth century, however, the stacks were open; readers could choose their own books and take them to a checkout librarian.

By the 1930s, public libraries were open to all, and each public school had its own library. The idea of serving the community of readers became firmly established as the library's primary role. This function went well beyond helping someone find a particular book. The "reference collection" of the average library held many hundreds of reference books. These atlases, encyclopedias, dictionaries, and other works held a great deal of factual information that readers needed to live in a complex, industrial society. Another part of the reference collection—bibliographies—helped readers find books and articles on different topics. The reference librarian assisted the reader in using all of these works effectively. Another responsibility of the reference librarian was to assist the patron in navigating the huge card catalog, which had at least one card for *every* item in the library. Public and school libraries had established themselves as places where access to all kinds of information and knowledge was provided.

Because this new service role for libraries was well established before the age of digital technology, Lerner feels that libraries will not become museums of old knowledge. Instead, their reference and service function will expand to include access to digital information. Just as we once needed the assistance of reference librarians to find everything from the meaning of a word to the location of a book, now we need them to guide us through the maze of resources available via the Internet.

Reviews can vary widely in content to accommodate the different kinds of work they discuss. Still, a good review, like this one, includes specific elements. The book under review here is identified at the very beginning. Then the author's **thesis** (about the growing impact of libraries on society) is made clear, and the overall scope of the work (the 2,000-year development of the public role of the library) is described. The author's qualifications are also mentioned in the introduction. The review then describes the stages in the development of writing, books, and libraries and the many cultures that have contributed to the process. All of these historical developments are part of the author's **evidence** for his thesis. The student reviewer does not assess the quality of the evidence, indicating that she has not become familiar enough with the subject to compare this work with others. However, if the course for which she wrote the review included other information on the history of libraries or on their impact on society, she probably would be expected to make such a comparison. For this same reason, the student closes with a summary of the book's conclusions rather than with her own assessment.

If your instructor asks for a particular kind of review, you should follow those directions. You might be asked to include some of the evidence that argues against the theme and to assess the author's ability to present that evidence fairly and respond to it effectively. Or you might be asked to comment on the author's personal or academic background and reasons for writing the book. This last point should certainly be included if there is significant debate among historians about the thesis of the book or if the book's preface or introduction refers to such disagreements. With a book of this kind, your instructor may ask you to comment on the debate and perhaps also ask you how the book affects your views on the subject.

It is usually unwise to emphasize your personal opinion in a review unless your instructor asks you to do so. If you are asked to express it, don't write simply, "I liked the way the author defended women's rights." Instead say, "I was impressed by the author's use of many concrete examples of actions by women to dramatize their demand for the right to vote. The fact that one day they chained themselves to the White House fence made clear how strongly they felt about their cause." Show that your opinion is the result of serious thought about the arguments made in the book.

If your assignment is a review that is longer than a few pages, you might want to quote a sentence or phrase from the book to support a point you are making. But don't use too many quotations. Your review should be written in your own words rather than those of the author.

Guidelines for Writing a Book Review

- At the top of the first page, put the name of the author, the title of the work, the publisher's name, and the date of publication.
- State the author's theme and thesis.
- Describe the evidence presented to support the thesis.
- If possible, assess the arguments and evidence used. (Are they clear or unclear, strong or weak, convincing or unconvincing?)
- If appropriate, describe the author's background and reason for writing the book.
- If required, compare the work to related course materials. (Does it agree or disagree? Does it add a new perspective?)
- If expected, close with your own assessment of the book's assumptions, arguments, and conclusions.

Writing Comparative Book Reviews

Not all review assignments are concerned with only one source. A comparative book review is more difficult than a review of only one book, because you must also be able to compare the content. You need to discover what the books have in common (consider theme, thesis, style, approaches to the subject, conclusions) and where they differ. The key to success in an essay of this type is to come up with a series of points of similarity or dissimilarity (or some of each) and to focus your essay on them. Don't spend too much time discussing each book separately. Build your essay around the connections between books. That is the purpose of a comparative book review.

Comparing Essays or Articles

If your assignment is to compare essays or articles rather than books, you probably will be expected to treat them in detail. The goals of this kind of assignment are the same as those for comparing books. What are the similarities or differences in the arguments presented? How do the authors make their points? What conclusions do they draw? Again, focus on comparing the works. Don't get bogged down with long descriptions of each one.

Comparing Primary Documents

Comparing documents is a difficult task, but many instructors use this kind of assignment to judge the depth of your knowledge and your interpretive ability. **Primary documents** provide the most direct contact we have with the past, and they are filled with evidence about life in times and places often very different from our own (for more on primary documents, see Chapter 1, pp. 10–16). To understand them, we must know a good deal about the times and places they describe and, if possible, about the people who created them.

Consider the following assignment: You are given access to a series of letters written by U.S. soldiers fighting in Vietnam. Some of the letters talk about the heat and exhaustion of fighting in dense jungles or rice paddies. Some express deep hostility toward the enemy, but others contain no references to the enemy at all. Some letters are filled with questions about what is going on in the soldiers' families and hometowns and hardly even mention the war. The most surprising discovery is that a few letters mention the desire to be wounded (but not seriously) so that the letter writers can be sent home. To make sense of these letters, you need to know a lot about the ground war in Vietnam and the state of mind of the ground troops who fought there. The more you know about the historical event depicted in any set of primary documents, the more they will reveal to you.

Now you are given another group of Vietnam War letters. Unlike the first group written by front-line foot soldiers, these are from bomber pilots. Their war seems different. The pilots' letters don't complain about difficult living conditions. In fact, their lives on air bases or aircraft carriers seem fairly comfortable. They say that they rarely see their targets because they fly so high. Like some of the foot soldiers, the pilots do not talk about the enemy. But unlike some of the ground soldiers, none mentions wanting to get out of the war. In fact, the pilots' morale seems high.

If you are asked to compare the letters from these two groups of soldiers, you will be expected not only to notice the different things they write about but also to have some idea of *why* their letters are different. In this case, an understanding of the difference between the ground war and the air war and between the different types of people who fought in each is needed. Interpreting and comparing primary documents requires you to go beneath their surface. You need to understand the historical **context,** or historical environment, that gave rise to them. As a result of the growing availability of written and nonwritten primary sources on the **World Wide Web,** these kinds of assignments are becoming more common.

Writing Short Essays

Writing a short essay requires you to do some research and analysis. You are assigned, or you may be expected to find on your own, the materials you need to prepare your essay. Many of the skills you need are similar to those you will use in researching and writing a lengthy research paper of the kind described in Chapters 4 and 5.

You might be asked to take a position in a historical controversy and to defend your position with historical evidence. You might be asked to compare a group of readings or primary documents and draw conclusions about the differences among them. Perhaps you will be asked to write about your own life experience or that of an older relative and connect the story to important historical events. You might be asked to keep a journal in which you will write regularly about your response to ideas and subjects that arise in class discussion.

Some interpretive essays are similar to **essay exams.** Your instructor gives you a list of **topics** to choose from. For example, in a course on the history of journalism, you are asked to write an essay that includes a variety of printed sources about the relationship between rising literacy and the growth of newspaper circulation in the United States during the nineteenth century. If you study your sources closely, you will discover that your essay cannot take the easy route: the thesis that newspaper circulation increased because more people could read. If things were that simple, your instructor would not have chosen the topic for this kind of assignment.

As you dig into your research, you come across evidence that knowing how to read doesn't automatically give a person the desire (or the money) to read a newspaper. You also learn from your sources that by the late nineteenth century, illustrations took up a large part of a newspaper page. That meant that even people who knew very few words of English might still enjoy "reading" a paper. The relationship between literacy and readership is not a simple one — few things in history are. Perhaps you will conclude from your research that rising literacy and rising newspaper circulation reinforced one another, that neither was the simple cause of the other.

How do you prepare for and execute an assignment like this one? Here is some advice for preparing a short essay.

Documenting Your Essay. Some assignments of this type require you to document (identify the sources of) the major facts and conclusions of your essay. Chapter 5 (pp. 133–45) presents examples of **citations** to various kinds of sources (books, magazine articles, newspapers, interviews, videos, etc.) You usually inform the reader about your sources in **footnotes** (at the bottom of the page) or **endnotes** (at the end of the essay). You may also need a **bibliography,** an alphabetical list of all the sources you used or consulted. The bibliography is placed at the end of your paper. See Chapter 5 (pp. 146–58) for advice on constructing a bibliography.

Organizing and Writing Your Essay.   If you choose your own topic for your essay, choose carefully. Ask your instructor if your choice is appropriate for the assignment and if it is clearly formulated. Make sure you have all the research materials you need to document your essay. Take careful notes from your research materials (see Chapter 4, pp. 108–10, on taking notes from your sources).

Then write a **rough draft.** Organize your essay so that it clearly introduces your theme. Then add paragraphs that pursue your theme, including all of the evidence you have gathered from your research to support that theme, utilizing clear, connected sentences that form clear and coherent paragraphs. Finally, write your conclusion, summarizing the main point or points you want to make. Briefly restate your theme, summarizing the most important evidence presented to support it. Proofread the essay for errors of grammar and spelling — even after you run the spell-checker.

Guidelines for Writing Short Essays

- Choose a topic carefully. If you have questions about your choice, speak to your instructor.
- Choose your research materials carefully so that they flesh out your theme. (If you are using primary sources, be sure you understand their context.)
- Organize your paper by placing research notes in the right order.
- Introduce your essay with a clear statement of your theme.
- Link sentences and paragraphs so that each new point follows clearly from the one before it. This is your rough draft.
- Read and revise your rough draft. Look for clarity, continuity, and evidence for your theme.
- Write a conclusion — a brief restatement of your theme and a summary of the most important evidence presented to support it.
- If the assignment requires them, include footnotes or endnotes and a bibliography.
- Proofread your revised draft, looking for grammar and spelling mistakes.
- Produce the final draft neatly, following all of the instructions given by your instructor.

A NOTE ON PLAGIARISM:
A SERIOUS OFFENSE

Whenever you prepare a written assignment while working from notes you have taken from books or other course materials, you must be careful how you use those notes. Otherwise, you run the risk of including in your paper sentences or extended phrases that you copied word for word from your sources. Even if you do this copying accidentally, you are guilty of **plagiarism.** Unless the phrases or sentences written by other authors are placed in quotation marks and their sources are identified in a **footnote** or **endnote,** you have committed a very serious breach of academic honesty. Plagiarism can lead to failing a course and even to suspension. Be sure to read the sections on avoiding plagiarism and on the art of paraphrasing in Chapter 4 (pp. 115–18).

CHAPTER

4

How to Research
a History Topic

In introductory history courses, you may be asked to do historical research. In advanced courses, you certainly will be asked to write **research papers.** Whether you are preparing a short essay, a book review, a long class presentation, or a term paper, you will need to know how to gather all the necessary materials, how to analyze your information, and how to organize the information into research notes.

The assignment to write a research paper requires you to gather your own sources of information and draw your own conclusions. It is one of the most creative tasks you will do as a history student; the paper you write is uniquely your own. Because a lot of independent work is involved, research is often the most challenging history assignment. The skills you gain from this kind of project (gathering, evaluating, and organizing **evidence**) are invaluable. Any professional or business career that you later pursue will call for one or more of these skills. In years to come, you may not remember the name of the secret research program that produced the atomic bomb during World War II (the Manhattan Project), about which you wrote a paper. But while you were engaged in the research process that produced the paper, you were strengthening important skills.

This chapter surveys sources of historical information and explains how to use these sources most profitably. It will help you to decide on a **topic,** narrow the topic to a **theme,** and then refine the theme into a **thesis.** You will be assisted in finding your way through your school library, which should serve as the home base for your research. You will learn how to evaluate sources so that you understand their content. This ability will ensure that you use college-level sources and that you know what each author is saying so that you can determine a source's relevance (if any) to your theme. You will learn how to use sources to support your thesis. Finally, you will learn how to record and organize relevant information so that you can easily find it when you begin to write your paper.

BEGINNING THE RESEARCH PROCESS

Choosing a Topic

Some instructors assign a topic — a broad subject area — for research, but most set out a range of possible topics and leave the choice to you. Choose your topic carefully. You will become bored if you have to spend weeks searching out and reading information about a subject that does not interest you. Select a topic that fits the course you are taking and about which you are genuinely curious. No matter what subject, person, or event you are interested in, it has a history. Every subject can be studied backward in time because every event was caused by events that preceded it. A history research project can be created out of almost anything. Perhaps in the neighborhood where you grew up there was a very old building and you always wondered when it was built and what it was used for. Finding out what the neighborhood was like when that building was new can be an exciting search.

An ideal topic is not only one about which you are curious but one about which you already know something. Perhaps you read a book about Socrates and want to know more about why he was condemned to death. Perhaps you saw a movie about the Great Depression and want to know what it was like to live through it. Instructors are eager to help students who show genuine interest in a topic. Your instructor can assist you in selecting a topic related to your interests that also suits the particular course you are taking.

Moving from a Topic to a Theme

A theme is more narrow than a topic. A topic is the general subject — for example, the influence of Islam on the kingdom of Mali; or the philosophy of Martin Luther King Jr. A theme is some important aspect of the topic that you wish to investigate. For a paper on King's philosophy, you may want to show that his "I Have a Dream" speech at the Lincoln Memorial in 1963 expresses several elements of his religious beliefs. In that case, your theme would be the connection between the speech and King's religious development. This connection would direct your research and writing. Without a theme, you will not have a clear idea of which sources of information to investigate, what notes to take from your sources, or how to organize your paper.

Narrowing a broad topic down to a theme is not always easy. The key is to find an aspect of the topic that falls within the scope of your course and will serve to orient your research effort. The theme also needs to fit the sources available to you and be one that you can satisfactorily research in the time available to complete the assignment.

The process of narrowing can produce both workable and unwieldy themes. A topic such as the Spanish conquest of the Aztec Empire might be narrowed to the theme "the correspondence of Hernán Cortés and King Ferdinand." For this theme to be workable, you would need access to copies of letters in which Cortés discussed the conquest of the Aztecs with the king. If this correspondence was not available in your library or on the **World Wide Web,** you would lack a crucial piece of the research material needed to explore this theme. In contrast, the theme "the factors that enabled the Spanish to defeat the Aztecs" would be workable because material on this subject is not difficult to find.

Even if resources are available, make sure that your theme is not overly broad. For a topic such as European exploration of Africa, you might come up with the theme "exploration of the Congo River." However, dozens of such explorations were made over many years, so this would not be a workable theme. If you began to research "exploration of the Congo River," you would soon be overwhelmed by the vast quantity of sources available, and you would quickly see that you have neither the time nor the space in your paper to do them justice. Additional narrowing of the theme would be necessary.

Narrowing Your Theme

Formulating a theme that is narrow enough yet not too narrow is tricky. To narrow a theme, it is often useful to pose some questions about the original topic. If your topic is Native Americans of the western United States, ask yourself a question you would like to know the answer to. Maybe some aspect of Native American life, such as the practices of medicine men or the conflict between a particular tribe and European settlers, has aroused your curiosity. You might ask yourself: "What did medicine men believe?" or "How did the Indians defend their lands?" These questions might yield themes such as "the practice of magic among the Cheyenne" or "efforts of the Nez Perce to protect their native lands in Oregon." If your topic is Canadian frontier communities in the nineteenth century, ask yourself what specific things you would like to know about them. Was the coming of the railroad of great importance to them? This question might lead you to the theme "the Canadian Pacific Railroad comes to Winnipeg, Manitoba."

Composing questions usually will help you arrive at and then narrow a theme. Be careful, however, that your questions are not too broad ("Why did the Roman Empire fall?"), too narrow ("Who was the first person to sign the Declaration of Independence?"), or too unimportant ("Why are Ping-Pong tables green?").

If you know very little about your topic, you will need to conduct preliminary research before you attempt to create and then narrow a theme. If your topic is the Mexican Revolution of 1910, check a brief history of the subject in a good **historical dictionary** or an **historical encyclopedia** (for example, *Encyclopaedia Britannica* or the *Encyclopedia of Latin America*). The description of the Mexican Revolution in these works will likely mention its principal leaders — Francisco Madero, Pancho Villa, Emiliano Zapata, and Venustiano Carranza. Perhaps your interest will then be triggered by the recollection of stories concerning Villa's daring raid on the U.S. border town of Columbus, New Mexico, in 1916 and how a U.S. Army force under General John Pershing marched into Mexico to capture Villa — but never did. Or perhaps you have seen the Hollywood movie *Viva Zapata,* which tells the story (not very accurately) of the peasant leader Emiliano Zapata and his fight to preserve the lands of the Indian villages in his native state of Morelos. If you have ever seen photographs of Zapata, you know his piercing eyes and look of determination.

If your interest in the Mexican Revolution is now focusing on Villa or Zapata, you should next turn to a biographical dictionary. Here you will discover that Villa's real name was Doroteo Arango and that he was a cattle thief as well as a brilliant military commander. Zapata, you will learn, led a peasant guerrilla army whose aim was to recapture village land seized by the owners of expanding sugar plantations. To flesh out a paper on Villa's military career or Zapata's land reform program (some elements of which Mexican peasants are still struggling to achieve today), turn to the list of specialized resources in Latin American and Caribbean history in Appendix A (pp. 220–21), to the reference section of your library, or to an online reference source such as Encyclopaedia Britannica online. These tools will lead you to individual historical works on the Mexican Revolution, and from the book and article titles (and any descriptions of their content) you will be able to identify works that may contain information on the theme you are considering.

Moving from a Theme to a Thesis

Your thesis is the central point or argument that you intend to make about your theme. Crafting a thesis is the last step in the narrowing process that takes you from a broad general topic to a narrow theme and finally to a specific thesis. Your thesis is not a description of your theme; it is a statement of the central argument or claim you intend to make about your theme. It should be based on your analysis of the sources you consulted.

Let's return to the topic about the Mexican Revolution of 1910. Your research has led you to consider the theme "the role of Emiliano Zapata in the Mexican Revolution of 1910." After further research, you narrow the theme to "the land reform program of Emiliano Zapata in the Mexican Revolution." The next step is to ask yourself a question about your narrowed theme — for example, "Was Zapata's land program an important element in the

Mexican Revolution?" A possible answer (suggested by more research) might be, "Zapata's land reform program was a central element in the Mexican Revolution." You have now arrived at a thesis.

It is usually not necessary to finalize a thesis until you complete your research. Until then, what you have is a tentative or working thesis. Just as you need to have a good background knowledge of your topic in order to create your theme, so you must wait until you have conducted some research on your theme before you can finally decide which particular question about your theme will serve as the basis of your thesis. (See "Preparing to Write: Why Your Paper Needs a Thesis" in Chapter 5, pp. 119–20.)

Making an Argument in Support of Your Thesis

The thesis is the central point or argument that you intend to make about your theme. In a courtroom, the district attorney argues the prosecution's case. He or she lays out evidence in order to convince the jury that the defendant is guilty. In your paper, you too will be arguing a case — to your readers. To argue that Zapata's land reform program was a central element in the Mexican Revolution, you need to gather and organize evidence that supports this thesis. Your research will most likely uncover the important fact that Zapata's land reform program attracted thousands of Mexican peasants whose land had been taken from them. You can use this fact to help you construct a strong **argument** in support of your thesis. Your research will turn up **primary sources** and **secondary sources** that you can use as evidence to support your thesis. Gathering that evidence is discussed in the "Conducting Research" section of this chapter (pp. 84–100).

As you conduct research, be careful not to get so carried away in looking for support for your argument that you ignore evidence at odds with your thesis. This kind of evidence is sometimes referred to as **counterevidence.** If your research turns up evidence that goes against your thesis, you will have to acknowledge this evidence when you write your paper. For example, if you come across a book or journal article whose argument is that Zapata's program was not an important element of the revolution, you will need to tell your reader that some authors disagree with your thesis. If your research uncovers a lot of counterevidence, your thesis is weak and you will have to change it.

Creating a Preliminary Research Plan

You will need to spend many weeks gathering evidence to formulate and strongly support your thesis. Because your search for this evidence needs to be organized, you should create a **research plan** at the outset. You would begin your research on the topic of the Mexican Revolution of 1910 by locating general information that would help you to narrow this topic to a theme such as land reform. You would then seek out more specific information in order to formulate a tentative thesis about the importance of Zapata's land reform program.

The following research plan indicates the kinds of tasks you need to carry out at different stages of your research. It includes an estimate (shown in italics) of the time needed to complete each task.

SAMPLE RESEARCH PLAN

Task #1: [Background] Gain a general knowledge of the Mexican Revolution from a good historical encyclopedia, textbook, or Web site. *(Approximately 2–3 hours in the course of 1 day.)*

Task #2: [Background] Gain a general idea about land reform before the revolution. An historical encyclopedia or a general history of Mexico in the nineteenth century. *(Approximately 2–3 hours in the course of 1 day.)*

Task #3: [Information about Zapata] Life in Ananecquilco, Morelos (village and state where Zapata grew up). A biography of Zapata and a book or articles examining changes in village life in Morelos in the decades before 1910. *(Approximately 6–9 hours over 3 days.)*

Task #4: [Specific information about land reform efforts in Ananecquilco] Books, articles, and documents (including online resources) about how the villagers lost their lands before 1910. *(Approximately 6–9 hours over 3 days.)*

Task #5: [Zapata's role in the effort to regain village lands] Sources that examine Zapata's early career as a village leader. *(Approximately 6–9 hours over 3 days.)*

Task #6: [The period of the revolution, 1910–1920] Sources examining the role of Zapata and his followers in the revolution. *(Approximately 8–12 hours over 4 days.)*

Task #7: [Specific land reform programs] Primary sources (perhaps in document archives on the Web) that contain copies of actual proposals made by Zapata. *(Approximately 4–6 hours over 2 days.)*

Task #8: [The fate of the programs] Read about the final years of the revolution and of the fate of Zapata (assassinated in 1919). *(Approximately 4–6 hours over 2 days.)*

Not all research plans can be this specific. A certain amount of exploring for sources may be necessary before you begin to prepare such a plan, and your actual research is likely to move back and forth between the various tasks on any given day in the library. In the early stages of research you may become aware that there is not enough information on your proposed theme and that it has to be changed. A thesis that seems promising at an early stage of research is likely to need revision. It may take you longer than you expect to find an important source or to discover that one that seemed promising actually deals with an area outside of your theme.

Time frames such as the ones in the sample plan can only be estimates. Deadlines will vary depending on the kind of project your instructor has assigned. In addition, keep in mind that the sample plan covers only the time needed for research and for note taking. You will need additional time to organize your notes, prepare a **writing outline,** and draft and revise your paper.

The information you find in the library will not be neatly divided into the tasks you have laid out. The reason for coming up with a preliminary research plan is to give yourself a sense of direction, from which you will benefit even if the actual process turns out to be messier than you anticipate. If you haven't thought about what kinds of sources to look for first, which to read first, and which to read later, you may try to take notes on specific land reform proposals before you even know who Zapata was or how long the Mexican Revolution lasted. Even if you cannot always stick to your research plan, just listing the tasks and having the plan in mind will help you as you do your research.

Don't begin serious research until you have a clear idea of what you will be looking for. You may change your theme and your thesis after some background reading, and you can always adjust your schedule. It is always better to have a research plan that you change than to have no plan at all.

Creating a Research Bibliography

A **research bibliography** is a list of all the sources you discover in the early stages of your research. It is a record of all the sources that you might use in your research. It is not necessary to have read them all at this point, but you should look at them closely enough to determine that they (1) are related to your theme, (2) are sources normally used in scholarly research, (3) are likely to be available to you, and (4) are sufficient in number to satisfy your assignment. As you begin to discover useful research materials, copy down exactly and fully all of the information about them — such as the author, title, publisher, and date of publication of a book. These are the sources that will help you understand your theme and that you will use to support your thesis. The information you record will enable you to document these sources in your paper. When you examine these sources more fully, you will be able to determine which of them should be included in your paper. Those are the works from which you should take careful notes. (See "How to Organize Your Notes," pp. 110–15.)

You will find useful research materials in a variety of places. Some may be in print form on the shelves of your library; others may be in electronic form in **databases** to which your library subscribes or in history-oriented **Web sites.** To locate useful sources, you need to know how to conduct research in your library and on the Web.

CONDUCTING RESEARCH

Begin your research efforts in the school library. No other place brings together all of the connections between your research project and the sources you will need to carry it out. Become familiar with the layout of the library. Take a formal tour of its resources or ask a librarian to point them out to you. Find out, for example, where the **library stacks** are — the shelves where bound books and journals (and audio and video materials) are stored. You also should be able to find areas such as the section where **reference books** (**historical encyclopedias, dictionaries, atlases,** etc.) are shelved, the microprint section (**microfilms** and **microfiche**), and any "special collections" that are in the library.

Don't make the mistake of thinking that the immense amount of information available on the **World Wide Web** will allow you to bypass the library and to set out on a "surfing" expedition. In many cases, access to the most useful research material on the Web is possible only through your school library. The library's **online catalog** will also filter Web sources. It will help you to find those that are serious research sites — and perhaps save you from drawing research materials from unreliable ones. (See "Using Internet Search Tools," pp. 95–97.)

Using the Library Online Catalog to Locate Resources

Once you have a sense of how your library is organized, explore the online catalog. Become familiar with the library's **home page.** It should tell you how to search for different kinds of material. Explore the home page carefully. It is your entry point not only to materials in your school's library but also to materials in other libraries and on the Web. Look first for the way to search for books, journals, and other scholarly sources that are in the library. Follow the directions on the home page for searching this kind of material by author, by title, or by subject. Then find the link from the home page to the library's collection of "electronic databases" or a similar term that identifies the entry point for the many books, articles, and reference sources that are not physically present in the library but are available on the Web. In most cases you can access these huge databases of research materials only through the library's online catalog. Your school pays for such access. (Appendix A, Resources for History Research, includes annotated entries for many of these electronic databases.) Make a list of databases that contain sources of historical information. At some schools, access to electronic databases is also available from other campus computers, including those in dorm rooms, or from PCs and laptops connected to the campus network. Checking out the level of electronic access is becoming important to conducting research effectively.

Figure 4.1 (p. 85) shows an example of a typical library home page. Annotations identify each important element of the page.

FIGURE 4.1   Annotated Example of a Library Home Page

① Links to the university home page and to other university libraries.

② Name of library; the sponsor of the site.

③ Search box with drop-down menu that can bring you to page(s) that describe each of the university's libraries and their major collections of books, journals, documents, etc.

④ Search box (with "advanced search" option) for finding books and other materials in <u>this</u> library or in other campus libraries.

⑤ Links to information about the operation of the library.

⑥ + ⑦ Important links to electronic information sources available to users of this particular library. Through these links, you can search a wide range of subjects and topics and, in particular, journal articles by subject, keyword, journal name, or article title.

⑧ Notice of new links from the library home page.

⑨ Links that aid students in using library resources.

⑩ Links to practical information for library users.

⑪ Links to very large databases of films, spatial and statistical data, documents, and images.

⑫ How to ask questions of research librarians.

⑬ Links, including a way of searching the site and moving to the university's home page.

SOURCE: *Used with permission of The University of North Carolina at Chapel Hill Libraries.*

Searching the Catalog by Author and Title. Author and title searches are usually simple as long as you know the proper commands and spell the names or titles correctly. If you are uncertain about the spelling, ask the reference librarian for help. For example, titles that begin with "A" or "The" can confuse the computer. The catalog's rules for title searching usually tell you which words in titles can cause trouble. Sometimes the spelling of an author's name can be tricky, especially if the name is spelled differently in English than in its language of origin. Be especially careful when using ancient or foreign names.

Author and title searches are fairly straightforward, but they require you to know in advance what person or book you are looking for. This is often not possible, especially at the beginning stages of research. For the most part, you will need to discover which sources by which authors are related to your theme. To do this, you must search the online catalog by subject or by keyword.

Searching the Catalog by Subject or Keyword. The principles behind subject searches and keyword searches are *not* the same, and unless you enter the right words or choose the right subject headings, the catalog will not provide you with the materials you need. In a library catalog, a **subject heading** is a term (or terms) that the library profession uses to describe all of the material listed under that heading. A **keyword,** in contrast, is a term that *you* choose because it seems to describe the kinds of sources that you think you need. In many instances, you will be able to search by both subject and keyword.

Subject Headings

If you want to search by subject heading in the most complete way, go to the official set of headings compiled by the Library of Congress. These headings are printed in the volumes *Library of Congress Subject Headings,* usually kept in the reference section of the library. The online catalog uses these headings in its own internal organization. If you are having trouble finding the proper subject headings for your search, do not hesitate to ask the advice of the reference librarian. Doing so can save you a great deal of time.

Searching the library catalog, a database, or the Web by subject calls for understanding what a *subject hierarchy* is. A subject hierarchy is a series of subjects that moves from the broadest to the narrowest category. The trick is to start with the broad category that is most likely to contain the narrower subject area that your theme is a part of. Sometimes common sense will do; at other times you will need to learn the logic behind the categories of the subject hierarchy. The following example will introduce you to the logic behind a subject hierarchy.

Suppose your theme is "women workers in the Lowell, Massachusetts, textile mills, 1820–1850." You might begin your search with a broader subject such as "textile industry" and then move down the hierarchy by choosing narrower subjects, such as "Massachusetts," then "Lowell," then "history of," and then "19th century." If that is the closest the subject headings get to your theme, your search would stop there. At that point the sources that resulted would be confined to the nineteenth-century Lowell, Massachusetts, textile industry. This procedure may seem simple, but at each step of the narrowing process you will have a series of sub-headings to choose from. A wrong choice could send you away from rather than toward your theme.

Keywords

In keyword searching, instead of trying to figure out which subject your topic is under, you ask the computer to search its records of books and other materials for certain words.

Again suppose your theme is "women workers in the Lowell, Massachu-setts, textile mills, 1820–1850." Your most promising keywords will be the nouns in your theme: *women, workers, Lowell,* and *textile mills.* Don't search by using any of these words by themselves. They are too general and will generate a long list of sources, most of them not related to your theme. For example, the keyword *textile mills* will produce sources on such topics as "textile mills in Japan during World War II." It is always best to do an "advanced" or "complex" search, in which you can combine a series of key-words, asking to see only those sources that have several of the keywords in a certain order. In this case, you might use the following: *"women" AND "workers" AND "textile mills."* The rules for advanced keyword searching are usually available through a link from the search page. If you need assis-tance with keyword searches, ask a librarian.

Locating Library Materials by Using Call Numbers. Don't sit at the com-puter monitor for long stretches trying to find that one subject heading or keyword that will give you everything you want. Once your searches have turned up a number of promising titles, record all of the information from the screen. You will need this information for your research bibliography and, eventually, for the **bibliography** to your written paper. (For informa-tion about organizing a bibliography, see pp. 146–58 in Chapter 5.) If the source on your list is a book or journal on the library shelves, be sure to take down the **call number.** The call number indicates a book's location in the library stacks. As you look over your list of call numbers, you will probably discover that many of the books and journals you listed have call numbers that begin with the same letters or numbers. Books with similar call num-bers are usually on related topics. When you get to the stacks, don't look only for the specific books you found in your computer search; look at all of the books on nearby shelves as well. You will likely find additional works related to your theme. If they seem promising, add them to your research bibliography.

Be sure to find out whether the material you want is on campus. The online catalog should make that clear. Getting material from a distant library can take time. The process by which your library borrows a book from another library is called **interlibrary loan.** Don't wait until it is too late to find out that a book you really need has to be borrowed from another library.

Using Print and Electronic Reference Sources

Reference sources can be found in print form in the reference collection of your library, on **CD-ROM** (though these are being phased out), or in electronic databases. (Appendix A, pp. 185–243, lists many of these kinds of printed sources, and additional resources can be found at <bedfordstmartins .com/benjamin>). Nonprint reference sources will be linked to the library home page under "Electronic Reference Sources" or a similar name. Some electronic reference sources are also available on the Web, but access to the most respected ones usually requires a password. Your reference librarian can help you to find open-access reference sources on the Web.

Reference sources can help you define your terms, gather background information on a topic, and locate specific facts, dates, and biographical and statistical material. Since many reference sources are large and have special ways of organizing their content, look for the place at the beginning of each source where advice is given about using the source. This will save you a lot of time. If you cannot find your way around one of these sources, ask a reference librarian for help.

Atlases, Dictionaries, and Encyclopedias. Atlases are collections of maps. Some atlases are very specialized, showing highly detailed maps of specific regions, towns, and so on. Some of these maps lay out topography (mountains, valleys, rivers, etc.); others display the economic, ethnic, weather, or navigational features of an area. Historical atlases display changes that have occurred in nations, regions, communities, and so on, over time. For example, a historical atlas of transportation might display the expansion of different railroad lines over a period of many decades.

You are already familiar with general dictionaries, but various historical dictionaries should also be available in your school library. They define terms of historical importance not usually found in a general dictionary. Suppose your research requires that you know a particular term from the history of China. A dictionary explaining this term (such as *China: A Historical and Cultural Dictionary)* might be available in your library. Important in the study of history are biographical dictionaries, which give brief descriptions of the lives of important individuals. Information about a Canadian explorer might be found in a source such as the *Dictionary of Canadian Biography.*

Some encyclopedias, such as *Encyclopaedia Britannica,* are general; others focus on historical topics. You could find, for example, a historical encyclopedia of slavery or of the French Revolution. Such an encyclopedia, whose articles might run from a few paragraphs to several pages, is a good place to begin research on a historical topic or theme.

Subject Bibliographies. **Subject bibliographies** list a variety of research materials — including books, book reviews, and journal articles — by subject. They may be in the reference section of your library, on CD-ROM, or accessible from the home page of the online library catalog via a link to electronic reference sources. Some subject bibliographies are openly available on the Web. A large number of print and electronic subject bibliographies are included in Appendix A and on this book's companion Web site at <bedfordstmartins.com/benjamin>.

Subject bibliographies are almost always the best sources to use when you are in the early stages of your research. Once you determine your research topic, seek out the subject bibliography that best fits. If you narrow your topic to a theme such as "the role of journalists in the Vietnam War," the print subject bibliography *The Wars in Vietnam, Cambodia and Laos, 1945–1982: A Bibliographical Guide* might lead you to many useful sources. Subject bibliographies usually list a great many sources. You will need to use good judgment to determine which ones are close enough to your theme to be worth pursuing.

Using Print and Electronic Periodical Databases

A **periodical** is a publication that appears on a regular basis—daily, weekly, monthly, quarterly. For example, newspapers usually appear daily, popular magazines weekly or monthly, academic **journals** quarterly. Students often search for books but skip over the valuable category of periodicals. Always seek out periodicals to locate articles related to your theme.

Some "directories" of periodicals can be found in print form in the library's reference section, but in most cases, the best way to search for periodicals is through the library's electronic databases, which can be accessed through the online catalog. Most of these databases are searchable by author, title, or keyword. A list of periodical indexes and databases can be found on pp. 195–97 in Appendix A and at <bedfordstmartins.com/benjamin>.

Locating Articles in Scholarly Journals. The periodicals most useful for historical research are scholarly journals. While the articles in these journals are written for scholars, most are accessible to students. The articles in these journals are "refereed," which means that one or more scholars in the appropriate field read each article *before* it is accepted for publication. The process of refereeing provides a kind of quality control, helping to ensure that the articles in scholarly journals can serve as reliable sources for scholarly research. There are a great number of scholarly history journals, covering many areas, such as *China Quarterly, Film and History, History of Religions, Journal of Environmental History,* and *Russian History.*

Journal Databases

Your library has scholarly journals in its stacks, and its subscriptions to online journal databases such as JSTOR and PROJECT MUSE will give you access to many others. Searching these databases is similar to searching the online catalog. Choose one of the journal databases that include a large number of history journals. Search these journals by subject or keyword, looking for articles that seem related to your theme. Pay attention to search rules, because they vary from database to database.

It is important to know that some journal databases contain "full text," which means that the entire article is available on the database. Other databases are "annotated" or "abstracted." Those databases do not have the articles themselves but contain summaries of their content that will help you decide whether or not to search out the full text. If your library has no full-text electronic access to the particular journal articles you want, the full text may be available in the library stacks or through interlibrary loan. Always seek out the articles that appear most useful in your research. Don't download or print out an article just because it is available in full text.

Even very large databases that allow you to search for articles in hundreds of journals have limitations you should be aware of. Some have articles only from *recent* issues of the journals they contain. Others have articles published only in *older* issues. In history research, the **date range** of a database is important to know; it can tell you what is *not* there and save you a lot of searching time.

Guidelines for Finding an Article in a Periodical Database

- Choose a database that includes a large number of history journals that deal with the general topic you are working within — for example, *Journal of African History* for a theme under the topic "apartheid in South Africa."
- Determine the content and range of your chosen database. What years does it cover for the journals you are interested in?
- Carefully choose two or three keywords that express the most important aspects of your theme. To search by subject, choose the large category that includes your theme.
- Scan the list of articles generated in response to your search. If the article titles do not seem close enough, refine your search terms.
- If an **abstract** (or brief description) accompanies an article, be sure to read it.
- If the abstract seems promising, take down *all* the information about the article so that you can find the full text.
- If the article is full text, read enough of it to be sure it is related to your theme. Don't download or print it until you have done this.

Journal Indexes

Electronic databases often contain the full text of an article, but journal **indexes** usually list only the basic information: author, title, journal, and date. Articles may or may not be annotated or searchable. Journal indexes usually organize articles by subject and period. You should be aware that most indexes list articles from a very large number of journals, including many not covered by journal databases. For example, *America: History and Life* currently covers about 1,700 journals and includes annotations.

Suppose you are researching the theme "women workers in the Lowell, Massachusetts, textile mills, 1820–1850." The article "Letters of a Lowell Mill Girl and Friends," published in the journal *Labor History* in 1976, could be useful to you. How could you discover the existence of this article? You might discover it while conducting a keyword search of one of the library's full-text or annotated journal databases, using "Lowell, Massachusetts" AND "textile mills." However, if the database does not include the journal *Labor History*, you will not find the article there. You might, however, discover the article in a journal index. Searching the subject headings of a large index such as *America: History and Life* is likely to turn up the article from *Labor History*. Of course, if you already know the author or title of the article you want, you can use the journal index to give you the name of the journal and the date. Your research should always include a search of the major journal indexes.

Many academic journals have their own indexes. For example, all of the articles in the *Canadian Historical Review* are included in *Index to the Canadian Historical Review*. Printed indexes to specific journals are kept in the library's reference section or in the stacks next to the bound volumes of the journal. Once you have looked at general journal indexes, you will probably discover that several articles related to your theme come from a small number of journals. If this is the case, find out if your library has print copies of these journals. If it does, go to the reference section or into the stacks and seek out the indexes to these specific journals.

Another way to find journal articles related to your theme is by looking at the documentation in the books and articles that you have already found. The **footnotes** and especially the bibliography in these sources will mention the books and articles that the author relied on, and many of them will also be relevant to your theme. From the footnotes or bibliography, write down the titles of any articles and books that seem relevant. In fact, whenever you find a good source, check its notes and bibliography against the sources you already have, and add any promising items to your research bibliography. Be sure to copy down all of the relevant information.

Locating Articles in Magazines and Newspapers. You search for magazine and newspaper articles in databases and indexes dedicated to these kinds of periodicals, such as *Index to Early American Periodicals* and *Reader's Guide*

Retrospective. Some magazine and newspaper databases are full text and contain every page, advertisements included; others list articles by title or subject.

Current issues of popular magazines (such as *People, Time,* and *National Geographic*) and of newspapers rarely contain serious historical studies. However, if your library has print copies of, or electronic access to, magazines and newspapers *from the period of your theme,* these can be valuable sources. For example, the *Lowell Courier* from the 1830s may very well have contemporary articles on women workers in the textile mills. This is a valuable source for the theme we have been talking about because it is also a **primary source** (see "Primary and Secondary Sources of Evidence" in Chapter 1, pp. 10–16). If you are seeking old issues of magazines and newspapers, make sure that the print copies or database goes back to the years encompassed by your theme. If your library does not have the particular newspaper or magazine you are looking for, try to find it on the Web or borrow it — via interlibrary loan — from another library.

Locating Primary Sources

Primary sources are as close to history as you can get. Such sources help you to imagine what the past was like for those who lived it. Numerous archives of primary sources can be found on the Web. Entire sites are dedicated to making primary documents widely available. These sites include not only printed and handwritten documents but visual and audio materials such as sound recordings, historical maps, artwork, photographs, and motion pictures. The largest such site for U.S. primary sources is "American Memory": <memory.loc.gov/ammem/index.html>. (A large number of primary source Web sites are included in the lists of General and Specialized Resources in Appendix A and on this book's website, <bedfordstmartins .com/benjamin>.) For a wide array of themes, you should be able to discover primary material on the Web. To assist you in finding such sources, your instructors may list important Web sites in the course syllabus or elsewhere. If so, be sure to follow their advice.

In many cases, access to Web sites for primary sources is free. This is one instance in which using the Web for research is highly recommended. Also check the databases of historical documents to which your library may have subscribed. To see an example of this kind of database, examine "Alexander Street Press": <www.alexanderst.com>. This site has a well-organized collection of letters, diaries, speeches, interviews, and so on.

Primary sources are also available in **archives** such as museums, historical societies, specialized libraries, and the private records of an institution or corporation, including the film and audiotape libraries of television and radio studios. If any of these archives are nearby, visit them to see if they

DOCUMENTING *the American South*

powered by **Google**

Search All Collections

Search

Highlights | About | Collections | Authors | Titles | Subjects | Geographic | Classroom | New Additions

Collections >> True and Candid Compositions >> Primary document

Print Page
XML/TEI File

About this E-edition | About the Primary Document | Editorial Practices

Document Summary

In a love letter to his cousin and fiancée, Halliburton apologizes for upsetting her with his recent letter and admits that students criticize him for being pro-Union but anti-Lincoln.

Letter from John W. Halliburton to Juliet Halliburton, March 6, [1861][1]

Halliburton, John Wesley, b. 1840

Page 1 page image

Chapel Hill
March the 6th

My Darling.

You have consented to let one <u>sunday</u> pass without giving to me the accustomed salute. I have not been well at ease since Ed's letter was recieved. He said that you were very sorry. My Darling is it always my fault to bring grief and sadness where smiles and bubling joy should reign? Am I so unfortunate as to always be the bearer of evil tidings to those most dear to me? My own darling that letter was not written to bedew your eyes with tears, twas not my intention to harrow up your tenderest sentiments by penning a cruel letter.[2] Oh! my darling why is it that we cannot be entirely happy? Why is it that so many things

Page 4 page image

as well satisfied as I was some weeks ago. I will not tell any more of my misfortunes.

I have seen Lincoln's inaugural. It declares that he will collect the revenue and hold on to UNS property.[5] It amounts to coersion. Still it does not make me a secessionist only an anti-Lincoln man. His life is of less value than the Union. I can hate him and still love the Union. We must not dissolve a Government because it has one traitor in its borders. Do away with the traitor and hold on to the Government. I have a hard time here about politics. I am assailed and attacked by all the boys that I meet, I verily believe that I am the only union man in College I have to fight for Tennessee myself and the Union. I strive hard. I am loth to be conquered. Daily am I engaged in a wordy war with some two or three and I just slash right and left, like Sir Amiot, and never loose or gain anything. I begin to think that we are all right, all of us. Our Segnior Speakin begins upon the 23rd of April. on the first day of may I will be done with books. Soon darling I'll see you. Cheer up love! Cheer up my darling! Give my love to all.

I want to kiss you darling

Cousie

FIGURE 4.2   Example of Locating a Primary Web Source

The student's theme is "antisecessionist opinion in the American South, 1860–1861." A list of Web sites with online documents related to this subject included the University of North Carolina Library. From that library's home page (see Figure 4.1 on p. 85), the student linked to the online collection entitled "Documenting the American South" by clicking on the photo next to "Digital Collections including DocSouth." The collection is divided into several subjects. The student clicked on "True and Candid Compositions: The Lives and Writings of Antebellum Students at the University of North Carolina." The home page for this collection separates the writings by date. The student chose 1861 in order to discover what students in the South were saying about the possibility of civil war right before the outbreak of hostilities. The list of these writings includes a letter written by a young man, John Halliburton, on March 6, 1861. Such a letter might be a useful source for the student's theme. The choice of this letter brought up a transcribed (printed) version of it. The overlapping screen shots show the document summary and the opening of the letter as well as the excerpt that was relevant to the student's theme.

SOURCE: Used with permission of Documenting the American South, The University of North Carolina at Chapel Hill Libraries.

have materials related to your theme. In fact, a visit to such a place could help you to come up with a theme. You would then know that primary materials relevant to your theme could be part of your research. Finally, it may surprise you to learn that most colleges, perhaps including your own, have archives of documents that chronicle the history of the school. Could these materials serve as primary documents for your research?

Written Primary Sources. Written primary sources allow you to read what someone who was part of a historical event or period felt and thought about the experience. You can read the diary of a young woman crossing the western United States by wagon train, a newspaper article describing Babe Ruth hitting a home run, or the minutes of a private meeting between President John F. Kennedy and his advisers during the Cuban missile crisis. These documents bring history onto the printed page you are holding or onto your computer screen.

Some written primary sources are printed and some are handwritten. A French newspaper from 1779 will have been printed. The diary of an Italian goldsmith from 1899 is probably handwritten. If the goldsmith became well known, the diary might later have been published as a printed book. Later still, the content of the book might have been digitized and placed in a database of written primary sources. Such databases, usually called "electronic archives," are available on the Web.

Figure 4.2 (p. 93) shows excepts from a written primary source that a student obtained by following links from the online library catalog.

Nonwritten Primary Sources. Another kind of primary source is something *nonwritten,* something you can hold in your hand or see in a museum exhibition — an **artifact,** a physical piece of history such as a tool used by peasants in ancient India or a jacket worn by President Jefferson. Other kinds of nonwritten sources are images and sounds captured in the past, such as a 1930's recording of Bessie Smith singing the blues or a photograph of Chinese workers building the transcontinental railroad in the western United States in the 1860s. Drawings and photographs of nonwritten primary sources are available in books, and many more are available on the Web.

Interviews as Primary Sources. If your theme concerns events that occurred within the last sixty or seventy years, you might be able to interview someone who lived through them. Members of your community or your own family members can be sources of historical information. You might be able to gain access to people who have been leaders in local or national affairs and have personal knowledge of important historical events. Perhaps you can prepare a list of questions about past events in which they were participants. You can write to these individuals or perhaps speak with them. They may have personal papers they are willing to show you. This kind of historical research is exciting and satisfying, and it may enable you to use primary historical material that no other historian has uncovered.

Older adults can recall their years in another country (if they are immigrants) or describe the America in which they grew up. They may not have been important historical figures, but they reflect the experiences of countless others and are thus the stuff of which history is made. Their recollections of how they felt and of what they and others did and said when Pearl Harbor was attacked, when they first saw television, when John F. Kennedy was assassinated, or when the Berlin Wall came down are priceless pieces of the historical puzzle. For information about how to conduct interviews with older people, see "How to Research Your Family History" in Appendix B, pp. 246–47.

One final point about primary documents in general: You need to have read a lot about your theme in order to understand primary sources. You won't know why the faces of the Italian family look so bewildered in the old photograph of immigrants arriving in America if you haven't learned about the mixture of confusion, fear, and excitement that was part of coming to the United States in the late nineteenth and early twentieth centuries. You won't know why the letters of Thomas Jefferson on the subject of slavery sound so uncertain unless you know about the battle going on in his mind about the place of Africans in a republic. Use primary sources if you can, but save them until you are well acquainted with your theme. For information about evaluating primary sources, see pp. 102–05.

Using Internet Search Tools

On the Web you can search for information in millions of Web sites. You can find reference sources, secondary sources, and primary sources (written and nonwritten). If you know how to explore the Web, you can add a world of information to the materials available on the shelves of your school library. If you know the correct electronic path, you can reach any of these sites in a matter of seconds. Even without a Web address — a **URL** — you can search the Web by keyword and subject. The extent and variety of sites is almost endless. Researchers like you can locate books, scholarly journals, magazines, newspapers, and primary documents such as photographs and audio and video files. While you will need to be careful to determine the quality of the information on a Web site (see "Special Problems of Evaluating Web-Based Sources" on pp. 105–06), you should be sure to spend some of your research time exploring this electronic world.

Another advantage of Web searching is that you can communicate with people as well as with computers. E-mail, **newsgroups,** and discussion groups put you in touch with Web users who are communicating with one another. There are many history-oriented newsgroups where you can post messages, ask questions, and join conversations on history topics of interest to you. (See "Electronic Discussion Lists in History" in Appendix A, p. 243.)

Your instructor may assist you in your use of the Web by recommending specific sites that fit your course and that have the content you need. If so, be sure to follow these directions. They will guide you to sites that are reliable and appropriate to college-level research. Such sites are not easy to find on your own.

If you are expected to find online sources on your own, you will need to be familiar with a variety of search tools. Knowing how to use these tools will save you a great deal of time and help ensure that you come up with the most relevant and valuable material.

Searching by Subject and Keywords. Most **search engines** — Google, for example — allow you to search by subject just as you would in a library online catalog. As noted earlier, a subject hierarchy is a long list of information sources that begins with the broadest subject category and allows you to narrow the choices on the screen until you reach a subject category that is close to your theme. For example, to get to information about Joan of Arc, the narrowing of subjects might go like this: *Humanities> History> Europe> France> Fifteenth Century.* The goal is to choose the most promising **link(s)** at each stage. If your choices move beyond your theme, go "back" a step and try a different route. Using the example of Joan of Arc, if you chose "Religion" after "France" instead of "Fifteenth Century," you might be led to sites about the building of cathedrals.

Another search option, as with the online catalog, is to search by keyword. In this case you plug the keywords into the **browser** of the search engine. The result is a list of all of the sites that contain your words. Most search engines allow you to do an "advanced" search in which you ask for pages that have your keywords in a certain order or in combination with certain other words. Different search engines use different searching techniques, so ask the librarian which word combination is preferable. Each site that the search engine brings to your screen will have only a brief description. Click on the site to be sure that it is related to your theme. If the list of sites is too long, change one or more of your keywords or connect your keywords in a different way.

Once you have a list of sites that seem promising, **bookmark** them, or record all of the information about each site so that you can find it again. Because of the dynamic nature of the Web, a search you conduct one day using a particular subject path or keyword may yield somewhat different results a week later, so you should be sure to carefully document the pages from which you have taken information, as well as the date on which you visited the site.

There is no one correct search term or path to the sites you need. If you reach dead ends, don't be discouraged. Each search you conduct will sharpen your skills at choosing subject paths and keywords and identifying promising links. Although major research projects cannot yet be done adequately by means of the Web alone, you need to become adept at finding useful research sites. In a few years, the Web is likely to be the principal avenue for finding nearly anything and anyone. Just as computer literacy has become essential for living in a modern information environment, so Web literacy will be essential for finding your way around that environment.

Guidelines for Conducting Internet Searches
• Choose your subject path or keywords carefully to help ensure that the sites you turn up are related to your theme. • Read the instructions on the search page carefully. Use the "advanced" search option whenever it is available. • Change your subject path or keywords if you get too many or too few hits or if you turn up many sites not meant for research or not related to your theme. If you are having trouble finding appropriate sites, ask the librarian for help. • Bookmark all promising sites. In addition, record the path of each subject search. Record also the URL of the *original* site if you ended up bookmarking a site that you reached by following *links.*

Evaluating Web Sites

Books in libraries, scholarly articles, or Web sites screened by your instructor have material appropriate for serious research. This is not true of Web sites in general. Anyone can "publish" on the Web. There is much excellent research material on the Web (especially primary sources), but nothing clearly separates the good sites from the bad, the serious from the silly. If you find something on the Web that you want to use in your research but you question its reliability, ask your instructor what he or she thinks of it. See also "Special Problems of Evaluating Web-Based Sources" on pp. 105–06.

To determine the quality of a Web site, you should consider the following factors. Always ask your instructor about anything that raises questions about the seriousness of a site.

Sponsor. The sponsor of a site determines the kind of information the site contains. Universities, libraries, museums, government agencies, and research organizations sponsor the Web sites most appropriate for student researchers. The domain name on the URL of these sites will likely be *edu, gov,* or *org.* These sites are well maintained, have serious content and reliable links, and are regularly updated. In contrast, many commercial sites are geared toward selling products or services, which makes their content less reliable. Numerous distracting advertisements on a Web site are a sign that its purpose is commercial rather than educational. If you are unsure about the seriousness of a site's sponsor, conduct a Web search using the sponsor name, and share the results with your instructor.

Quality of Links. Even if you are satisfied that you have found a serious site, keep in mind that not all of the material linked to the site may have been evaluated by the sponsoring agency. At times, even a trustworthy site contains links that lead to less trustworthy sites. Make sure that any site you take material from is as serious as the site through which you found it. If you go "offsite," know the kind of territory into which you have ventured. Also, be sure to record the URL of the *new* site to document any sources that you take from it.

Currency. The currency of a site can tell you a lot about its quality. A site that has not been updated in a long time will not contain recent materials. On a serious site, both the date the site was first created and the date of its last update should be easily available. Following a few of the links from the site will tell you if the links too are current. If a lot of them are "dead," then the sponsor of the original site does not review the status of links; this is not a good sign.

Audience. The intended audience for a site is an important clue to its seriousness. The site's content and the way it is displayed indicate the audience for which the site was intended. This audience should be scholars, college-level researchers like yourself, or anyone with a serious interest in the subject to which the site is dedicated. Beware of sites that seem too entertaining or that have lots of ads.

Bias. If you do your Web searching after reading some background information about your theme, you should be able to detect the presence of strong **bias** on a site. The sources of the information on the site should be recorded there. If sources are not clear, if only a narrow range of perspectives is offered, or if the declared purpose of the site seems one-sided, you need to be very careful about using information found there.

To find some examples of biased Web sites, you can search for "9/11" and see what sites are listed. Several of the sites will be "conspiracy" sites, dedicated to proving that one or more branches of the U.S. government were responsible for the attacks on the World Trade Center and on the Pentagon. Some of these sites appear to be well organized and are filled with documents. But a close look will enable you to see that the information is one-sided and dedicated to making a point that is highly controversial.

Statement of Purpose. In many cases, the perspective of a site is recorded on its home page or on a clear link from the home page. It usually takes the form of a statement of purpose made by the sponsoring organization. Pay close attention to this statement. If it is not consistent with serious research, do not use the site. A well-known and well-respected site such as that of the Library of Congress, a major university, an important library, or a serious research organization may not need to include a statement of purpose. For other sites, however, the absence of a statement of purpose is not a good sign.

Relevance to Theme. Be sure that the sources you intend to use are relevant to some aspect of your theme.

Guidelines for Evaluating Web Sites

- Who or what is the sponsor of the site? This information should be in a statement of purpose or under an "about" link. Is the sponsor a university, library, museum, or research organization? If the sponsor is an individual, try to determine that person's credentials.
- Click on some of the links. Do they take you to sites as respectable as the home site? If you use a source from one of these linked sites, be sure to record the site's URL.
- Is the material on the site current? Has it been kept up-to-date? Are most of the links "live"? A site with many "dead" links is not well maintained.
- What is the intended audience for the site? Are its contents meant to serve college students, faculty, other professionals? Is it filled with commercial links and advertisements or with links to sites that are concerned with entertainment rather than research?
- Does the sponsor of the site have a bias that influences the kind of material on the site? Are a variety of views expressed on the site? Does the information on the site, or on most of the links from the site, sound argumentative? Does the site attempt to inform rather than convince?
- If the site seems promising, are the materials there relevant to your theme? Does the material include the information you need to document your work?
- Do you have any questions about the relevance or reliability of a site? If so, check with your instructor.

Navigating Web Sites

A large Web site can be a complex environment. Like the home page of your library's online catalog, it will have many, many links and often more than one search box. Such a site will (or should) have a series of menus or other kinds of options that will take you to particular places on the site. It should also have a site map. A serious, well-maintained site with a serious sponsor should be clearly organized; it needs to be. The purpose of the following discussion is to help you learn to "navigate" such a site — that is, to use its "internal" links to find the primary history sources that it contains and to use its "external" links to discover related sites and sources.

Many serious sites have collections of documents that are searchable, but not all of the documents will be full-text documents that can be read, printed, or downloaded from the site. If a site does provide access to serious historical sources, you must find the place on the site where those sources can be found.

Many large sites, such as those of a library, a museum, or a professional organization, are designed to serve several functions. They may contain archives of documents, but the home pages serve the needs of several kinds of users. One section of a library or museum site might be for people who want to search its collection of books and other materials. A catalog of such sources may be helpful to you in preparing a research bibliography. However, if you come to the site for access to copies of these materials, you will need to find links to the "digital" or "research" sections of the site. There you will find the portion of the organization's documents that have been digitized—that is, those whose content can be read by your computer. Digitizing sources is expensive and time-consuming. Many archives with huge collections of documents or images (photographs, art, maps, etc.) have digitized only small portions of their holdings.

A large site with many kinds of sources is likely to place them in separate "collections" in different parts of the site. If that is the case, searching the site is usually more productive than following its internal links. Of course, as you already know, a successful search requires the careful choice of subjects or keywords. If your search yields strange results, click on the "site map," which will bring you to a subject list of the different parts of the site. Choosing the most promising links here should bring you closer to the materials on the site that are relevant to your topic.

Internal links need to be chosen with care, but external ones—links to sites other than the one you are using—require even more attention. Most important, you must be sure that any external links take you to sites that are as respectable and useful for research as the site with which you began.

Do not let these cautions about navigating large research sites discourage you from visiting them. Using sites (or portions of sites) chosen by your instructor and consulting the lists of reliable digital resources in Appendix A will help you to avoid unreliable Web sites.

EVALUATING SOURCES

There are many factors to consider when you evaluate a book or article, a nonwritten source, or a Web-based source. You need to know if it is a proper source for college-level work and if it fits your theme. You need to figure out the perspective of the author or creator. You cannot make proper use of a source unless you understand the points the author is trying to make.

Evaluating Secondary Sources

Most history books and articles fall into the category of **secondary sources,** because they are written by someone who did not observe or participate in an event but investigated primary evidence of it. (For more on primary and secondary sources, see "Primary and Secondary Sources of Evidence" in Chapter 1, pp. 10–16.) Among the factors affecting the quality of a book or article is the background of the author. You may find a description of this background on the front or back cover or on the cover flaps. If not, you need to find out about the author on your own. A search of the library catalog may turn up other books by the same person, or you can search the author's name on the Web. A book or article need not be written by a professor or some other serious writer in order to be useful for your research, but these kinds of authors are especially likely to produce reliable sources.

An examination of a book's table of contents and preface or introduction should tell you much about the background of the author and the quality of the work. Examine, as well, the footnotes and bibliography of a book or article. Their absence is a strong indication that the work is not a scholarly one. If there is a bibliography, make sure that some of the works listed are serious sources.

Pay attention to the audience for whom the source seems to have been written. The article you printed out from a Web site may have been intended for a high school reader. Note also if the book or article is meant to entertain rather than inform. A book on the highlights of the 1956 World Series most likely falls into the realm of entertainment, but it may still be a useful source if your topic is baseball history.

The name of the publisher or the journal may be a clue to the seriousness of a book or article. University presses are reliable producers of serious academic books. Some commercial publishers, such as Penguin Books, publish works intended for a sophisticated audience, but the majority publish books that are intended for a general audience and that may not be as useful in your research. Often the title provides a clue. A scholarly book might have a title such as *Hindu Fundamentalism and the Destruction of the Mosque of Babur in Ayodya,* whereas a popular book on the same subject might be titled *Massacre at Ayodya: The True Story!* You should be able to distinguish *Changing Images of Female Beauty in Renaissance Art* from *How to Look like a Renaissance Beauty: Twelve Easy Steps.*

Any **bias** on the part of an author or work that you are considering will tell you a lot about a work's seriousness. Bias — an author's perspective on a topic — can be modest or very strong. Strong bias is indicated by an unwillingness to consider or acknowledge other interpretations and by the use of harsh language to characterize authors with different perspectives. A book with a strong bias is unlikely to be a useful source, unless your theme requires an examination of biased works, as would a paper on the anti-Semitism expressed in nineteenth-century French accounts of the Dreyfus trial.

Moderate bias, however, is a characteristic of all scholars. Every author has a perspective on his or her subject and, like you, is making an argument in support of a thesis. A history of World War II written by an English author is likely to have a different viewpoint from one written by a German author. Many historical developments and their interpretation are topics of profound controversy, and it is almost impossible for a historian to investigate one of these controversial areas without being affected by his or her own biases. A particular attitude toward a topic is to be expected. Historical problems are highly complex, and without a sense of which aspects of a problem are most important, a historian will be unable to develop a thesis.

It is important for you to become familiar with the biases and perspectives of the authors you read so that you do not unknowingly accept their viewpoints. If you agree with someone's point of view, it is natural for you to favor his or her work in your own research. If you do not understand the points of view of the authors whose work you read, you will not know why you agree with some authors more than with others. Furthermore, you will not be able to make a clear presentation of these points of view in your own written work.

Guidelines for Evaluating Secondary Sources

- Is the author a scholarly writer or an expert on your theme? (If you're not sure, conduct a Web search to find out more about the author.)
- To obtain an overview of the subject of the work, read the table of contents, preface, and other introductory materials. For this purpose, examine also the footnotes and bibliography.
- Is the intended audience scholars, serious readers, and college-level students?
- Who is the publisher? It is a good sign if the work is published by a major commercial publisher or a university press.
- Is the bias (the perspective) of the author moderate or strong? Be careful when using the work of an author who uses strong language against people who disagree with him or her or who ignores other perspectives.
- Is the source relevant enough to your theme to merit inclusion in your research bibliography? If your theme covers recent events, does the date of publication indicate that the source covers the period that you are focusing on?

When examining a book, journal article, or Web document, you need to find out if it contains the kind of information on your theme and working thesis that you are looking for. A book on Charles Lindbergh that you intend to use in your paper on "Charles Lindbergh's role in the isolationist movement" may be about his celebrity status in 1927 as a result of his solo flight across the Atlantic. The essay "The Kidnapping of Charles Lindbergh's Infant Son in 1932," which you found on a Lindbergh Web site, is unlikely to say much about his political views. The date of publication may determine the relevance of a source to your theme. A book published in 1950, even if it examines aspects of race in American history, cannot include information about the theme "the integration of public schools as a result of the Supreme Court ruling on school segregation in 1954."

Evidence of a book's relation to your theme can also be found in the introduction and the table of contents. In the preface or introduction, the author may explain the background of the book, describe the kinds of questions it addresses, and preview some of its conclusions, and the chapter titles listed in the table of contents may indicate how broadly or narrowly a topic is covered. There is no substitute, of course, for reading sections of the text to see if the author directly addresses your theme.

Evaluating Primary Sources

Some of the ways of evaluating primary sources are similar to those that you use to evaluate secondary sources, but others are not. As you do with a secondary source, you need to determine for a printed primary source the perspective of the author. Doing so, however, may be difficult because the author may have lived centuries ago or may have been an "ordinary" person, the facts of whose life were not recorded. In such a case, understanding the historical and cultural context of the author's life is very important. In addition, you need to consider the reliability of the author. Did she or he correctly understand and interpret events? Who was the intended audience of the document: an entire nation (in the case of a rebel leader or a president)? a single person (in the case of a personal letter)? What was the author's intended purpose in writing?

If the source is nonwritten—a drawing, a physical object (**artifact**), or a preserved picture or sound—new questions need to be asked. In addition to identifying the creator and context, you need to discover how the physical object was made and what it was used for. What technology was used to make a bowl, take a photograph, or record a sound? How were such bowls, pictures, or sounds used by consumers? For example, what kinds of machines did people use to listen to sound recordings in the 1920s? What kind of music was recorded? What records were the most popular?

Written Primary Sources. Written primary sources were created at the time of the events that they describe. The author of a primary source is someone who took part in or who witnessed those events. The journal in which Ibn Batuta describes his travels from North Africa to India and China in the fourteenth century is an example of a primary document. Written primary sources record the reaction of someone who lived through a particular event and felt its effects, but it is important to be aware that recorded memories can be faulty.

Primary evidence can be found in newspaper articles, written interviews, diaries, letters, and notebooks (like the one you may be creating for a course). Official documents such as speeches, political platforms, **statistics,** and laws are also primary sources. Literary works such as novels, poems, and stories are primary sources that can be particularly useful for understanding social or cultural history.

If you will be using written primary documents in your research, you need to become aware of their historical and cultural context—that is, the circumstances surrounding an author at the time a particular document was written. For example, to understand an American woman's diary from the nineteenth century, you need to know something about the world in which the writer lived. Was she an urban or rural resident? How old was she? Was she married, divorced, or single? Was her family rich or poor? What was her religion, her attitude toward the subjects she mentioned in her diary, and so on? Understanding the meaning of her diary entries rests on knowing something about this woman, the society she lived in, and her position in that society.

Written primary evidence is not always reliable. The views of participants or observers (like the views of any author) may be biased; the writers may have misunderstood what they saw or experienced. Ancient eyewitness testimony may claim that the god of war spread great flames across the valley in what was actually the eruption of a volcano. Primary evidence can also be intentionally deceptive. The edict of a Chinese emperor may have been intended to hide the truth from his subjects. Of course, a historian may want to study the influence of the emperor's edict even if it was intended to deceive.

Nonwritten Primary Sources. Nonwritten primary sources such as physical objects, paintings, photographs, and sound or video recordings raise additional issues. For these kinds of primary sources, you need to know something about the technical process by which they were produced as well as the intent of the maker. Changes in the size and weight of cameras and in the time it took to develop a picture in the nineteenth century affected the subject matter of photographs, for example. Nonwritten primary sources require kinds of interpretation that are different from those used to evaluate written sources, whether primary or secondary. Still, for certain themes, nonwritten primary sources may prove central to your argument.

Nonwritten primary sources are quite varied. Physical objects, or artifacts, can take many forms. Some, such as clothing, jewelry, furniture, and tools, were made for personal use. Others are art objects such as paintings, drawings, or sculpture. Recorded pictures and sounds (photographs, films, records) comprise one of the major categories of nonwritten primary sources.

Nonwritten sources have to be analyzed for what they "say" even though they do not use words. (For more information, see "How to 'Read' Nonwritten Materials" in Chapter 2, pp. 25–36.) How would you analyze a statue of Thomas Jefferson? First you would need to describe its original location and its physical appearance — what it is made of, its size, its style.

Who was the sculptor? What image of Jefferson was he or she trying to portray? How did people respond to the statue when it was first created, and how do they respond today?

Finally, you need to determine if a primary source, whether written or nonwritten, is directly related to your theme. Suppose your theme is "the breakup of Poland in the eighteenth century." A *political* map of Poland showing its boundaries and the neighboring states of Prussia, Austria, and Russia would be a relevant source. A *topographical* map showing such features as mountains and rivers would not be a relevant source. (Also see the section "Incorporating Visual Materials into Your Paper" on pp. 129–30 in Chapter 5.)

Neither written nor nonwritten primary sources can be taken at face value. You must look behind them, so to speak. Whenever you intend to use a primary source as evidence, be sure to take the time to learn about the context in which it was created and the impact that it had on its original audience.

Special Problems of Evaluating Web-Based Sources

Certain aspects of evaluating Web sources and printed sources are similar, but some special characteristics of Web documents make their evaluation more difficult. Authors of scholarly books and journal articles have had their work reviewed by editors and by experts in the field. Because of this process, much of what gets into print is of high quality. For the most part, the Web is unedited. *Anyone* can become the author of a Web document. This accessibility is one of the marvels of the Web, but it makes separating serious authors from less informed ones difficult. Nevertheless, if you take care to conduct your Web research in stable, scholarly sites, you can minimize the problems noted below. (See also "Evaluating Web Sites," pp. 97–99.)

Before you download or print a possible source from a Web site, find out as much as you can about the author, either from the site itself or by conducting a Web search. If you cannot figure out who wrote the material you are interested in or how it got to the site, you would be wise not to use it.

If you can identify a Web author, you then need to ascertain the author's bias. Examine the document and the site at which you found it to determine the author's perspective on your topic. Some sites and the authors whose work they include are as serious as any university publisher or scholarly journal, but many sites are created to disseminate the viewpoint of a particular group. In the latter case, all of the documents on the site as well as those on any linked sites are likely to share a similar perspective, and you will need to be aware of this bias. If you cannot find out much about the author or the origins of a Web document, and if the site does not include a statement describing its purpose, then assessing bias will be difficult and you need to be cautious about using the document as a

Guidelines for Evaluating Web Sources

- Try to identify the author of the source. Do a Web search for any author or sponsor name that is on the site or on the source that interests you.
- Look for signs of bias on the site or in the document: dramatic presentation, one-sided arguments, lack of documentation for statements made.
- Try to track down the original print version of a Web-based document, so that you can check to see whether the electronic version was altered.
- Check reliable resources such as the online library catalog to see whether there are more recent versions or translations of a source that may be more accurate than the version or translation you found on the Web.
- Try to ascertain whether any nonwritten materials—still photographs, sound recordings, films—that you found on the Web were altered in any way.
- If you cannot determine the seriousness of an author or site sponsor, or the quality of the documents that interest you, discuss these issues with your instructor.
- If the site and document appear to be respectable, properly documented, and in a stable form, add the source to your working research bibliography.
- Because of the many problems concerning Web sources, be sure to fully document any source that you place in your notes.

source. In such a case, you should be sure to show the document to your instructor before including it in your research.

You should also be aware of potential problems concerning the accuracy and authenticity of Web sources. Sometimes the fact that only part of a document is included on a site is not made clear. If a document has been translated, the translation may not be accurate. If a document is an early version of something that was later revised, you may be missing important changes made by the author. The text of a written document may have been altered. Similarly, a photograph can be altered or a recording spliced. Your best assurance of accuracy is to confine your research to sites about whose seriousness you feel confident, and to inform your instructor about any questionable Web-based sources.

If you decide to use a source from the Web that was copied from an original print source, you should attempt to track down the print version, so you can cite it directly in your paper. Sometimes print documents are reformatted to fit the needs of the Web, in which case, the "pages" of the electronic version are different from the pages of the original. If you cannot obtain the original printed source, you should record the page numbers that appear in the Web document, taking care to make that fact clear in any notes you take from the document and in the footnotes to the document that you create for your paper. The reader must know both that the version of the document you used came from the Web and that the page numbers you cited are not those of the original print version.

A well-maintained site is a stable site; documents won't disappear from it without notice. The content of some well-respected Web sites, however, changes regularly, and material from poorly maintained sites can vanish from the site where you found it. For these reasons, you should be sure to record the date on which you took information from a Web document.

Because of the unstable nature of Web-based documents, you must tell the reader what site a document came from, the title of the document, and the path from the site's home page to the document's page. You also need to provide the URL and the date you looked at the site. (For information on documenting sources from the Web, see pp. 142–44 in Chapter 5.)

You need not be overly cautious about using Web sources, especially if you discuss questionable ones with your instructor. However, you should observe the preceding guidelines for evaluating Web-based documents.

INTERPRETING SOURCES AND TAKING NOTES

When you evaluate a source, you determine whether it should be part of your research. When you interpret a source, you make judgments about its content. To make such judgments, you need to understand what you are reading. You also need to have a clear view of your theme so that you take the notes that you need to take and are able to place them in the proper order. In order to avoid **plagiarism,** your notes need to make clear when the words you are recording are those of your source and when they are your own.

How to Read Your Sources

Reading scholarly books, journal articles, and Web documents can present challenges. Until you gain experience in reading serious historical studies, the going is likely to be slow. Some of the vocabulary may be new to you. A work on the French Revolution will contain words such as *Jacobin, Thermidor,* and *Girondin.* A study of the atom bomb will talk about *implosion* and *fission* and places such as Tinian and Eniwetok. If possible, keep a good dictionary (and an encyclopedia) handy. Another challenge is the academic or scholarly style of writing found in specialized works. Ease into your topic by reading the least specialized works first. Read difficult sentences slowly, and look up any unfamiliar words. As you become familiar with your theme, you will learn the meanings of terms that scholars use, and you will become increasingly comfortable with their style and terminology.

Your main task is to understand the points an author is trying to establish. In particular, you need to identify the author's thesis. Good historical writing does more than lay out a series of historical events and then combine them into an understandable story of what occurred. Professional historians want to prove a point — a thesis — to show that a series of historical events means one thing rather than another.

A history of the rise of Adolf Hitler, for example, won't merely tell you that the National Socialist Party (Nazi), which he led, increased the number of its representatives in the German Reichstag (parliament) from 12 to 107 in the election of 1930. It will attempt to describe the conditions that led to such an outcome and to explain the impact of the election on later events. Perhaps the author will discuss unemployment, German nationalism, the cartelization of German industry, the Treaty of Versailles, the growth of the German Communist Party, anti-Semitism, the structure of the German family, the philosophy of Nietzsche, or the insecurity of the lower middle class. The author will probably deal with some of these subjects more extensively than others and will attempt to show how the emphasized factors offer a better explanation of the subject than the others. The argument for a particular explanation of the rise of Nazism will most likely be the author's thesis. Although almost all historians will agree on the number of National Socialist members of the 1930 Reichstag, each will construct the causes and effects of that fact in different ways — sometimes in very different ways. Each will argue a somewhat different thesis to explain the outcome.

If you wish to understand a particular author's interpretation of an event, you must know how the author arrived at that interpretation and what significance he or she believes it to have. Only a careful reading of the entire work and close attention to its main arguments can give you such knowledge. Remember, history works are a selection of facts and interpretations constructed to explain a particular writer's understanding of a historical subject. If your own research relies heavily on a particular book, you will need to know its perspective and its thesis.

How to Record Information from Your Sources

The first rule of note taking is to know in advance what you are looking for. This is especially difficult at the outset of your research, when your understanding of your theme is still somewhat vague. Nevertheless, it is important to define the scope and content of your research, as well as a preliminary thesis, as quickly as possible. In order to avoid either taking note after note that you will never need or failing to jot down things that you will need, you should have a clear understanding of your theme and the kinds of evidence you are seeking. Otherwise, your research and note taking will wander, and you will lose valuable time.

There are three standard ways to take notes. You can *summarize* information from a source. Doing this allows you to draw upon ideas spread across several pages in the source. You restate these ideas briefly in your own words. You can *paraphrase* information so as to capture the meaning of a few sentences from a source. (For this type of note, a short sentence will do.) You can *quote* a sentence word for word, carefully placing quotation marks around the author's words when recording them in your notes.

Using Direct Quotation. As you go through a source, you may find passages that you want to repeat word for word in your own research paper. Although overreliance on **quotations** can be a weakness, if you feel that a quote is necessary to make a very important point about your theme, be careful to copy the words exactly *and to enclose them in quotation marks.* If you quote, be sure that the meaning of the words you take from the author will be clear when they appear in your paper. Also be sure that you do not alter the author's point by quoting it out of context.

Suppose you wish to use a quotation to demonstrate that Robert E. Lee was an excellent military strategist — a point that is important to your thesis. The quotation "Lee was more admired by the average soldier than any other commanding officer" would not make that point because it refers to Lee's popularity, not his generalship. Moreover, if the next sentence in the text you are quoting from were "However, his strategic decisions were not usually equal to those of Union army commanders," then you would have altered the author's point by ignoring the original context.

Before you use a quotation, make sure you understand the author's meaning. Do not quote more material than is necessary to convey the desired point clearly and accurately. Never quote something in your notes simply because you find it difficult to say in your own words. You will have to express the idea in your own words when you write your paper, and it is best to think about the meaning of your research material now, while you are taking notes.

Suppose the material you wish to quote from a source is itself a quotation from another text. You will need to make that clear in your own notes. If you think you might want to quote this material in your own paper, you should locate the source that the quote comes from and quote that source directly.

Suppose a quotation is very long and some parts of it are not related to your thesis. You may omit portions of the original quote from your notes as long as you indicate the omission by an **ellipsis** mark — three dots (. . .) — in the quoted material. If the portion omitted includes the end of a sentence, insert four dots — three to indicate the omission and the fourth to mark the end of the original sentence. In this case, the closing quotation mark would follow the fourth dot. But suppose the quotation is "Feudalism, despite later idealizations of it, was maintained by an oppressive social order." If you wanted to omit "despite later idealizations of it," you would use three ellipsis dots and quote the sentence like this: "Feudalism . . . was maintained by an oppressive social order."

Never use an ellipsis mark if doing so would change the meaning of the author's words. If, in the previous example, the quoted sentence had read "Feudalism in its later stages in Moravia was maintained by an oppressive social order," you would have to quote the entire sentence; otherwise, the author's meaning would be seriously altered.

Using Paraphrase and Summary. When you want to record an author's general arguments and conclusions, you will need to write a **paraphrase** or a **summary** of particular points. As stated earlier, a summary is a brief re-statement, in your own words, of a point made by an author over the space of several pages. A paraphrase records a more limited point made by an author. Both should reflect the author's point accurately — but in your own words, not those of the author. (See "Avoiding Plagiarism," pp. 115–18.)

Suppose an author spends several pages connecting the nineteenth-century decline in Spanish-Mexican trade to Mexican independence from Spain. You may want to summarize the findings simply by noting that the author feels that the diminishing economic tie between colony and mother country was one of the major factors leading to Mexican independence. If you wish to record some of the evidence itself, you may want to paraphrase the author's description of the decline in trade with several sentences of your own that include the main factors of this decline.

Be aware that paraphrasing can lead to plagiarism. It is extremely important for you to know how to paraphrase without using an author's own words or anything close to those words. Your paraphrase must contain words and sentences that are distinct from those of your source. Also, be sure *not* to retain the sentence structure or whole phrases from the original. (See "The Art of Paraphrasing," pp. 116–17).

How to Organize Your Notes

As you approach the end of your research, you will have taken a large number of notes. It is important for you to organize your notes effectively as you create them so that you can find the information you need when you are ready to write your paper. Be sure to give each note card or file a **subject heading** that indicates what aspect of your theme it will help you to document and what part of your paper it will most likely appear in. When you complete your research, you will use these headings to help you place each note with other notes to which it is related.

Taking Notes on Note Cards. A long established and effective system of note taking uses paper index cards. For an example, see Figure 4.3 (p. 111). For each source you take notes from, you create a series of cards. On the first card, called a **source card,** you record *all* of the information you will need to cite the work if you decide to use it in your paper, such as the library call number and the author, title, publisher, and place and date of publication for a book. (For information about how to cite a variety of sources, see the "Documenting Your Paper: Citing Your Sources" section of Chapter 5, pp. 130–58.) Each card in the series contains a quotation, paraphrase, or summary of information from the source that you might

First note card on each source must include a full citation for use in footnotes/endnotes and bibliography.

GT 2869.M56

Sugar comes to
the New World

Subject heading.

Sidney W. Mintz
Sweetness and Power: The Place of Sugar
in Modern History
N.Y.: Penguin Books, 1985

Library call number in case you need to locate the book again.

Sugar cane brought by Columbus in 1493. First grown
in Spanish Santo Domingo. First shipment to Europe
around 1519. " . . . it was Spain that pioneered sugar
cane, sugar making, African slave labor, and the
plantation form in the Americas." (32)

Student's summary comments set context for quoted material.

Page number from source to use in footnote.

Mintz — Sweetness
pp. 38–39

Rise of English
sugar production

Subject heading.

Short author and title.

British plantations in the Caribbean grew coffee,
chocolate, nutmeg, and coconut but sugar most
important crop. The main plantations were in Barbados
and Jamaica. English learned how to make sugar from
the Dutch. Production on Barbados began in 1640s.
When British took Jamaica from Spain, sugar
production greatly expanded. Jamaica was much
bigger than Barbados.

Student's summary.

2

Number keeps several notes from same source in order.

FIGURE 4.3   Example of the First Two Note Cards for a Source

use in your paper and, if helpful, any comments of your own about the source. At the top left corner of the second and later cards will be the author's last name, a short version of the full title (which you recorded on the source card), along with the page or pages where you found the information. The top right corner will contain a word or phrase — a subject heading — that describes the aspect of your theme and thesis to which the information on the card is related. Subject headings will prove crucial when you begin the process of arranging your notes as you prepare to write your paper (see "Organizing Your Paper" in Chapter 5, pp. 120–25). If a source could relate to more than one aspect of your theme, be sure to note this as well.

Taking Notes on a Computer. Computerized note-taking programs provide a new way to create and organize notes. You enter information from your sources directly into the note-taking program by placing it into a digital note "card." Before you use such a program, be sure that you fully understand how it operates.

A note-taking program lets you create a folder for each of your sources. For an example of a digital source folder, see Figure 4.4 (p. 113). Be sure that each source folder has all the information you will need to document the source if you decide to use it in your paper. Each digital note "card" that you file within the source folder should indicate whether the information it records is a quotation, paraphrase, or summary. An example of a digital note "card" appears on page 114 (Figure 4.5). Each note "card" also should have a subject header that describes its content. This is the essential arranging tool that will enable you to organize your notes by content and, eventually, by the part of your theme to which they relate. If you need to reorganize your notes, the subject headers will make doing so relatively easy.

Be sure to keep all of your digital source folders and the note "cards" filed within them in a labeled folder separate from the folder you will create for the drafting of your paper. Be sure to give these folders different names that cannot be confused with one another so that you do not enter notes or draft text into the wrong folder.

If you copy and paste material from a digital source directly into a note "card" file, be sure to immediately add to the file the full source information of the pasted material. To prevent the possibility that you might later mistake the contents of this file and paste it into a draft of your paper, change the font or color of the pasted text and surround it with quotation marks.

A quick way to obtain text from some digital sources is to e-mail the text to yourself. Do not manually or digitally enter this text into a note "card" file without including the full source information and without placing the text itself within quotation marks. Although it is likely that if you use any of these notes in your paper you will change the quoted material into a paraphrase or summary, the presence of quotation marks will assure that you never lose track of the fact that the notes contain quoted material. As with all computer files, save your notes regularly and create a back-up file.

TOOLBAR: `..Folder Name..` `..Sort Option..` `..Search Options..`

Part of an advanced note-taking program.

SOURCE: University of North Carolina, "Documenting the American South," "The Lives and Writings of Antebellum Students at the University of North Carolina," Chapter 6: 1860-69 (Primary Documents). **SHORT SOURCE NAME:** Letters of UNC students.

Be sure to use proper note style.

WHERE FOUND: http://docsouth.unc.edu/true/ (2/5/2006)

URL & Path / Library Catalog #/ Name of Database / Etc.

THEME: Anti-Secessionist Opinion in the American South, 1860-1861.

THESIS: (Tentative) During this period many Southerners opposed secession.

LIST OF SUBJECT HEADERS FOR THIS SOURCE: Student Opinion. Reaction of Secessionists to Unionists. Backgrounds of Unionists.

Use "Search" and "Sort" to organize.

COMMENTS ON THIS SOURCE: An Archive of letters by UNC students (1795-1869).

LINKS:

a. To List of Cards for This Source
b. To List of Sources
c. To Draft Bibliography
d. To Draft Outline
e. To Draft Folder of Your Paper.

In advanced programs these would be live links.

2/5/06   Date Created

FIGURE 4.4   Example of a Digital Source Folder
This source folder is for a collection of digital documents containing letters by students at the University of North Carolina. Note that these letters are part of a larger collection of documents called "Documenting the American South." The source folder page includes a series of "subject headers," one of which will appear on each digital note "card" so that cards with similar headers can be found through a search.

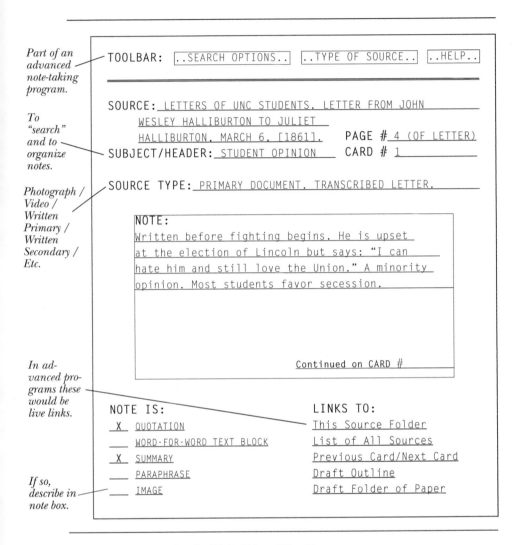

Part of an advanced note-taking program.

To "search" and to organize notes.

Photograph / Video / Written Primary / Written Secondary / Etc.

In advanced programs these would be live links.

If so, describe in note box.

TOOLBAR: [..SEARCH OPTIONS..] [..TYPE OF SOURCE..] [..HELP..]

SOURCE: LETTERS OF UNC STUDENTS. LETTER FROM JOHN
        WESLEY HALLIBURTON TO JULIET
        HALLIBURTON. MARCH 6. [1861].   PAGE # 4 (OF LETTER)
SUBJECT/HEADER: STUDENT OPINION   CARD # 1

SOURCE TYPE: PRIMARY DOCUMENT. TRANSCRIBED LETTER.

NOTE:
Written before fighting begins. He is upset
at the election of Lincoln but says: "I can
hate him and still love the Union." A minority
opinion. Most students favor secession.

                              Continued on CARD #

NOTE IS: LINKS TO:
 X QUOTATION   This Source Folder
 __ WORD-FOR-WORD TEXT BLOCK   List of All Sources
 X SUMMARY   Previous Card/Next Card
 __ PARAPHRASE   Draft Outline
 __ IMAGE   Draft Folder of Paper

FIGURE 4.5   Example of a Digital Note "Card"
This digital note "card" identifies the source of the note, records the subject
header the note is related to, and indicates the source type. A note from a
different letter in the *same* collection would be filed in the same source
folder. A note from a document in another part of the "Documenting the
American South" collection would require a new source folder.

Figures 4.4 and 4.5 show how you might use a note-taking program to
produce both a source "folder" that describes a source and a typical "card"
for notes taken from that source.

Photocopying, Downloading, or Printing Sources. It is possible to download or print out source material that you find in a database or on the
Web, and you can take a book or article from the library shelf over to the

copy machine. Whenever you come across a source that you feel may be very important to your research, photocopying it, downloading it, or printing it may seem preferable to note taking because it will save time. But don't fool yourself. At some point you will have to read and take notes on all those copied, downloaded, or printed pages. Also, don't copy, download, or print anything without reading enough of it to know that it contains material central to your theme. Finally, be sure that you have all of the source information for such documents.

AVOIDING PLAGIARISM

As a beginning researcher, you may be tempted to use the sophisticated language of the trained historians you are reading. In most cases, their expertise enables them to make their points clearly, and it is easy to fall into the dangerous habit of using their words instead of your own. Remember that your instructor is also a historian and can tell the difference between the language of someone who has spent years researching a topic and that of the average history student. Moreover, thinking is learning. If you substitute the simple task of copying the author's words for the more difficult but rewarding one of learning to understand the point she or he is making and then expressing it in your own words, you are doing yourself a disservice. Finally, **plagiarism** is **cheating** — a very serious violation of college rules. The penalty can be severe, sometimes leading to expulsion.

When taking notes, never copy an author's words unless you think you might need to quote them in your paper. In that case, be sure to put very clear quotation marks on your note card or digital note file at the beginning and end of each word-for-word passage. In all other instances, paraphrase or summarize the author's ideas and information *in your own words*. Moreover, your own words should not even come close to the words of the author, and all ideas taken from your sources must be documented when you write your paper, even if you are not using direct quotations. You will need to footnote even your summaries of an author's ideas in order to tell the reader where the ideas originally came from.

One of the very few times you can use information from a text without documenting it is when you are sure that the information is common knowledge that can be verified in a wide range of sources. Proper names, dates, and other very widely known facts can generally be used without documentation. If a source says: "Joseph Stalin, born in 1879, was a great Russian leader," you can put the date of Stalin's birth in your paper without citing a source. However, you cannot say he was "a great Russian leader" without using quotation marks and a footnote, because this characterization of Stalin represents the author's ideas, not yours.

Of course, the points that you record from your sources and incorporate in your paper should accurately reflect your sources. However, all of the words in your paper that are not in quotation marks must be your own, and you must document any information that you take from your sources unless it is common knowledge.

The Computer and Plagiarism

The increasing use of computers in note taking and writing intensifies the difficulty of avoiding plagiarism. If you enter your research notes directly into a computer, be sure to put your notes into folders and files that are different from the folders and files that you are using (or will use) for drafts of your paper. Never cut and paste words from a source into any draft of your paper. In your note files, clearly distinguish between words that you are quoting, paraphrasing, or summarizing. Always put quotation marks around quoted material. Also indicate the source of any paraphrase or summary, because you will have to acknowledge the origin of the ideas when you use them in your paper. When you create your notes, it is also wise to change the color or the font of material taken from your sources. (See "How to Organize Your Notes," pp. 110–15.)

The computer revolution has also created a new temptation — downloading an entire paper from the Web. People trying to make money and students overwhelmed by the task of conducting independent research and writing come together at Web sites where thousands of papers are available. Submitting such work as your own is dishonest and also foolish. Software that allows you to search the Internet for papers to plagiarize can also be used by your instructor to search for the source of "your" paper. Don't play this dangerous game. It has serious consequences.

The Art of Paraphrasing

A paraphrase directly reflects the ideas of an author. When you write your paper, you may use paraphrases as long as you footnote them. Even so, paraphrasing must be done carefully. Take care that your paraphrase does not come too close to being a loose quotation. If it does come that close and is not in quotation marks, you are guilty of plagiarism.

To avoid this form of plagiarism, compare the following passage from J. Joseph Hutchmaker and Warren I. Sussman, eds., *Wilson's Diplomacy: An International Symposium* (Cambridge, MA: Schenckman, 1973), 13, with the two paraphrasings that follow it. Paraphrase A constitutes plagiarism; paraphrase B does not. The subject is the diplomacy of Woodrow Wilson. Here is the original text:

> Wilson took personal responsibility for the conduct of the important diplomacy of the United States chiefly because he believed that it was wise, right, and necessary for him to do so. Believing as he did that the people had temporarily vested their sovereignty in foreign affairs in him, he could not delegate responsibility in this field to any individual. His scholarly training and self-disciplined habits of work made him so much more efficient than his advisors that he must

have thought that the most economical way of doing important diplomatic business was for him to do it himself. Experience in dealing with subordinates who sometimes tried to defeat his purposes also led him to conclude that it was the safest method, for he, and not his subordinates, bore the responsibility to the American people and to history for the consequences of his policies.

PARAPHRASE A <u>Wilson took personal responsibility</u> for conducting diplomacy because he believed it was right <u>for him to do so</u>. Believing that the <u>people had vested their sovereignty in foreign affairs in him,</u> he couldn't delegate this responsibility. <u>His scholarly training and self-discipline made him more efficient than his advisors</u>. He thought that <u>the most economical way of doing important</u> business was to <u>do it himself</u>. <u>Experience in dealing with subordinates who sometimes tried to defeat his purposes led him to conclude that it was the safest method</u> because he <u>bore responsibility to the American people for the consequences</u>.

PARAPHRASE B Wilson felt personally responsible for major diplomacy because he believed that the voters had entrusted him with such matters. He felt he was more capable than his advisors in this area. He, and not his advisors, was responsible to the people.

Paraphrase A is too close to the original. The underlined phrases are almost the same as those of the source. If they were used in a paper without quotation marks, they would constitute plagiarism. Rather than recording the main points of the passage, this paraphrase repeats much of the text word for word. It is time-consuming to take such lengthy notes, and, more seriously, the unacknowledged use of the author's wording constitutes plagiarism.

Paraphrase B records only the principal point of the passage — that Wilson decided major foreign policy issues on his own because he felt personally responsible to the people in such matters. It does not copy phrases from the original text. This type of note taking saves time, avoids plagiarism, yet conveys the central idea of the passage. Remember, however, that paraphrase B still needs to be footnoted, because it incorporates ideas taken from a source.

Paraphrasing that reduces your readings to their essential points and uses your own words is not easy to do at first. But by mastering this technique, you will avoid plagiarism and produce a finished paper that is truly yours.

Plagiarism and Group Work

Working with other students can be an enjoyable and rewarding experience. Still, group work can lead to forms of plagiarism different from those arising from individual research. If the work of your team is evaluated as a whole, each member of the group is responsible to see to it that no part of the group's work has been taken improperly from research sources. Do not let the fact that your work is a group product lessen your concern for this vital matter.

Guidelines for Avoiding Plagiarism

- When taking notes from sources, rarely use the exact words of the source. If you do use them, always place the words within quotation marks. It is best to paraphrase or summarize source material. Indicate in your notes whether the words are exact quotations, paraphrases, or summaries.
- If you enter research notes directly into a computer, be sure to put your notes in a folder separate from the folder you are using for draft versions of your paper.
- If you download quoted material from a source directly into your note files, change the color or font of the quotation to avoid confusion with your own words.
- When you paraphrase a source, do not use either the sentence structure or the exact words of the author.
- When writing your paper, be certain to acknowledge your sources and to correctly document paraphrased material as well as direct quotations.

CHAPTER

5

How to Write
a Research Paper

PREPARING TO WRITE

Why Your Paper Needs a Thesis

Before you begin to write, you need to have narrowed your **topic** to a **theme,** to have fully researched that theme, and to have developed a **thesis** (see Chapter 4, "How to Research a History Topic"). A thesis is the point about your theme that you want to make the central **argument** of your paper. Never begin to write until you are clear about your thesis.

In some cases, it might become necessary even after you have completed your research to modify your thesis. Look over your notes carefully. Perhaps they cannot fully support the kind of argument you want to make. If necessary, refine your thesis so that you will not need to modify it again. Since your thesis will determine the organization of your paper, it must be clear in your mind. With a clear idea of what your **conclusion** will be, you can determine the order in which you want to introduce different parts of your research.

Your **research paper** needs to begin with a clear statement of your thesis. Suppose your topic is "the Japanese attack on Pearl Harbor" and the narrower theme you wish to investigate is the fact that the Japanese were able to sink a large part of the American navy based in Hawaii. Your research should have focused on **evidence** that accounts for Japan's success. If your research showed that the United States was not prepared for the attack, you might have asked yourself why that was so. (Millions of Americans asked that same question in the weeks after the attack on December 7, 1941.) By turning that question into a statement such as "The United

States' focus on events in Europe explains why America was unprepared for the Japanese attack on Pearl Harbor," you created a thesis. You made a clear statement about your theme that you can argue in your paper. If this thesis helped you to organize your research, then your notes should have the information needed to support your explanations as to why the United States was unprepared. Your writing should present the necessary information and do so in an organized way. The **introduction** to your paper should tell your reader what your thesis is—for example:

> This paper will examine several factors that led to the success of the Japanese attack on Pearl Harbor. It will discuss the strength of Japan and its policy in the Pacific, how the issue of Japanese control of China increased tensions between Japan and the United States, and how events in Europe influenced U.S. policy in Asia. The thesis of this paper is that the influence of events in Europe best explains the lack of United States preparation for the Japanese attack.

Just as narrowing your theme to a thesis helped to clarify the kind of research you had to do, stating your thesis at the very beginning of your paper will help you to organize your notes and to organize your writing as well. (If your instructor does not require a formal thesis statement, then begin your paper with a description of the specific points about your theme that you will be making.)

ORGANIZING YOUR PAPER

During the process of research you were aided by your **research plan,** which helped you to determine what sources to seek first and in what order to read them (see "Creating a Preliminary Research Plan" in Chapter 4, pp. 81–83). Now that your reading is finished, it is time to arrange all the notes you have taken on your sources so that you can create your paper out of them. It is time to prepare a **writing outline.**

Preparing a Writing Outline

Suppose your topic is the conflict between Israel and its Arab neighbors and you have narrowed it to the theme "the origins of the 1947 partition of Palestine." Several major points should have appeared in your reading and should be reflected in your notes and in the headings on your note cards or computer files. The claims of three parties (Arab, Jewish, and British) concerning the future of Palestine were no doubt mentioned in many of your readings. As a result, you should have notes concerning Arab nationalism, Zionism, and British colonial policy. These three perspectives are natural sections of your paper, each with a place in the writing outline. The shifting state of opinion within the United Nations (the body that would vote on the partition of Palestine) and the role of the United States (the most important power outside the region) should have appeared in your research and in your notes as well. This suggests two more possible sections for your paper. If your notes reflect what your research uncovered about your theme, you should have more notes, say, on the British decision to withdraw from Palestine than you do, say, about British policy in India. You might mention Britain's role in India; it does have an indirect relation to your theme. However, the British decision to withdraw from Palestine is much closer to your theme and thus deserves a major section in your paper rather than a sentence or two. Be guided by your notes. If your research has been broad and thorough and your notes contain material closely related to your theme, you will end up with more notes on some points than others.

Once you have a general plan for the parts of your paper, the next question is: In what order should you include them in your paper? Suppose your theme is "the impact of the Great Depression on African Americans" and you want to organize your paper so as to effectively present and support the thesis that African Americans were more seriously affected by the Depression than other groups.

You may decide to deal with your theme chronologically and separate your paper into sections dealing with the period before 1929, the administration of Herbert Hoover (1928–1932), and the period of the New Deal (1933–1940). Or perhaps you want to cover the subject topically, setting up separate sections on (1) African American reactions to economic discrimination, (2) the efforts of the National Association for the Advancement of Colored People (NAACP) to counter racial segregation, (3) the participation of African Americans in the labor force, and (4) New Deal legislation affecting African Americans. Or perhaps you will want to examine the reactions to the Depression by major African American writers. With this perspective in mind, you could create sections of your paper dealing with the writings of E. Franklin Frazier, Richard Wright, W. E. B. Du Bois, Langston Hughes, Zora Neale Hurston, and Claude McKay. As with any theme, you can organize your evidence and support your thesis in a variety of ways. The two most common ways are chronological and topical.

A paper that has a **chronological organization** begins with events that predate those that are the main focus of the paper. It then moves, step by step, through stages that group together spans of time. These spans may be in years, decades, or—for a very broad theme—centuries. Each time span is later than the one preceding it, and spans generally do not overlap. Time spans do not have to be the same length. It is best to use larger time units when discussing events that occurred long before the main events covered in the paper and to use smaller ones when covering the period closest to the main events. A different rule applies to the length of each section of the paper: The portions dealing with periods removed from central events should be more brief than the portions close in time to such events.

A common problem with chronological organization is determining how far back in time to begin. Do you start ten or a hundred years before the time of the main events of the paper? A similar problem is determining where to stop. Do you stop with the main events themselves, or do you add short sections covering later events that help to support your thesis? There is no hard-and-fast rule, but it is wise not to cover too much ground. Don't start too long before or end too long after the principal events of your theme. A paper on a topic that spans a long time period is best handled by another form of organization.

A **topical organization** is best suited for more general themes—those that deal with ideas, social changes, or other complex phenomena that involve a mixture of political, social, economic, cultural, and intellectual developments. In this form of organization, the task is not so much to build a historical sequence leading up to a particular event, but to weave a fabric composed of the many separate lines of historical development that demonstrate the main points of the theme and the evidence behind the thesis.

In some cases, the same theme can be organized in several different ways. To give you an idea of how the same theme might be organized both chronologically and topically, here are sample outlines showing each method. The student's research dealt with the topic of the United States and Vietnam and was narrowed to the theme "How did the United States become involved in the war in Vietnam?" The student's thesis was that this involvement was a result of the Cold War.

CHRONOLOGICAL ORGANIZATION

Introduction: The World War II Era (1940–1945)

U.S. policy toward Southeast Asia in World War II
U.S. aid for anti-Japanese guerrillas in Vietnam
The U.S. military and the Vietnamese nationalist movement

U.S. Attitude toward the Return of French Colonial Control of Vietnam (1945–1949)

Defeat of Japan (1945)
Creation of a nationalist-communist government in Vietnam under Ho Chi Minh
Tensions between U.S. and France regarding goals in Vietnam

Impact of the Cold War (1949–1954)

The victory of communist forces in China and its impact on U.S. foreign policy
War in Korea and the effort to "contain" communism
France defeated by the Vietnamese communists and nationalists
The reaction to the defeat by China, the Soviet Union, and the United States

The United States and the Republic of Vietnam or "South Vietnam" (1954–1963)

The failure of reform efforts in the South
The rise of a nationalist-communist insurgency in the South
Aid to the insurgency by the government of Ho Chi Minh or "North Vietnam"

United States Defends the South from "Aggression" by "North Vietnam" (1960–1963)

Instability in the government of "South Vietnam"
The role of U.S. advisers in Vietnam

Growing U.S. Military Involvement (1963–1968)

U.S. ground troops sent to Vietnam
The escalation of the air war
Military stalemate in Vietnam
Growing domestic opposition to the war

Conclusion: The Cold War and U.S. Involvement in Vietnam

Anticommunism in the United States
Support of "North Vietnam" by the Soviet Union
U.S. foreign policy and the "containment" of communism

Note that in the chronologically organized outline the sections are in almost perfect chronological order. Don't expect to write your paper in fixed time compartments, however. There are bound to be sections that run into each other. In fact, to tie your paper together, some overlap between sections is necessary.

Here is a writing outline organized by topic for a paper with the same theme and thesis:

TOPICAL ORGANIZATION

The Cold War and Anticommunism in the United States

The Soviet Union as a threat to America
The "loss" of China — the domestic political debate
Stalemate in Korea — the domestic political debate

U.S. interests in Southeast Asia

Strategic positions and economic investments
The "domino theory"

Debate over U.S. involvement in Vietnam

The debate within the executive branch of the U.S. government
The debate in Congress
The debate in the universities

Conclusion

The forces that drew the United States into Vietnam

The topically organized paper covers some of the same ground as the chronologically organized one. Nevertheless, the topical organization leads to a different paper.

In the final analysis, the outline that you create will reflect the nature of your interest in your theme, the kind of research materials you have uncovered, and the way they have influenced your thinking. (For another example of organizing a paper, see "Example of a Research Paper" beginning on p. 161 in this chapter.)

To summarize, the purpose of preparing a writing outline is to help you organize your research notes and to determine the order in which you will write about each element of your theme. You need to decide what organization will work best to support your thesis or main argument. Preparing a writing outline will also help you determine how you can best use the information from the sources that you have recorded in your notes to develop and support your main argument.

Plugging Your Research Notes into Your Outline

The note cards or computer files and the kinds of information they contain have helped you to create a writing outline for your paper. Now that the outline is done, go back to your notes and decide which section of the paper they are most relevant to. For example, the notes concerning the impact of the Korean War on U.S. involvement in Vietnam, which you took from a book about the Cold War in Asia, should become the basis for the section in the chronologically organized paper named "War in Korea and the effort to 'contain' communism" or the section in the topically organized paper named "Stalemate in Korea — the domestic political debate." Mark the notes in each group (usually in the upper right-hand corner) with the name of the section of the outline to which they are most directly related (see "How to Organize Your Notes" in Chapter 4, pp. 110–15). Some groups of notes will not neatly fit in just one section. In that case, mark two or more section headings in the corner. If you have taken notes on a computer, you should be able to organize them according to the section of your paper that they relate to. If you cannot find any place in your outline where certain notes go, then something is wrong. Either don't use this group of notes, because they are not dealt with in the outline, or change the outline to accommodate them.

If you discover that your sources make an important point that you had not intended to cover, you must make room for it in your outline so that it appears in your paper. Another reason for changing an outline is finding material that differs strongly with one of the points you have intended to make. Always make room in your paper for **counterevidence** — points made by authors who disagree with part (or all) of your thesis. Having done so, be sure to explain why you believe the evidence in support of your thesis is stronger. You should not claim that your ideas are the *only* correct ones. You should show, however, that there is solid evidence for your interpretation.

Make sure that you have enough information on each section of your outline to do it justice. If, looking at your notes, you see a mismatch between a section of the outline and the notes needed to support it, you must alter or eliminate that section or, more likely, reread the relevant sources and take notes more directly connected with the point covered in your outline. Notes and outlines are rarely in perfect harmony at the outset. Be sure you have the notes you need. Don't wait until the paper is half written to discover that an important part lacks the kind of documentation it should have.

Now, finally, you are prepared to write. The goal of your writing should be to (1) state your thesis clearly and briefly, (2) support it in a series of well-documented sections, and (3) draw clear and brief conclusions concerning what you have said about your thesis.

WRITING THE TEXT

Chapter 3 discusses the importance of writing skills. As you prepare your paper, you may find it helpful to review the sections in Chapter 3 titled "The Components of Clear Writing" and "Building an Essay" (pp. 58–67).

As you write, keep the following basic points in mind. Don't let parts of your paper drift away from your theme. Stay focused on the central arguments that support your thesis. Be sure that you can document the points you are making.

If your instructor does not require a formal thesis statement, then be sure to begin your paper with a statement that clarifies the specific points you intend to make about your theme.

The Rough Draft

Your **rough draft** will change, perhaps several times, so don't worry too much about the exact wording when you write it. The introductory paragraph of your first draft, in which you lay out your thesis, will also need changing. Many a thesis needs fine tuning before a rough draft is finished. Nevertheless, you need a direction to your writing even at this early stage. By introducing at the outset of your paper the points you intend to make, as well as a clear statement of your thesis, you will find it easier to direct your writing to points that develop your thesis.

If you are writing the rough draft of a paper on the independence of Texas and your theme is "the role of Sam Houston in Texas independence," you will need to focus tightly on Houston's role. Moreover, if your thesis is that Houston's actions were vital to the success of Texas independence, you need to state this in your introduction. Doing so will keep your writing on track. Of course, other people will appear in your paper (the Mexican general Antonio López de Santa Anna, for example), but a clear focus on Houston and his leadership role in your introduction will keep you from writing a long section of your paper on Santa Anna or having too much to say about the defense of the Alamo (Houston was not there). As your writing proceeds, always use the test of relevance to the thesis so that the direction set out in your introduction will be maintained.

Writing the central sections of your draft raises the practical question of how long each section of your paper should be. There is no correct length, of course, but each section should be long enough to make the point you want to cover. As you write the rough draft of each section, keep in mind the information you want to include. Develop each section from the notes that support it, but don't feel obliged to use all of these notes. When you have made the point you intended to make, stop. Then begin the next section. Be sure to write a **linking sentence** — either at the end of one section or at the beginning of the next — that introduces the next point you intend to make. Now you are prepared to repeat the process in the next section of your paper, and in the next, until you reach your conclusion.

Keep the overall length of the paper in mind as well. If your paper is limited to twenty-five pages and your outline has seven points, don't start out with a section ten pages long. Of course, sections may be of unequal length; some points are more important than others or take more space to document. Here is a very general guide: For a paper of about twenty-five pages, it is best to have no more than six to eight sections. You will need about two or three pages in each section to make your point. You also need to leave about one page at the beginning for your introduction and another at the end for your conclusion. **Footnotes** or **endnotes** and your **bibliography** are not usually counted as part of page length. It is best to clarify this point with your instructor. Keep your overall limit in mind; otherwise, you can end up with too many (or too few) pages.

The last section of your paper is, of course, the conclusion. It is rarely possible to write a conclusion for a draft. Even if your thesis does not change significantly as you write, changes to any part of your paper from one draft to another will require a modified conclusion. Still, it is worth pointing out here that the goal of your conclusion is to summarize briefly the points you have made concerning your thesis. In the paper about Sam Houston's leadership, for example, you would briefly refer to the evidence (both supporting and countering your thesis) about his leadership and why you concluded that it was vital to Texas independence.

Clear Writing: A Matter of Continuity

As you write the rough draft of each section, keep in mind the information you wish to include and the points you wish to make. If your theme is "German aid to the forces of General Franco in the Spanish civil war," then the section that deals with the reasons behind German support might begin by briefly describing the circumstances surrounding Franco's appeal to Hitler in 1936. The main body of the section would explain in some detail Hitler's reasons for giving aid (for example, strategic and economic considerations, ideological and diplomatic factors) and would conclude by relating these reasons to the subject of later sections, such as the actual aid given and its effect on the course of the war. Your principal concerns as you construct each section of your paper should be: Does this section follow logically from the one preceding it? Does it adequately support and develop the theme and thesis? Does it establish the necessary background for the section that follows?

As each section mirrors the overall structure of the paper by containing an introduction, a main body, and a transition to the next section, so each paragraph of which the section is composed contains a similar structure. A well-constructed paragraph begins with a sentence that introduces the information to be developed and concludes with a sentence that leads to the next paragraph. If each paragraph is developed in this way, and if sentences explaining the relationship between paragraphs are included where necessary, then the paper as a whole becomes a tightly knit series of related statements rather than a random group of facts that do not seem to move in any clear direction. The key to tight construction is for each sentence to have two components: It must be related to the one preceding it, and it must continue the development of the thesis to which it is related. Not all themes and not all writing styles can accommodate so tight a structure. Still, the closer you can come to this kind of organization, the better a paper you will write.

The best way to ensure that there are no gaps in logic between your sentences is to construct each paragraph taking into account the knowledge of the average person who might read your paper. Very often, a disconnected set of sentences may seem clear to you because as you write them you unconsciously fill in the gaps with your own knowledge. Your reader most likely is not familiar with your theme and has to depend entirely on the words you write. If these are not enough to make your point clearly, you must be more explicit. Refer back to Chapter 3 for detailed help on writing.

Quotations: When and How to Use Them

Good general rules are: Don't quote too often, don't quote too much, and rely on your own words unless there is a good reason for quoting those of your source. Unless it is necessary to use the *very same* words found in a source to make a point that is crucial to your thesis, don't use a **quotation.** Paraphrasing the point made in a source or summarizing it are usually preferred (see "The Art of Paraphrasing" in Chapter 4, pp. 116–17). However, if your source says something highly controversial or extremely important to supporting your thesis, you may want to make clear to the reader that you have not misinterpreted the source. In this case a direct quotation may be useful. If you do quote, be sure to include enough of the original statement to make its meaning clear. Don't make a quote any longer than is necessary. Finally, enclose quoted words in quotation marks. (A common error is forgetting one set of quotation marks.)

Quotation Form.   In most cases a **paraphrase** or **summary** of your source, properly footnoted, is sufficient. If you need to quote, however, the following rules will help.

If a quotation is brief, taking up no more than two or three lines of your paper, then it should be written as a part of your text and enclosed in quotation marks. Introduce the quotation by clearly identifying the speaker. The reader will always want to know who is speaking and in what context. Don't say: *The strikers were "a dangerous mob."* Say: *According to D. H. Dyson, the plant manager, the strikers were "a dangerous mob."* If you do not wish to quote a whole statement, it is necessary to insert an **ellipsis** mark—three dots (. . .)—wherever words have been omitted. You must always let your reader know when part of a quotation has been left out. Of course, never omit part of a quotation if doing so would change its meaning. (See Chapter 4, "Using Direct Quotation," pp. 109–10.)

SHORT QUOTATION EXAMPLE The early settlers were not hostile to the Native Americans. As pointed out by the Claxton *Banner* in 1836: "Our Sioux neighbors, despite their fierce reputation, are a friendly and peaceable people."[1]

SHORT QUOTATION EXAMPLE WITH OMISSION As pointed out by the Claxton *Banner* in 1836: "Our Sioux neighbors . . . are a friendly and peaceable people."[1]

If your quotation is very long, it must be set off from the sentences that precede and follow it. It should be indented ten or more spaces and appear in single-spaced type. Do not put quotation marks around a long quote. Even though you are quoting, indenting a quote makes this fact clear to the reader.

LONG QUOTATION EXAMPLE The early settlers were not hostile to the Native Americans. As pointed out by the Claxton *Banner* in 1836:

> Our Sioux neighbors, despite their fierce reputation, are a friendly and peaceable people. No livestock have been disturbed, and the outermost cabins are unmolested. We trust in God that our two peoples may live in harmony in this territory.[1]

Remember that all quotations must be footnoted.

A problem that many students face is being sure that quotations actually support the point being made. For example, the first quotation below does *not* support the point that the early settlers got along with the Native Americans; the second quotation does support the thesis.

IMPROPER QUOTATION EXAMPLE The early settlers were not hostile to the Native Americans. As pointed out by the Claxton *Banner* in 1836: "Our Sioux neighbors are peaceable but only when they are penned up in closely guarded reservations."

PROPER QUOTATION EXAMPLE The early settlers were not hostile to the Native Americans. As pointed out by the Claxton *Banner* in 1836: "We have always respected our Sioux neighbors. There has never been warfare between us."

Incorporating Visual Materials into Your Paper

Ask your instructor about the usefulness of visual material. Be sure to find out if the space taken up by visuals will be counted as part of the assigned length of the paper or if it will be an addition to this limit. If visuals are acceptable, you should try to find ways to include them. Illustrating important points in your paper with visual material such as maps, **charts, tables,** drawings, and photographs can strengthen your argument. Some points — the way something looks, a very important comparison between numbers (as in a chart) — can best be made by *showing* your reader a visual of it.

Computers have made it easier to integrate visuals into your text. You can create your own charts and tables on your computer or download drawings and photographs to illustrate an important point about your theme. Be sure not to pad your paper with visuals, however. Ask your instructor about the quantity that is appropriate.

You can place the visuals on or near the page containing the text they illustrate, or you can put all visual material at the end of the paper in an **appendix.** If you use an appendix, you need to place a note in the text that directs your reader to the page where the corresponding image is located — for example, "See Figure 3.2 on page 14." If your visuals are within the body of the paper, make sure that they are cleanly separated (perhaps by a top and bottom line) from the surrounding text. Even more important is formatting them so that they end up where you want them when your paper is printed out. Each visual, regardless of its position (within text or in an appendix), should have a title above or below it that tells readers what it refers to. Finally, except for visuals that you create, be sure to note at the bottom of each where you found it. Doing this is as necessary as documenting printed sources with footnotes or endnotes.

For a paper about the importance of Sam Houston's leadership to the success of Texas independence, a variety of visuals might be relevant. You could use a map showing his army's successful, strategic retreat before a large Mexican army in 1836. You could create a bar **graph** comparing the size of the two armies. (The Texans were often heavily outnumbered.) Or you could use a dramatic painting of Houston at the Battle of San Jacinto, where a Texas army under his command defeated a much larger Mexican army. Indeed, Houston's forces captured the Mexican commander, López de Santa Anna, who was also the president of Mexico, and in doing so effectively gained independence for Texas. Each of the visuals would illustrate some aspect of Houston's leadership — that is, each would support the thesis that his leadership was important to achieving Texas independence.

Be sure that any visual you use will reproduce clearly. More important, be sure that the visual is accurate and that it illustrates and supports your thesis. Your map of the retreat of Houston's army must get the place-names and the movement of the armies correct. Your graph must be calibrated accurately. The painting of Houston at San Jacinto needs to be consistent with claims in your paper that Houston's generalship at the battle was excellent. For example, the picture may show Houston in the midst of the battle when, in fact, he was well behind the lines. A visual may seem "real" simply because it looks that way. Don't treat visuals as facts until you have examined them as carefully as you would any other source used in your paper. Again, be sure to document any visuals. (See model footnotes and endnotes for multimedia sources on pp. 140–42; also see the source notes in the sample research paper on pp. 180–82 at the end of this chapter.)

Guidelines for Incorporating Visuals

- Look for visual materials on your theme when you do your research; they can strengthen your argument.
- Be sure that the visual actually is what you say it is and means what you say it means. You can misinterpret a visual just as you can misinterpret a printed source.
- Learn about your word processing program's ability to download, store, and insert visuals into your paper.
- Do not pad your paper with visuals.
- Format your visuals correctly by clearly separating them from the surrounding text. Identify them correctly, and make sure that in the final draft of your paper the visual appears where you want it to.
- In addition to a proper identification of a visual on the page where it appears, you need to document its source as you would any other source. You need to tell the reader where the visual came from.

DOCUMENTING YOUR PAPER: CITING YOUR SOURCES

Documentation tells your reader where the material in your paper comes from. Documentation usually takes the form of **footnotes** or **endnotes,** but it can also be included in the captions for illustrations, diagrams, photographs, or any special material that you place in your paper to support your thesis.

When and How to Use Footnotes and Endnotes

Footnotes are forms of documentation that appear at the bottom of the page; endnotes appear at the end of the paper. They include the same information. (A sample endnote page can be found on p. 180.) If your instructor has no preference, you can choose to put your documentation in either place, but you must be consistent throughout the paper. You must number your notes consecutively. (When **proofreading,** be sure that the number in the text matches the number of the note.) Because footnotes and endnotes have the same form, the following discussion that describes how to write them uses the word *footnotes* to refer to both types.

If you quote from, paraphrase, or closely summarize your research sources, you must tell your reader where the original information can be found. In this way, the reader can check the accuracy of your quotes and statements, judge the **bias** and credibility of your sources, or carry out research of his or her own. On occasion, you may also want to use footnotes to make brief comments that qualify or supplement statements in your paper. These are called "explanatory" footnotes.

The question that troubles students the most is: Which of the statements that I make in my paper need footnotes? There are only a few hard-and-fast rules to guide you. However, four types of statements *must* be footnoted: (1) direct **quotations,** (2) **paraphrases,** (3) controversial facts or opinions, and (4) statements that directly support the main points made in your paper. Another group of statements — those that constitute a **summary** of important points from your sources — should also be footnoted and *must* be if they are used to sustain an important part of your argument. Finally, **statistics** are almost always footnoted.

Here is some clarification concerning what is meant by "controversial facts or opinions" and "statements that directly support the main points made in your paper." Controversial facts or opinions are those on which your sources disagree or those that will surprise your reader. Suppose, in your paper on the theme "the treatment of slaves on Mississippi plantations," you write that some slave owners were kind to their slaves. This statement may surprise the reader and thus must be footnoted. Suppose, while researching the theme "European discoverers of America," you find that your sources all agree that Vikings visited the New World long before Columbus. If you suspect that most people believe that Columbus was the first European to see the New World, then it is necessary to show the reader the source of your information with a footnote. Finally, statements of fact or opinion that directly support main points of your argument should be footnoted. If your theme concerns the Protestant Reformation and you argue that nationalism was a major factor in the break with Catholicism, then your references in the text to nationalist forces should be footnoted. But if you treat the wealth of the Catholic Church as a very minor factor, then your brief references to that point may not need to be footnoted.

The number of footnotes to use is another thorny problem. As a rule of thumb, if your paper goes on for several pages without any footnotes, you are not documenting as much as you should. If you are writing five or more footnotes per page, you may be overdoing it.

Here is a final point about what to footnote. Using a footnote does not give you permission to plagiarize. If the words in your paper are the same, *or very nearly the same,* as the words in your source, you have committed **plagiarism** even if you include a footnote. (For more on plagiarism, see Chapter 4, pp. 115–18.) You should not use sentences or even phrases from your sources unless you put them in quotation marks.

Directory to Footnote/Endnote Documentation Models

BOOKS

1. Basic Format for a Book (First Reference), 133
2. Book (Second Reference), 134
3. Two or Three Authors, 134
4. Four or More Authors, 134
5. Organization as Author, 134
6. Book by an Unknown Author, 135
7. Translated Book, 135
8. Book with One or More Editors, 135
9. Selection in an Edited Work or Anthology, 136
10. Edition Other Than the First, 136
11. Multivolume Work, 136
12. Encyclopedia or Dictionary, 136

PERIODICALS

13. Journal Article (First Reference), 137
14. Journal Article (Second Reference), 137
15. Article in a Journal Paginated by Volume, 137
16. Article in a Journal Paginated by Issue, 137
17. Article in a Magazine, 138
18. Article in a Newspaper, 138
19. Article by an Unknown Author, 138
20. Editorial, 138
21. Letter to the Editor, 138
22. Book or Film Review, 139

PUBLIC DOCUMENTS

23. U.S. Legislative Branch Committee Report, 139
24. U.S. Treaty, 139
25. U.S. Supreme Court Decision, 140
26. Canadian Legislative Branch Committee Report, 140

MULTIMEDIA SOURCES

27. DVD or Videocassette, 140
28. Musical Composition, 140
29. Sound Recording, 140
30. Work of Art, 140
31. Slide, 141
32. Map, 141
33. Chart, Graph, or Table, 141

ELECTRONIC SOURCES

34. Small Web Site, 142
35. Large Web Site, 142
36. Material from an Information Service or Database, 143
37. Article from a Database of Full-Text Journal Articles, 143
38. Online Book, 143
39. Article from an Electronic Journal, 143
40. Computer Software, 143
41. E-mail Message, 144
42. Listserv Message, 144
43. Newsgroup Message, 144
44. Synchronous Communication, 144

OTHER SOURCES

45. Pamphlet, 144
46. Unpublished Dissertation, 145
47. Dissertation Abstract, 145
48. Lecture or Public Address, 145
49. Interview or Oral History, 145

How to Write Footnotes and Endnotes

When a footnote or endnote is necessary, place a number at the end of the sentence that contains the information to be documented. Occasionally, you may want to footnote two different sources in the same sentence. In this case, place each number right after the word or phrase that you want to reference in the notes, especially if it is an important fact or a quotation. If you are documenting a general idea or opinion, place the number at the end of the paragraph or paragraphs that discuss it. All footnote or endnote numbers in the text should be in superscript — that is, a half line above the line of the type. The number should not be put in parentheses and should be inserted *after* any punctuation except a dash.

Footnotes are placed at the bottom of the page containing the text to which they refer. Endnotes are gathered together in numerical order and placed after the text of the paper, and this page (or pages) should be headed "Endnotes." The first line of an endnote (or footnote) is indented five spaces; the other lines begin at the left margin. (See the footnote and endnote examples that follow and the endnotes in the sample research paper on pp. 180–82.) Both footnotes and endnotes are single-spaced. Remember to use only footnotes or only endnotes within the same paper.

Footnote or Endnote Form. The following examples of footnotes and endnotes show the different forms required for citing different types of sources. These forms are drawn from *The Chicago Manual of Style,* Fifteenth Edition (Chicago: University of Chicago Press, 2003), which is the documentation style generally preferred by historians.

The wide variety of electronic sources available on the Web comprise a relatively new and constantly evolving medium. For help documenting the exact place on the Web where you found material that you wish to use in a paper, see the guidelines for documenting electronic sources on pp. 142–44. These guidelines differ from Chicago style in a few cases in order to provide the most accurate and efficient method of recording the location of an Internet source.

Books

1. BASIC FORMAT FOR A BOOK (FIRST REFERENCE)

The first time you refer to a book, include the author's full name, followed by a comma; the book title in full (including subtitle after a colon), italicized or underlined; publication information enclosed in parentheses — place of publication (followed by a colon), name of publisher (followed by a comma), date of publication; and the page number(s) cited (followed by a period).

1. Robert Darnton, *George Washington's False Teeth: An Unconventional Guide to the Eighteenth Century* (New York: Norton, 2003), 64.

2. BOOK (SECOND REFERENCE)

If you cite the same book again, your note need only include the author's last name and the page number.

> 2. Darnton, 102.

If, however, you cite *more than one* book (or article, etc.) by the same author, any second or later reference must include a shortened form of the title in order to make clear to the reader which of the works you are citing.

> 3. Darnton, *George Washington's False Teeth,* 68.

Some book notes are more complex. If a book has several authors, a translator or editor, or multiple editors, or if a book was published in several volumes or editions, then the footnote or endnote has to include such information as in the following examples.

3. TWO OR THREE AUTHORS

When there are two authors, both names are listed, in the order in which they appear on the title page.

> 4. Catherine Clinton and Christine A. Lunadini, *The Columbia Guide to Women in the Nineteenth Century* (New York: Columbia University Press, 2000), 48.

If there are three authors, include all three names separated by commas, in the order in which they appear on the title page.

> 5. Ronald Inden, Jonathan Walters, and Daud Ali, *Querying the Medieval: Texts and the History of Practices in South Asia* (New York: Oxford University Press, 2000), 22.

4. FOUR OR MORE AUTHORS

If there are more than three authors, the footnote or endnote includes the name of the author listed first on the title page followed by "and others" or by "et al." (from the Latin, meaning "and others").

> 6. James L. Roark and others, *The American Promise: A History of the United States,* 3rd ed. (Boston: Bedford/St. Martin's, 2005), 452.

5. ORGANIZATION AS AUTHOR

When writing a note for a source with organizational authorship, use the name of the corporation, government agency, or other organization as the author's name.

> 7. Congressional Quarterly, *Congressional Quarterly's Guide to Congress,* 5th ed., vol. 2 (Washington, DC: Congressional Quarterly, 2000), 122.

6. BOOK BY AN UNKNOWN AUTHOR

If the author of a work is unknown or is listed as "Anonymous" on the title page, skip the listing of the author in your footnote or endnote and begin the reference with the title of the work.

> 8. *Through Our Enemies' Eyes: Osama Bin Laden, Radical Islam and the Future of America* (Washington, DC: Brassey's, 2002), 134.

If a work is anonymously written but has a known editor, you may treat it as a book with an editor (see section 8).

7. TRANSLATED BOOK

When a work has been translated, put the name of the translator after the title of the work, preceded by the notation "trans."

> 9. Mahatma Gandhi, *An Autobiography: Or the Story of My Experiments with Truth,* 2nd ed., trans. Mahadev Desai (Ahmedabad: Navajivan Press, 1956), 74.

If the book was translated and edited by the same person, follow the title by "trans. and ed."

> 10. Giovanni Boccaccio, *Famous Women,* trans. and ed. Virginia Brown (Cambridge, MA: Harvard University Press, 2001), 88.

8. BOOK WITH ONE OR MORE EDITORS

If a work has both an author and an editor, keep the author's name at the beginning of the reference, and put the name of the editor after the title, preceded by the notation "ed." (for either a single editor or multiple editors).

> 11. George Fox, *The Journal,* ed. Nigel Smith (New York: Penguin Books, 1998), 44.

In an edited work that has no author, the editor's name, followed by "ed.," appears where the author's name normally would. If you want to cite only one part of an edited work, see section 9, "Selection in an Edited Work or Anthology."

> 12. T. Douglas Price, ed., *Europe's First Farmers* (Chicago: University of Chicago Press, 2000), 200-04.

In a work with multiple editors and no author, use the same format as for multiple authors, but follow the names with "eds."

> 13. Camron Michael Amin, Benjamin C. Fortna, and Elizabeth B. Frierson, eds., *The Modern Middle East: A Sourcebook for History* (Oxford: Oxford University Press, 2006), 326.

For four or more editors, write only the full name of the first one followed by "and others" or "et al." to indicate the other editors, and conclude with "eds."

14. Esther Breitenbach and others, eds., *The Changing Politics of Gender Equality in Britain* (New York: Palgrave, 2002), 18-21.

9. SELECTION IN AN EDITED WORK OR ANTHOLOGY

If you are using only a part (chapter, essay, document, etc.) of an edited work, begin the note with the name of the author of the part used, followed by the title of the selection, the title of the edited work (preceded by the word "in"), the name of the editor (preceded by "ed."), and publication information.

15. Paul R. Jones, "The Two Field System," in *Europe's First Farmers*, ed. T. Douglas Price (Chicago: University of Chicago Press, 2000), 26.

10. EDITION OTHER THAN THE FIRST

If you are using a later edition of a work, the number of the edition is placed after the title.

16. John Charles Chasteen, *Born in Blood and Fire: A Concise History of Latin America*, 2nd ed. (New York: Norton, 2005), 225.

For a revised edition, use "rev. ed."

17. Cornel West, *Race Matters,* rev. ed. (Boston: Beacon Press, 2001), 52.

11. MULTIVOLUME WORK

When there is more than one volume to the work and the volumes all have the same name, then put the volume number directly before the page number, followed by a colon.

18. Fernand Braudel, *The Mediterranean and the Mediterranean World in the Age of Philip II*, trans. Sian Reynolds (Berkeley: University of California Press, 1996), 1:46.

When, however, there is more than one volume to the work and each volume has its own title, then the volume title and the number of the specific volume used come first, followed by the general title and the publication information.

19. Robert A. Caro, *Master of the Senate,* vol. 3, *The Years of Lyndon Johnson* (New York: Knopf, 2002), 85.

12. ENCYCLOPEDIA OR DICTIONARY

Facts of publication for well-known reference books are usually omitted. However, you must cite the edition if it is not the first. When a reference work is organized alphabetically, the item being defined or described is preceded by "s.v." (short for the Latin *sub verbo*, meaning "under the word").

20. *The Columbia Dictionary of Quotations*, s.v. "Lincoln, Gettysburg Address."

If an encyclopedia tells you the *author* of the entry, then list the author at the end of your footnote or endnote.

21. *Handbook of American Women's History*, 2nd ed., s.v. "Willard, Frances E. (1839-1898)," by Anita M. Weber.

Periodicals

13. JOURNAL ARTICLE (FIRST REFERENCE)

The first reference to a journal article should include the author's full name followed by a comma; the title of the article followed by a comma, all in quotation marks; the title of the journal, italicized or underlined; the volume number of the journal; the year of the volume in parentheses, followed by a colon; and the page number(s) cited, followed by a period.

22. Wendy Goldman, "Stalinist Terror and Democracy: The 1937 Union Campaign," *American Historical Review* 110 (2005): 1435.

14. JOURNAL ARTICLE (SECOND REFERENCE)

If you cite the same article again, use only the author's last name and the page number.

23. Goldman, 1440.

If, however, you cite *more than one* work by the same author, any second or later reference must include a shortened form of the title in order to make clear to the reader which of the author's works you are citing. This is true even if one work is a book and the other is an article.

24. Goldman, "Stalinist Terror," 1429.

15. ARTICLE IN A JOURNAL PAGINATED BY VOLUME

Journals often have multiple issues per year, generally indicating each year by a volume number and then specifying individual issues within that volume. Sometimes the journal carries over the numbering system throughout the year (that is, throughout the several issues of a volume). If a journal paginates by volume, there is no need to identify the issue number in your citation.

25. E. Lawrence Abel, "And the Generals Sang," *Civil War Times* 39 (2000): 45.

16. ARTICLE IN A JOURNAL PAGINATED BY ISSUE

If a journal paginates by issue (that is, each issue begins with page 1), then it is necessary to include both volume number and issue number (the latter indicated by "no.") so that the reader can easily find your reference.

If a journal paginates by issue but does not have issue numbers, then include the season or month of the issue before the year in the parentheses.

26. Daniel Horodsky, "How U.S. Merchant Marines Fared during WWII," *Insight on the News* 16, no. 1 (2000): 46.

17. ARTICLE IN A MAGAZINE

Reference to a popular magazine (rather than to a scholarly journal) requires author, title of article, title of magazine, date, but no volume or issue number. It is not necessary to include page numbers, but if you do they should be preceded by a comma rather than a colon.

27. Greg Grandin, "Latin America's New Consensus," *Nation*, May 1, 2006, 24.

18. ARTICLE IN A NEWSPAPER

Reference to a newspaper article requires day, month, and year as well as author, title, name of paper, and section number or name (if applicable). If the newspaper has sections, mark the section with "sec." Page numbers can be omitted, as they may vary over the different daily editions of a paper.

28. Steven R. Weisman, "South Korea, Once a Solid Ally, Now Poses Problems for the U.S.," *New York Times,* January 2, 2003, sec. A.

19. ARTICLE BY AN UNKNOWN AUTHOR

If the magazine or newspaper article has no listed author, the citation begins with the name of the article.

29. "Australia's Aborigines: A Dispute over Mistake Creek," *Economist,* December 14–20, 2002, 37.

20. EDITORIAL

The editorial page of a newspaper generally has pieces written by a member of the paper's editorial board as well as by invited columnists. If an author has signed the editorial, then cite the editorial as you would an article in a newspaper. If the editorial is unsigned, write "Editorial" in the place normally reserved for an author's name.

30. Editorial, "The Price of Guessing Right," *Wall Street Journal*, December 27, 2002, sec. A.

21. LETTER TO THE EDITOR

For a letter to the editor in a journal, put the author's name first, "letter to the editor," then the name of the journal, the volume, date, and the page number.

31. Paul J. Herr, letter to the editor, *Foreign Affairs* 79, no. 2 (2000): 180.

If the letter appears in a popular magazine or newspaper, then the date and page or section number should appear as in the magazine or newspaper format.

> 32. Eric Chivian, letter to the editor, *Boston Globe,* January 21, 2003, sec. A.

22. BOOK OR FILM REVIEW

A reference to a book or film review includes the author of the review, the title of the review article if there is one, followed by the words "review of," the title of the work being reviewed, the name of the author of the reviewed work, the journal or newspaper in which the review appears, and the relevant publication information.

> 33. Harold Kinkaid, "Scientific Historiography and the Philosophy of Science," review of *Our Knowledge of the Past: A Philosophy of Historiography,* by Aviezer Tucker, *History and Theory* 45 (2006): 125.

Public Documents

For government publications, begin the citation with the name of the country, state, city, county, or other government body that created the document you used as a source. If there is also a subagency, this smaller body (say, a "committee" of the U.S. House of Representatives, as in the first example), should come next. Then the collection (if applicable) from which the document comes, followed by the title of the document in italics. If the document or the collection has its own author, that person's name comes next. The publisher need be included only if it differs from the issuing agency. The Government Printing Office (GPO) publishes many U.S. government documents. Finally, include the date and page or other number identifying the document. If the government document is online, include the URL.

The following items are models for different kinds of government documents. They are not intended to be exhaustive, but simply to give a sense of how to apply the guidelines to different situations.

23. U.S. LEGISLATIVE BRANCH COMMITTEE REPORT

> 34. U.S. Congress, House, House Select Committee on Assassinations, *Final Report of the House Select Committee on Assassinations* (Washington DC: GPO, 1979): 84.

24. U.S. TREATY

> 35. U.S .Department of State, "The Paris Peace Accords," January 27, 1973, *United States Treaties and Other International Agreements* 24, pt. 1.

25. U.S. SUPREME COURT DECISION

36. U.S Supreme Court, *Brown v. Board of Education of Topeka, Kansas*, Case # 347US483,May 17, 1954.

26. CANADIAN LEGISLATIVE BRANCH COMMITTEE REPORT

37. Canada, House of Commons, Standing Committee on Canadian Heritage, *Interim Report on the Canadian Film Industry* (Ottawa: June 2005): 24.

Multimedia Sources

27. DVD OR VIDEOCASSETTE

The citation for a DVD or videocassette should include the title of the film or episode, followed by the name of the series if applicable, the type of medium, the name of the director, and the publication information.

38. "The Challenge of Freedom," *Slavery and the Making of America*, DVD, directed by Leslie D. Farrell (New York: Ambrose Video, 2005).

28. MUSICAL COMPOSITION

To cite a printed musical score, list the composer, the title of the piece, the editor ("ed.") or arranger ("arr.") if applicable, and the publication information. If the score is part of a series, list the volume number and title of the series after the title of the score.

39. Luciano Berio, *Alternatim: per clarinetto, viola e orchestra* (Vienna: Universal Edition, 2001).

29. SOUND RECORDING

The content of a footnote or endnote for a sound recording depends on whether the recording is of a musical composition, a speech, or a reading. For the performance of a musical composition, list the name of the composer, the title of the piece, the performer(s), the recording company, the number of the recording, and the type of medium (compact disc, audiocassette, etc.).

40. Bernard Rands, *Le Tambourin, Suites 1 and 2*, Philadelphia Orchestra, New World Records 80392, compact disc.

If the recording is of a speech or reading, list the speaker, the title of the recording, the publication information, and the medium.

41. Martin Luther King Jr., *Martin Luther King at Zion Hill* (Los Angeles: Duotone Records, 1962), audiocassette.

30. WORK OF ART

If you found an illustration or photograph in a printed work, begin with the name of the artist, followed by the title of the work of art, the title of the book or article in which you found it, and the publication information and page number.

42. Alexis Preller, "Hieratic Women," in *A History of Art*, ed. Sir Lawrence Gowing, rev. ed. (Ann Arbor: Borders Press, 2002), 973.

If the artist is unknown, begin with the title or description of the work.

43. "A Chavin Hammered Gold Plaque," in *A History of Art*, ed. Sir Lawrence Gowing, rev. ed. (Ann Arbor: Borders Press, 2002), 479.

If you saw the photograph, painting, or sculpture in a museum, an archive, or a private collection, tell the reader where you saw it. Include the name of the artist, the title of the work, the type of medium, the date the work was created, and where it can be found.

44. Ansel Adams, *The Golden Gate before the Bridge, San Francisco, California*, gelatin silver print, 1980, National Gallery of Art, Washington, DC.

31. SLIDE

A citation for slides should include the compiler of the collection, the title of the collection, the name of the editor if any, the publication information, and the indication that the medium is "slides."

45. Elizabeth Hammer, *The Arts of Korea: A Resource for Educators*, ed. Judith G. Smith (New York: Metropolitan Museum of Art, 2002), slides.

32. MAP

If a map is in a printed work, treat it as you would an illustration or photograph. Begin with the name of the map designer if known, followed by the title of the map in quotation marks, the title of the book or edited work in which the map was found, the author or editor of the work, the publication information, and the page number.

46. "Spanish Military Frontier, Northwest New Spain," in *Cycles of Conquest: The Impact of Spain, Mexico, and the United States on the Indians of the Southwest, 1533-1960,* by Edward H. Spicer (Tucson: University of Arizona Press, 1962), 286.

33. CHART, GRAPH, OR TABLE

If a chart is in a printed work, treat it as you would a map or an illustration. Include the title of the chart, graph, or table, usually found beneath it, the publication information for the work in which it appeared, and the page number.

47. "Estimated World Population," in *A Student's Guide to History*, 9th ed., by Jules Benjamin (Boston: Bedford/St. Martin's, 2004), 30.

Electronic Sources

34. SMALL WEB SITE

The Internet is an unstable place in which new Web sites regularly
come into existence while others disappear or change their addresses.
Moreover, the information on a site can be removed or changed. Your citation to an online source needs to be as complete as possible because of
the changing nature of digital information.

If you are documenting a small Web site whose creator you can identify,
or a site in which one person compiled or created all of the information,
then you can treat that person as the "author." Your note should list the
author's name, the name of the document (or other source) you are referring to, the name of the site (if the two are different), the URL, and the
date on which you visited, or accessed, the site.

> 48. Barbara Landis, "Carlisle Indian Industrial School History,"
> http://home.epix.net/~Landis/histry.html (accessed May 10, 2006).

35. LARGE WEB SITE

A large Web site is likely to be more stable than a small one. Nevertheless, it will contain a great many documents (and other information
sources), and the author of a particular document may not be clear. If this
is the case, begin with the sponsor (or other group responsible for the
site) and the name of the site. Then record the name of the text, illustration, photograph, streaming video, audio, and so on that you are documenting and its date of origin if available. Finally, record the URL and the
date of access.

If the document is difficult to find because of the complex nature of
the site, include the name of the section (and subsection) where it is located. Be sure to check the accuracy of all of the segments of the URL.
Be aware that the home URL of the site will be different from the URL
of the section of the site on which you found your source. The source itself may have yet another URL. If the URL of your source is very long, it
is preferable to tell your reader the home URL and the path of links (or
search terms) you took to arrive at your source. (See the path example
below.)

> 49. Library of Congress, American Memory, Map Collections: 1500-2004,
> U.S Railroad Maps, 1828-1900, "Map of Pennsylvania Railroad with its connec-
> tions. . ." (Philadelphia; Friend & Aub., 1851), http://memory.loc.gov/
> cgi-bin/query/D?gmd:29:./temp/~ammem_R98A:: (accessed August 20, 2006).

> *Home URL plus path*:
> http://memory.loc.gov/ammem/ ⇨ Browse Collection: Maps ⇨ Railroad Maps ⇨
> Browse Geog. Loc. ⇨ U.S. ⇨ Map#37.

36. MATERIAL FROM AN INFORMATION SERVICE OR DATABASE

When citing an information service or database, list the service, agency, or corporation responsible for collecting the information as the author, followed by the name of the compilation or survey (or other type of information) in quotation marks, the name of the database italicized, and the URL.

50. United Nations Population Division, "World Population Prospects: The 2004 Revision Population Database," *United Nations Population Information Network*, http://esa.un.org/unpp/.

37. ARTICLE FROM A DATABASE OF FULL-TEXT JOURNAL ARTICLES

Cite the article as you would one from a printed journal. Then add the name of the online database and the URL. In some instances, the name of the database is included in the URL.

51. Stephane Castonguay, "Naturalizing Federalism: Insect Outbreaks and the Centralization of Entomological Research in Canada, 1884–1914," *Canadian Historical Review* 85 (2004): 14. http:/muse.jhu.edu/journals/canadian_historical_review/v085/85.1castonguay.html.

38. ONLINE BOOK

To cite a printed book that has been digitized and placed on the Web, state the author, the title (in italics), the place and date of the publication of the printed book (in parentheses), and the page number. Also include the title of the collection of online books in which you found it, the URL and the date on which you accessed it.

52. George Rawlinson, *History of Phoenicia* (London: Longmans, Green and Co., 1889), 116, Project Gutenberg, http://www.gutenberg.org/etext/2331 (accessed May 15, 2006).

39. ARTICLE FROM AN ELECTRONIC JOURNAL

Cite an article from an online journal as you would an article in a printed journal. If the journal was part of a database, include the title of the database, the creator of the database if available, the URL of the article, and the date you accessed it. If you read the journal on the journal's own Web site, then use the URL of that site, as in the following example.

53. Scott Gac, "Jazz Strategy: Dizzy, Foreign Policy, and Government in 1956," *The Journal of American Popular Culture* 4 (Spring 2005), not paginated. http://www.americanpopularculture.com/journal/articles/spring_2005/gac.htm (accessed January 21, 2006).

40. COMPUTER SOFTWARE

To cite a software program, list the name of the software, the version used, the company that produced it, and the location of the company.

54. *U.S. History: The American West*, CD-ROM, ver. Windows NT, Fogware Publishing, San Jose.

41. E-MAIL MESSAGE

You should ask permission to use the content of an e-mail message from the person who wrote it. In the citation, give the author's name, the subject heading if there is one, the date when it was posted, the fact that it was an e-mail message ("personal e-mail message"), and the date on which you read it. Do not include the author's e-mail address.

55. Lynn Temple, "Re: Question about the Bedford flag," personal e-mail message, March 26, 2003.

42. LISTSERV MESSAGE

A listserv citation is similar to that for an e-mail message, except that you need to add the e-mail address of the listserv.

56. Ruth Rosen, "Question about recent feminist history," listserv message, January 31, 2006, h-women@h-net.msu.edu.

43. NEWSGROUP MESSAGE

A newsgroup citation is similar to that of a listserv or e-mail message, except that you should include the location of the newsgroup.

57. Domenico Rosa, "Vietnam's Women of War," newsgroup message, January 19, 2003, soc.history.war.vietnam.

44. SYNCHRONOUS COMMUNICATION

Synchronous communications over the Internet should be cited by listing the author of the message or the sponsor of the group, the title of the group if any, or the indication that this was an instant message, the date on which the group was created (if applicable and known), the URL for accessing the group or messenger, and the date on which the communication occurred. A difficulty in citing this kind of material is that the author of a message may use a pseudonym. If you know that the name is a pseudonym, you may put "(pseud.)" after the name.

58. Absolute MUSH, absolute.spod.org:6250 (accessed January 9, 2003).

Other Sources

45. PAMPHLET

Treat a pamphlet like the first reference to a book in your footnotes or endnotes.

59. Pat Nyhan and Helen Epstein, *Kenya's Unfinished Democracy: A Human Rights Agenda for the New Government* (Washington, DC: Human Rights Watch, 2002), 14.

46. UNPUBLISHED DISSERTATION

When citing a dissertation in footnotes or endnotes, list the author of the dissertation, the title in quotation marks, then in parentheses "PhD diss." followed by the university at which the dissertation was written, and the date, all separated by commas. Finally, outside the parentheses, list the page number or numbers.

> 60. Nadja Durbach, "Disease by Law: Anti-Vaccination in Victorian England, 1853–1907" (PhD diss., Johns Hopkins University, 2001), 69–80.

47. DISSERTATION ABSTRACT

To cite a dissertation abstract, list the work as you would a dissertation, but indicate where the abstract was found, including volume number and date, if applicable, before the page number.

> 61. David Charles Engerman, "America, Russia and the Romance of Economic Development" (PhD diss., University of California, Berkeley, 1999), abstract in *America since 1607* 678 (1999): 308t.

48. LECTURE OR PUBLIC ADDRESS

If a lecture or public address has been published, cite the published source in which you found it, following the appropriate form. If the lecture or public address has not been published, list the speaker, the title of the speech, and then, in parentheses, information about the group to which it was presented, the location, and the date.

> 62. Eva Bremner, "From Heldenkaiser to Hausvater: Wilhelm I as the King of Christmas" (paper presented at Young Scholars Forum, "Gender, Power, Religion: Forces in Cultural History," at the German Historical Institute, Washington, DC, March 31, 2001).

49. INTERVIEW OR ORAL HISTORY

If an interview has been published, you should cite it by listing the person interviewed, the title of the interview, the name of the interviewer, the publication, date, and page number.

> 63. Herman J. Viola, "Viola Records the View of the American Indian," interview by Stephen Goode, *Insight on the News,* January 3, 2000, 37.

If you are citing an unpublished interview or oral history, include the name of the speaker, the interviewer, the location of the interview, the date, and, if the interview is kept in an archive, the location of the transcript or recording. The following footnote is to an interview conducted by a student during research for a class assignment.

> 64. John Smith, interview by Mary Jones, San Francisco, January 8, 2004. Transcript in possession of this writer.

Directory to Bibliography Documentation Models

Organizing a Bibliography

A bibliography is an alphabetical listing of the sources you used when writing your paper. It must include *all* of the sources that appear in your footnotes or endnotes. However, do not include *all* of the sources you looked at in the course of your research. For a bibliography that is long, you might separate it into several categories, such as primary sources, books, articles, and nonprinted sources (tables, pictures, Internet pages, etc.). Each list is alphabetized according to the *last* name of the author. If a work has no author (or editor or translator), alphabetize it according to the first word (except for "A," "An," "The") of the title. Begin each entry at the left margin and indent any additional lines five spaces. Each item in a bibliography is single-spaced. Use double-spacing between items. If a work has more than one author, alphabetize according to the last name of the first author mentioned on the title page of the book or article. That name should be followed by the names of all of the other authors listed with their *first* names first. You should note that, while in many instances the parts of a footnote are separated by *commas,* in a bibliography they are usually separated by *periods.* (See the bibliography for the sample research paper on pp. 183–84.)

Bibliographic Form. The following examples of bibliography entries show the different forms required for citing different types of sources. These forms are drawn from *The Chicago Manual of Style,* Fifteenth Edition (Chicago: University of Chicago Press, 2003).

For help documenting the exact place on the Web where you found material that you wish to use in a paper, see the guidelines for documenting electronic sources on pp. 155–57. These guidelines differ from Chicago style in a few cases in order to provide the most accurate and efficient method of recording the location of an Internet source.

Books

1. BASIC FORMAT FOR A BOOK

A bibliographic reference for a book refers to the book as a whole. An entry in a bibliography for a book should include the author, last name first, followed by a period; the full title of the work (including any subtitle after a colon), italicized or underlined, followed by a period; the place of publication, followed by a colon; the name of the publisher, followed by a comma; and the date of publication, followed by a period. (If there is a "Jr.," "Sr.," or numeral after the author's name, put it after the first name, preceded by a comma — as in: Mansfield, Harvey C., Jr.) The reference should look like this example:

Darnton, Robert. *George Washington's False Teeth: An Unconventional Guide to the
    Eighteenth Century.* New York: Norton, 2003.

2. MULTIPLE WORKS BY THE SAME AUTHOR

If your paper includes more than one source by the same author, use three hyphens or dashes instead of repeating the name. List the works in alphabetical order by title.

Darnton, Robert. *George Washington's False Teeth: An Unconventional Guide to the Eighteenth Century.* New York: Norton, 2003.

———. *The Great Cat Massacre and Other Episodes in French Cultural History.* New York: Vintage Books, 1995.

3. TWO OR THREE AUTHORS

Bibliographic format is the same for books with two or three authors except that the names of the second (and third) authors are not inverted. Put a comma after both the last and the first names of the first author listed, and place the authors in the order in which they appear on the title page.

Inden, Ronald, Jonathan Walters, and Daud Ali. *Querying the Medieval: Texts and the History of Practices in South Asia.* New York: Oxford University Press, 2000.

4. FOUR OR MORE AUTHORS

If there are more than three authors, the bibliographic reference (unlike the form for footnotes) usually includes the names of all of the authors.

Roark, James L., Michael P. Johnson, Patricia Cline Cohen, Sarah Stage, Alan Lawson, and Susan M. Hartmann. *The American Promise: A History of the United States.* 3rd ed. Boston: Bedford/St. Martin's, 2005.

5. ORGANIZATION AS AUTHOR

If the author of the work you are citing is a corporation, group, agency, institution, or some other organization rather than a person, put the organization's name in the space for the author.

Congressional Quarterly. *Congressional Quarterly's Guide to Congress.* 5th ed. Vol. 2. Washington, DC: Congressional Quarterly, 2000.

6. BOOK BY AN UNKNOWN AUTHOR

If the author of a work is unknown or is listed as "Anonymous" on the title page, skip the listing of the author and begin the reference with the title of the work.

Through Our Enemies' Eyes: Osama Bin Laden, Radical Islam and the Future of America. Washington, DC: Brassey's, 2002.

If a work is anonymously written but has a known editor, you may treat the book as an edited volume.

7. TRANSLATED BOOK

In a bibliography, the name of the translator appears after the title and is introduced with "Translated by" and finished with a period.

Gandhi, Mahatma. *An Autobiography: Or the Story of My Experiments with Truth.* 2nd
  ed. Translated by Mahadev Desai. Ahmedabad: Navajivan Press, 1956.

If a work was edited and translated by the same person, indicate this in the reference.

Boccaccio, Giovanni. *Famous Women.* Translated and edited by Virginia Brown. Cambridge, MA: Harvard University Press, 2001.

8. BOOK WITH ONE OR MORE EDITORS

If a work has both an author and an editor, keep the author's name at the beginning of the reference, and put the name of the editor after the title, preceded by the notation "Edited by" and concluding with a period.

Fox, George. *The Journal.* Edited by Nigel Smith. New York: Penguin Books, 1998.

In an edited work that has no author, the editor's name, followed by "ed.," appears (last name first) where the author's name normally would.

Price, T. Douglas, ed. *Europe's First Farmers.* Chicago: University of Chicago Press,
  2000.

In a work with multiple editors and no author, use the same format as for multiple authors, but follow the names with "eds." (Only the first name listed should be in inverted order—last name first.)

Amin, Camron Michael, Benjamin C. Fortna, and Elizabeth B. Frierson, eds. *The Modern Middle East: A Sourcebook for History.* Oxford: Oxford University Press,
  2006.

For four or more editors, write only the first name followed by "and others" or "et al." to indicate the other editors, and conclude with "eds."

Breitenbach, Esther, and others, eds. *The Changing Politics of Gender Equality in
  Britain.* New York: Palgrave, 2002.

9. SELECTION IN AN EDITED WORK OR ANTHOLOGY

A reference for a selection (chapter, essay, document, etc.) from a larger edited work begins with the name of the author, followed by the title of the selection in quotation marks, the name of the entire work (preceded by the word "In"), the name of the editor (preceded by the words "edited by"), and standard publication information.

Jones, Paul R. "The Two Field System." In *Europe's First Farmers*, edited by T. Douglas
  Price. Chicago: University of Chicago Press, 2000.

10. EDITION OTHER THAN THE FIRST

If you are using a later edition of a work, the edition number is placed after the title and is followed by a period.

> Chasteen, John Charles. *Born in Blood and Fire: A Concise History of Latin America.* 2nd ed. New York: Norton, 2005.

For a revised edition, use "Rev. ed."

> West, Cornel. *Race Matters.* Rev. ed. Boston: Beacon Press, 2001.

11. MULTIVOLUME WORK

If you are citing one volume of a multivolume work and the volumes all have the same title, then put the volume number after the title.

> Braudel, Fernand. *The Mediterranean and the Mediterranean World in the Age of Philip II.* Vol. 1, translated by Sian Reynolds. Berkeley: University of California Press, 1996.

When, however, the volume has its own title, then the volume title and the number of the specific volume used come first, followed by the general title and the publication information.

> Caro, Robert A. *Master of the Senate.* Vol. 3, *The Years of Lyndon Johnson.* New York: Knopf, 2002.

When your bibliographic reference is to all of the volumes of a work, then you should note the number of volumes within the citation.

> Schama, Simon. *A History of Britain.* 2 vols. New York: Hyperion, 2000–2001.

12. ENCYCLOPEDIA OR DICTIONARY

A reference work from which only basic facts have been taken does not need to be included in a bibliography. However, if you footnoted an authored article appearing in an encyclopedia, you need to list it.

> Weber, Anita M. "Willard, Frances E. (1939–1898)." In *Handbook of American Women's History,* edited by Angela M. Howard and Frances K. Kavenik. 2nd ed. Thousand Oaks, CA: Sage, 2000.

Periodicals

13. JOURNAL ARTICLE

An entry in a bibliography for a scholarly journal article should include the author, last name first, followed by a period; the title of the article followed by a period, all in quotation marks; the title of the journal, italicized or underlined; the volume number of the journal and, in parentheses, the year of the volume, followed by a colon; and the pages on which the article begins and ends, followed by a period.

Goldman, Wendy. "Stalinist Terror and Democracy: The 1937 Union Campaign."
American Historical Review 110 (2005): 1427–1453.

14. ARTICLE IN A JOURNAL PAGINATED BY VOLUME

Journals often have multiple issues per year, generally indicating each
year by a volume number and then specifying individual issues within that
volume. Sometimes the journal carries over the numbering system
throughout the year (that is, throughout the several issues of the volume).
If the journal paginates by volume, there is no need to identify the issue
number in your citation.

Abel, E. Lawrence. "And the Generals Sang." *Civil War Times* 39 (2000): 45–50.

15. ARTICLE IN A JOURNAL PAGINATED BY ISSUE

If a journal paginates by issue (that is, every issue begins with page 1),
then it is necessary to include both volume number and issue number
(the latter indicated by "no.") so that the reader can easily find your reference. If a journal paginates by issue but does not have issue numbers,
then include the season or month of the issue before the year in the
parentheses.

Horodsky, Daniel. "How U.S. Merchant Marines Fared during WWII." *Insight on the
News* 16, no. 1 (2000): 46–49.

16. ARTICLE IN A MAGAZINE

Reference to a popular magazine (rather than to a scholarly journal)
requires author, title of article, title of magazine, and date, but no volume
or issue number. It is not necessary to include the pages encompassing
the entire article, as they may be separated by irrelevant material such as
advertisements.

Grandin, Greg. "Latin America's New Consensus." *Nation*, May 1, 2006.

17. ARTICLE IN A NEWSPAPER

Individual articles from daily newspapers are not usually listed in a bibliography. Instead, the name of the newspaper should be listed, along with
the range of years (but not the specific dates) of any articles cited.

New York Times, 1999-2003.

18. ARTICLE BY AN UNKNOWN AUTHOR

If a magazine or newspaper article has no listed author, the citation begins with the name of the article.

"Australia's Aborigines: A Dispute over Mistake Creek." *Economist*, December 14–20,
2002.

19. EDITORIAL

Newspaper editorials are not included in bibliographies. As with newspaper articles, record only the name of the newspaper and the year (but not the date) of any editorial cited. If, however, you are citing an editorial in a magazine, list the name of the editorial writer if known, the title of the editorial, the name of the magazine, and the date. If the editorial is unsigned, write "Editorial" in the space normally reserved for an author's name.

> Editorial. "TRB from Washington: A Century of Insight." *New Republic,* January 3, 2000.

20. LETTER TO THE EDITOR

For a letter to an editor in a magazine or journal, put the author's name first, then "Letter to the editor" (without quotation marks), then the name of the publication and the date. If the letter appears in a scholarly journal, then the volume, date, and page number should appear as in the journal article format.

> Herr, Paul J. Letter to the editor. *Foreign Affairs* 79, no. 2 (2000): 180.

If the letter appears in a magazine, then the date should appear as in the magazine format.

> Burnett, Christina D. Letter to the editor. *Harper's Magazine,* November 2002.

21. BOOK OR FILM REVIEW

A reference to a book or film review includes the author of the review, the title of the review article, the title of the work being reviewed, the name of the author or director of the reviewed work, and the relevant publication information.

> Kinkaid, Harold. "Scientific Historiography and the Philosophy of Science." Review of *Our Knowledge of the Past: A Philosophy of Historiography,* by Aviezer Tucker. *History and Theory* 45 (2006): 124–133.

Public Documents

The bibliography format for a government publication can be complex. In most cases, treat the government agency that produced the publication as the author. If there is a subagency, this smaller body (such as a committee of the House of Representatives, as in the first example) should come next, followed by the title of the document in italics. Any information indicating the collection of which the document is a part comes next, followed by the report number or other identifying information and the date. The publisher of the document or collection need be included only if it differs from the issuing agency. The Government Printing Office (GPO) publishes many U.S. government documents.

22. U.S. LEGISLATIVE BRANCH COMMITTEE REPORT

U.S. House of Representatives. House Select Committee on Assassinations. *Final Report of the Select Committee on Assassinations.* Washington, DC: GPO, 1979.

23. U.S. TREATY

U.S. Department of State. "The Paris Peace Accords." January 27, 1973. *United States Treaties and Other Agreements* 24, pt. 1.

24. U.S. SUPREME COURT DECISION

U.S. Supreme Court. *Brown v. Board of Education of Topeka, Kansas.* Case # 347US483. May 17, 1954.

25. CANADIAN LEGISLATIVE BRANCH COMMITTEE REPORT

Canada. House of Commons. Standing Committee on Canadian Heritage. *Interim Report on the Canadian Film Industry.* Ottawa: June 2005.

Multimedia Sources

26. DVD OR VIDEOCASSETTE

A citation for a DVD or videocassette should include the title of the film or episode, the name of the series (if applicable), the type of medium, the name of the director, and the publication information.

"The Challenge of Freedom." *Slavery and the Making of America.* DVD. Directed by Leslie D. Farrell. New York: Ambrose Video, 2005.

27. MUSICAL COMPOSITION

To list a printed musical score, note the composer, the title of the composition, the editor or arranger if applicable, and the publication information. If the composition is part of a series, list the volume number and title of the series after the title of the score.

Berio, Luciano. *Alternatim: per clarinetto, viola e orchestra.* Vienna: Universal Edition, 2001.

28. SOUND RECORDING

For the performance of a musical composition, list the name of the composer, the title of the piece (italicized), the performer(s), the recording company, the number of the recording, and the type of medium (compact disc, audiocassette, etc.)

Rands, Bernard. *Le Tambourin, Suites 1 and 2.* Philadelphia Orchestra. New World Records 80392. Compact disc.

If the recording is of a speech or reading, list the speaker, the title of the recording, the publication information, and the medium.

King, Martin Luther, Jr. *Martin Luther King at Zion Hill.* Los Angeles: Duotone
   Records, 1962. Audiocassette.

29. WORK OF ART

If you found an illustration or photograph in a printed work, begin with
the name of the artist, followed by the title of the work of art, the title of
the book or article in which you found it, and the publication information
and page number.

Preller, Alexis. "Hieratic Women." In *A History of Art,* edited by Sir Lawrence Gowing.
   Rev. ed. Ann Arbor: Borders Press, 2002.

If the artist is unknown, begin with the title or description of the work.

"A Chavin Hammered Gold Plaque." In *A History of Art,* edited by Sir Lawrence Gowing. Rev. ed. Ann Arbor: Borders Press, 2002.

If you saw the photograph, painting, or sculpture in a museum, an
archive, or a private collection, tell the reader where you saw it. Include
the name of the artist, the title of the work, the type of medium, the date
the work was created, and where it can be found.

Adams, Ansel. *The Golden Gate before the Bridge, San Francisco, California.* Gelatin
   silver print. 1980. National Gallery of Art, Washington, DC.

30. SLIDE

A citation to slides in a bibliography should include the compiler of the
slide collection, the title of the collection, the name of the editor if any, the
publication information, and the indication that the medium is "slides."

Hammer, Elizabeth. *The Arts of Korea: A Resource for Educators.* Edited by Judith G.
   Smith. New York: Metropolitan Museum of Art, 2002. Slides.

31. MAP

If a map is in a printed work, treat it as you would any other printed visual. Include the map designer if one is recorded, the title of the map followed by "in," then the title of the work in which the map was found, the
author or editor of the work, and the usual publication information.

"Spanish Military Frontier, Northwest New Spain." In *Cycles of Conquest: The Impact
   of Spain, Mexico, and the United States on the Indians of the Southwest, 1533-
   1960,* by Edward H. Spicer. Tucson: University of Arizona Press, 1962.

32. CHART, GRAPH, OR TABLE

If a chart is in a printed work, treat it as you would a map or an illustration. Include the title of the chart, graph, or table, usually found beneath
it, and the publication information for the work in which it appeared.

"Estimated World Population." In *A Student's Guide to History,* 9th ed., by Jules
   Benjamin. Boston: Bedford/St. Martin's, 2004.

Electronic Sources

33. SMALL WEB SITE

The Internet is an unstable place in which new Web sites regularly come into existence while others disappear or change their addresses. Moreover, the information on a site can be removed or changed. Your citation to an online source needs to be as complete as possible because of the changing nature of digital information.

If you are documenting a small Web site whose creator you can identify, or a site in which one person compiled or created all of the information, then you can treat that person as the "author." Your bibliographical entry should list the author's name, the name of the document (or other source) you are referring to, the name of the site (if the two are different), the URL, and the date of access if the material is time sensitive.

> Landis, Barbara. "Carlisle Indian Industrial School History." 1996.
>
> http://home.epix.net/~Landis/histry.html (accessed May 10, 2006).

34. LARGE WEB SITE

A large Web site is likely to be more stable than a small one. Nevertheless, it will contain a great many documents (and other information sources), and the author of a particular document may not be clear. If this is the case, begin with the sponsor (or other group responsible for the site) and the name of the site. Then record the name of the text, illustration, photograph, streaming video, audio, and so on that you are documenting, its date of origin if available, the URL, and the date of access if the materal is time sensitive.

If the document is difficult to find because of the complex nature of the site, include the name of the section (and subsection) where it is located. Be sure to check the accuracy of all segments of the URL. Be aware that the home URL of the site will be different from the URL of the section of the site on which you found your source. The source itself may have yet another URL. If the URL of your source is very long, it is preferable instead to tell your reader the home URL and the path of links (or search terms) you took to arrive at your source. (See the path example included in footnote 49 on p. 142.)

> Library of Congress. American Memory, Map Collections: 1500-2004. U.S. Railroad
>
> Maps, 1828-1900. "Map of Pennsylvania Railroad with its connections. . . ."
>
> Philadelphia: Friend & Aub., 1851. http://memory.loc.gov/cgi-bin/query/
>
> D?gmd:29:./temp/~ammem_R98A::

35. MATERIAL FROM AN INFORMATION SERVICE OR DATABASE

When citing an information service or database, list the service, agency, or corporation responsible for collecting the information as the author, followed by the name of the compilation or survey (if applicable) in quotation marks, the name of the database (if applicable) italicized, and the URL.

> United Nations Population Division. "World Population Prospects: The 2004 Revision Population Database." *United Nations Population Information Network.* http://esa.un.org/unpp/.

36. ARTICLE FROM A DATABASE OF FULL–TEXT JOURNAL ARTICLES

Follow the proper format for an article in a print journal. Then add the name of the online database and the URL. In some instances, the name of the database is included in the URL.

> Castonguay, Stephane. "Naturalizing Federalism: Insect Outbreaks and the Centralization of Entomological Research in Canada, 1884-1914." *Canadian Historical Review* 85 (2004): 1–34. http://muse.jhu.edu/journals/canadian_historical _review/v085/85.1castonguay.html.

37. ONLINE BOOK

For an online book, follow the format for a printed book and include the title of the collection of online books in which you found the source, the company that created the database, the URL, and the date of accession.

> Rawlinson, George. *History of Phoenicia.* London: Longmans Green Co., 1889. Project Gutenberg. http://www.gutenberg.org/etext/2331 (accessed May 15, 2006).

38. ARTICLE FROM AN ELECTRONIC JOURNAL

Cite an article in an online journal as you would an article in a printed journal. If the journal was part of a database, include the title of the database, the creator of the database if different, the URL of the article, and the date you accessed it. If you read the journal on the journal's own Web site, then use the URL of that site, as in the following example.

> Gac, Scott. "Jazz Strategy: Dizzy, Foreign Policy, and Government in 1956." *The Journal of American Popular Culture* 4 (2005). http://www.americanpopularculture .com/journal/articles/spring_2005/gac.htm (accessed March 4, 2006).

39. COMPUTER SOFTWARE

To cite a software program, list the name of the software, the version used, the publisher, and the location of the publisher.

> *U.S. History: The American West.* CD-ROM. Ver. Windows NT. Fogware Publishing, San Jose.

40. E-MAIL MESSAGE

In a bibliographic reference to an e-mail message, list the author and the subject header, indicate that the source is a personal e-mail, and put the date on which the e-mail was sent.

Temple, Lynn. "Re: Question about the Bedford flag." Personal e-mail message,
March 26, 2003.

41. LISTSERV MESSAGE

A listserv citation is like that for an e-mail message, except that you need to add the e-mail address of the listserv.

Rosen, Ruth. "Question about recent feminist history." Listserv message, January
31, 2006. h-women@h-net.msu.edu.

42. NEWSGROUP MESSAGE

A newsgroup citation is similar to that of a listserv or e-mail message, except that you should include the location of the newsgroup.

Rosa, Domenico. "Vietnam's Women of War." Newsgroup message, January 19, 2003.
soc.history.war.vietnam.

43. SYNCHRONOUS COMMUNICATION

Synchronous communications over the Internet should be cited by listing the author of the message — adding "(pseud.)" after the name if you know it to be a pseudonym — or the sponsor of the group, the title of the group (if any) or the indication that this was an instant message, the date on which the group was created (if applicable and known), the URL for accessing the group or messenger, and the date on which the communication occurred.

Absolute MUSH. absolute.spod.org:6250 (accessed January 9, 2003).

Other Sources

44. PAMPHLET

In a bibliography, a pamphlet is cited in the same format as a book.

Nyhan, Pat, and Helen Epstein. *Kenya's Unfinished Democracy: A Human Rights
Agenda for the New Government.* Washington, DC: Human Rights Watch, 2002.

45. UNPUBLISHED DISSERTATION

When citing a dissertation in a bibliography, put the author of the dissertation first, followed by the title in quotation marks. Then write "PhD diss.," the university at which the dissertation was written, and the date, all separated by commas.

Durbach, Nadja. "Disease by Law: Anti-Vaccination in Victorian England,
1853–1907." PhD diss., Johns Hopkins University, 2001.

46. DISSERTATION ABSTRACT

To cite a dissertation abstract, list the work as you would a dissertation, but indicate where the abstract was found, including volume number and date, if applicable.

> Engerman, David Charles. "America, Russia and the Romance of Economic Development." PhD diss., University of California, Berkeley, 1999. Abstract in *America since 1607* 678 (1999): 308t.

47. LECTURE OR PUBLIC ADDRESS

If a lecture or public address has been published, cite the published source as your reference and follow the appropriate bibliographic form. If the lecture or public address has not been published, list the speaker, the title of the speech, the group to which it was presented, the location, and the date.

> Bremner, Eva. "From Heldenkaiser to Hausvater: Wilhelm I as the King of Christmas." Paper presented at Young Scholars Forum, "Gender, Power, Religion: Forces in Cultural History," at the German Historical Institute, Washington, DC, March 31, 2001.

48. INTERVIEW OR ORAL HISTORY

If an interview has been published, you should cite it by listing the person interviewed, the title of the interview, the name of the interviewer, the publication, and the date.

> Viola, Herman J. "Viola Records the View of the American Indian." Interview by Stephen Goode. *Insight on the News*, January 3, 2000.

If you are citing an unpublished interview or oral history, include the name of the speaker, the interviewer, the location of the interview or oral history, the date, and, if the interview is kept in an archive, the location of the transcript or recording. The following example is for an interview conducted by a student doing research for a class assignment.

> Smith, John. Interviewed by Mary Jones. San Francisco, January 18, 2004. Transcript in possession of this writer.

REVISING AND REWRITING

Leave time in your writing schedule for revising your paper. Before writing your final draft, put the paper aside for a day or two (another reason to leave time) and then reread it. This way, you will gain a fresh perspective and may detect weaknesses that you hadn't noticed before.

A rough draft always needs smoothing out. As you reread your paper, look for any places where it seems to wander away from a direct focus on the theme. Be certain that the thesis is stated clearly at the outset and that each part of the paper contains information that supports the thesis. Does each part of the paper seem clearly connected to the part that follows it? Be sure that footnotes appear whenever they are needed.

While you examine the overall structure of the paper for defects, you also need to look closely at the language itself. If you repeated yourself, eliminate the repetition. If you included material that is unrelated to your theme, discard it. Check the connections between paragraphs to see whether the reader will be able to follow your argument. Make sure that you have accomplished what you set out to do in your introduction, that you have sufficiently supported your thesis, and that your conclusion makes it clear that you have done so. Check the footnotes (or endnotes) for proper style and accuracy. Do the same with the entries in the bibliography.

Finally, examine your writing for errors in spelling and grammar. Proofread carefully and slowly. At normal reading speed your eyes can go right by major errors. You are so familiar with your paper that you may not see what is on the page. Reading your paper aloud will help you catch unclear phrases. Showing it to a friend will let you know where your readers might have problems.

Guidelines for Revising and Rewriting

- Revising a rough draft takes time. Be sure to include that time in your writing schedule.
- Wait a day or two after completing the rough draft to prepare the final draft. This will help you to look at your rough draft with a fresh perspective.
- Examine the overall structure of the rough draft. Is it clearly focused on your intended theme and thesis?
- Be sure that the introduction states your thesis and that the major arguments behind your thesis are supported in the body of your paper.
- Check to see if the parts of the paper follow one another in a clear and direct way.
- Rewrite or eliminate any points that are weak, are repetitive, seem out of order, or are unrelated to your thesis.
- Examine the placement, form, and accuracy of the footnotes. Check the bibliography for form and accuracy as well.
- Proofread your paper carefully, looking for errors of grammar and spelling. Check the format of the paper, looking at margins, spacing, and the insertion of any visual material.
- Have a friend read your paper; rewrite any points that your friend has trouble understanding.

Sometimes **peer reviewing,** or reading a draft of another student's paper, is part of the work for the course. If your instructor gives specific guidelines for this assignment, follow them. (Refer to the peer-reviewing guidelines listed in Chapter 2.)

Word Processing: Advantages and Dangers

The ease of changing what you have written, because it is wrong or because you think of a better way to say it, is the greatest advantage of composing with a computer. Read each sentence as you are writing it. Looking at the screen, keep the larger picture in mind. Ask yourself: Is this sentence clear? Does it say what I want it to say? Will my reader understand it? Does it advance my thesis? If you see a problem, immediately revise your writing; don't wait until you have written more. If you wait, your weak sentence will become embedded in the text and difficult to revise later. When you scroll back to change the weak one, you probably will have to rework surrounding sentences too, to maintain **continuity.**

This advice for sentences holds true for paragraphs. Don't write too many paragraphs without rereading to see if they make sense together. Remember, you can see only one screen at a time, so you may have a tunnel-like vision of your paper. The paragraph on the screen may read well, but the one that just scrolled off the top of the screen may not be logically connected to it. Every few paragraphs, scroll back to earlier paragraphs (or to even earlier pages) to ensure that the sections of your paper hold together. If you lose a sense of the structure of any part of your paper, print it out and read it on the printed page. Don't let big pieces of your writing go by without rereading them — *and saving them.*

When you have finished a draft, print it out and read it as a whole. When you return to the computer, use an editing function such as Markup that clearly indicates changed text. If this kind of function is not available, save any changes to disk right away. If you don't do this, you may lose track of which changes you have and have not made. Because rewriting is so easy on a computer, what is on your disk can quickly jump ahead of what you have printed. Be vigilant; otherwise, your "final" hard copy may not reflect all the changes that are on the disk.

Using Spell- and Grammar-Checkers.   It is a good idea to run these checking programs every time you finish a section of your paper. However, they are *not* replacements for your own proofreading of your work. They catch only spelling errors that are not other words — writing "no" when you mean "know" will satisfy the checker every time. Also, grammar-checkers balk at some words and phrases that are just fine. Only you know what you mean to say, and only your eyes and brain can spot all of the spelling and grammar problems. Print out and carefully read each page of your work.

Formatting Your Paper. Pay attention to the format of your paper—how it looks to the reader. Your instructor may require a special format. If not, here are some generally accepted standards. You should create margins of about one inch on all four sides of each page. On your title page (which is *not* numbered), put (1) your name, (2) the course name and number, (3) the name of your instructor, (4) the date of your paper, and (5) the title of your paper. The body of the paper should be double-spaced—except for long (indented) quotations and footnotes, which are to be single-spaced. All pages following the title page should be consecutively numbered—including pages with illustrations, maps, graphs, and anything else. If you include visuals, mention them by number in your text—for example, "See Figure 6." Immediately below each visual, place the number, a brief description, and the source.

EXAMPLE OF A RESEARCH PAPER

As a final aid in preparing your **research paper,** this chapter ends with a full-scale example. The examination of the research paper begins with a discussion of how the **topic, theme,** and **thesis** were chosen and then moves on to the **writing outline** that the student developed. Finally, there is the paper itself, including **endnotes** and a **bibliography,** all of which follow the rules and suggestions made earlier in this chapter.

Several aspects of the sample research paper are designed to aid students. Annotations in the margin help you to see what the text is trying to accomplish. Also in the margin are a series of subtitles to the paper. Note how each one represents a stage in the unfolding story and is related to part of the writing outline. Finally, a comment in the margin of each endnote tells you what point in the paper is being supported. As you read the paper, ask yourself about the point the author is making and how she is accomplishing the goal. Pay special attention to the way in which the parts are put together and how each section adds strength to the effort to describe and support the thesis. Read through the endnotes also to determine why a citation is full or shortened and to see the form used for writing citations. Note also the form of the bibliography. If anything is unclear, refer back to the discussions of writing in Chapter 3 and to the "Writing the Text" section of this chapter (pp. 125–30).

This sample research paper can help you in two important ways. First, you can read the paper as a whole *before* you write your own. This will give you a clearer sense of what your paper should look like, how it should be developed, and the kind of **documentation** it should have. Second, you can refer to the paper *while* you are writing your own in order to answer specific questions about issues such as the introduction, continuity between paragraphs, the form of quotations and endnotes (or footnotes), the bibliography, and the conclusion.

How the Theme and Thesis Were Chosen

The theme chosen for this paper would fit a variety of courses: Pre–Civil War U.S. History, American Labor History, Women's History, and the History of Industrialization, among others. Within the framework of one such course, the student became curious about the lives of workers in the earliest factories. This curiosity led to a *topic* about industrialization in New England, where the student had grown up. Preliminary research indicated that textiles were the first goods to be made in factories, so the topic was narrowed to workers in that industry. When the student discovered that many of the earliest workers were young women who were the same age as she was, she decided to look at their lives in particular. At this point, her topic, "early industrialization in New England," had been narrowed to "women workers in early industrialization in New England." The largest number of these women worked in mills in Lowell, Massachusetts, so that town was chosen. (The student's research also made it clear that there were numerous sources that discussed Lowell mill workers.) The time period to be covered was the one during which women workers were the principal workforce in Lowell. Finally, the student discovered from preliminary research that in the early nineteenth century there was great concern about the impact of industrial work on American society and especially on women.

All of this narrowing led the student to her thesis: Women workers in Lowell, though working under difficult conditions, used this work experience to increase their independence. Finally, the student chose a title that introduced the reader both to her general theme, "women workers in the Lowell, Massachusetts, textile mills, 1820–1850," and to the question she intended to answer: whether their work represented "wage slavery or true independence." (See the sections on coming up with a theme and a thesis for your paper in Chapter 4, pp. 78–81.)

The Writing Outline for the Thesis

The writing outline was created from the student's **research plan** and subsequent research notes. (See "Creating a Preliminary Research Plan" in Chapter 4, pp. 81–83.) The research phase had made clear that several important aspects of the thesis had to be examined in the paper. Several sources gave detailed accounts of the experiences of the women workers, showing both positive and negative aspects of their working lives. It became clear that this subject should have an important place in the paper. Sections 4, 5, and 6 of the outline focus on this subject. Section 4 talks about work life, section 5 social life, and section 6 the women's response to changes in the mills. Having decided on the importance of the work experience, the student found it necessary to give the reader an understanding of how these women came to be mill workers in the first place. Section 3 examines this subject. Showing how the women came to be mill workers required an explanation of where the mills themselves came from. This was necessary because the mills represent the first stage of industrialization in America. Sections 1 and 2 deal with industrialization. Section 7 covers the end of the period during which women workers predominated in textile work. The other two sections, of course, are the introduction and conclusion.

The subheadings within each section are divisions of the larger subject and indicate the order in which a section will be developed. For example, section 4, "Life in a mill town," examines, in order, adjusting to life in a mill town, a typical workday, the work itself, the pay received, and the mill-owned boarding houses where the girls lived. Look at each part of the outline to see the function it serves and how the whole of the outline fully covers the important parts of the thesis. Try to be sure that your own outline sets the stage for writing your paper the way this one does.

SAMPLE WRITING OUTLINE

Wage Slavery or True Independence:
Women Workers in the Lowell, Massachusetts,
Textile Mills, 1820–1850

Introduction (thesis statement)
1. Attitudes toward industrialization in the United States
   a. Prejudice against industry by Americans
   b. Early industrialization in England
2. The origins of the textile industry in eastern Massachusetts
   a. The pre-industrial economy in America
   b. Slater-type mills
   c. Plans for a textile mill in Lowell, Massachusetts
3. Recruiting women workers
   a. The choice of a female workforce
   b. Overcoming the prejudice against women working outside the home
   c. Building a "moral" community
   d. Why young women chose to work in the mills
4. Life in a mill town
   a. Adjusting to life in the mills
   b. Typical workday
   c. Nature of work
   d. Rate of pay
   e. The boarding house
5. Social life
   a. Leisure hours
   b. Female companionship
   c. The *Lowell Offering*
6. Women workers' resistance to factory discipline
   a. "Turnouts"
   b. Slavery or independence?
7. Declining conditions of work in the Lowell mills
   a. End of paternalism
   b. The coming of the Irish workers
Conclusion
   a. Young women's experience of early industrialization

Turning Research into Writing: A Sample Research Paper

The full-scale example of a student research paper that concludes this chapter follows the rules and suggestions put forth earlier in the chapter. The **topic** ("women workers in early industrialization in New England") and **theme** ("women workers in Lowell, Massachusetts, textile mills, 1820–1850") were narrowed to form the **thesis.** This thesis — that women in Lowell used their difficult working conditions to gain independence — is reflected in the paper's title and writing outline and is supported throughout the paper.

Pay attention to the marginal comments that run down the sides of the pages of this sample paper. Compare them to the writing outline that you have just read. Note that each major section of the outline has a corresponding place in the paper itself. When you finish reading the paper, look at the marginal comments down the sides of the pages that contain the endnotes. Here you will see that each of the main points made in the paper is documented: Each point has one or more accompanying notes that tell the reader where the information came from. (See the section "Documenting Your Paper: Citing Your Sources" in this chapter, pp. 130–58.)

Wage Slavery or True Independence:

Women Workers in the Lowell, Massachusetts,

Textile Mills, 1820–1850

Unless your instructor has a special format, your title page should look something like this one. Whatever layout you choose, be sure to include: paper title, course name and number (and section, if necessary), instructor name, your name, and the date.

American History 200

Section 4

Professor Jones

Jane Q. Student

May 22, 2006

1

Introduction.

Statement of theme.

Statement of thesis.

Attitudes toward industrialization in the United States.

Superscript numbers refer to endnotes.

Background information.

This paper will examine the development of the textile industry in Lowell, Massachusetts, and the young women who served as its principal workforce between 1820 and 1850. It will describe how these women came to accept what was for them an unusual and difficult form of labor, but it will argue that they shaped this experience to serve their own purposes. Such a story helps to explain much about early industrialization in America and particularly about the role of women in the early factory system. The paper argues that these women workers were not mere laborers exploited by the mill owners but were actively engaged in expanding the constricted opportunities for women.

Until the early nineteenth century, the vast majority of Americans grew up in farm families. As the industrial revolution spread across England, rural Americans felt certain that the dark and dreary factory towns that were beginning to dot the English countryside would not arise in America. News coming from England contained reports that a permanent class of exploited workers was being created there. America, with its commitment to opportunity, would not, people were sure, experience such a fate. New England had been in the forefront of the struggle against British rule. Rural people in that region were especially proud of their independence and suspicious of anything that seemed to copy the ways of the English.[1]

New Englanders watched the rise of industrialization in England with concern. Changes in production there were most noticeable in the making of cloth. As late as the 1760s, English textile merchants were still making cloth by the age-old "putting out" system. They bought raw wool and hired women to spin it at home. When the wool had been spun into yarn, the merchant then sent it to weavers who also worked in their homes. In that decade, however, new machinery (the carding cylinder, spinning jenny, and most important, the water frame) was developed that made possible the shift of spinning and weaving from homes to what were called "factories." By 1800, many such factories had been established in England, usually employing children to do most of the

2

work. Many of these children were orphans or "paupers" from families so poor that they could not even afford to feed them. Conditions in these factories were very bad, and stories of these dark
and dangerous mills (some accurate, some exaggerated) filtered
back to America reinforcing the prejudice against England and industry.[2]

The economy of New England early in the nineteenth century
was tied to commerce and agriculture, not industry. The wealth of New
England merchants had been made in foreign trade, and few of them
saw the need to turn to other pursuits. Some worried that the development of American manufactures would cut down on the need to import
foreign goods. Until the War of 1812, which cut the United States off
from trade in English goods, most wealthy merchants in the Northeast
were content to stay in the business that had made their riches.[3] Moreover, where would American factory workers come from? England had a
large class of peasants who served as a pool of potential factory labor.
In America, however, when land wore out or harvests were poor, Yankee farmers could move west to the vast territories being taken from
Native Americans.

While great changes in the production of textiles were taking
place in England, most New Englanders still spun yarn at home and
some also wove their own cloth. In most cases they were simply making clothes for their families. Much of this work was done by women. A
spinning wheel was a possession of almost every household.[4] Despite
their anti-industrial prejudice, however, New England farmers witnessed, in the first two decades of the nineteenth century, a slow shift
in the way cloth was made in America. Home production gradually gave
way to "putting out" and that system was eventually replaced by factory production. Why did this change occur?

Unlike most merchants in America, a few, like Samuel Slater and
Francis Cabot Lowell, were impressed by the mechanization of English
textile production and began to think about an American textile industry. Men like these noted the massive increase in productivity in
the English textile industry. At first, Slater, and others who followed
his lead, built small mills in rural villages and employed not children

*The origins of
the textile indus-
try in eastern
Massachusetts.*

3

as in England but whole families. The building of Slater-type mills did not directly challenge the New England way of living. Most villages already contained small mills run by water power (streams pushing paddle wheels) that ground corn or wheat. Since the textile mills hired whole families who already lived in the villages, family and village life was not greatly altered.[5]

Transition sentence introduces discussion of new type of mill.

One new development in textile production, however, did raise troublesome questions about the impact of industrialization on America's rural way of life. This change came from a new type of mill. The first of its type was built in Waltham, Massachusetts, in 1813 by Francis Lowell and a small group of wealthy Boston merchants.[6] Three years earlier, Lowell had returned from a long trip to England. The British government would not allow the plans for the new power looms to be taken out of the country, but Lowell had paid close attention to their construction on his many tours of English mills and returned to America with enough knowledge in his head to eventually reproduce a machine comparable to the English power loom.[7]

In Waltham, Francis Lowell built a large mill that carried out both the spinning and weaving processes. In fact, every step of the production process was done in a series of connected steps. Waltham was not a village with a textile mill in it; it was a "mill town" in which the factory dominated the economic life of a rapidly growing city. Most significantly, Lowell's system of production brought important changes in the lives of his workers. He hired them as individuals, not as families, and many came from great distances to live and work in the new mill town. When Lowell died in 1817, the small group of Boston businessmen who had invested in his mill at Waltham spread the new factory system to other places. Their biggest investment was in the small village of East Chelmsford about twenty-seven miles from Boston and lying along the swift-flowing Concord and Merrimack Rivers. There they built what was soon the biggest mill town in the nation with more than a dozen large integrated mills based upon mechanical looms. In honor of their friend, they called the new town Lowell. (See Figure 1, a map of Lowell in 1845.)[8]

4

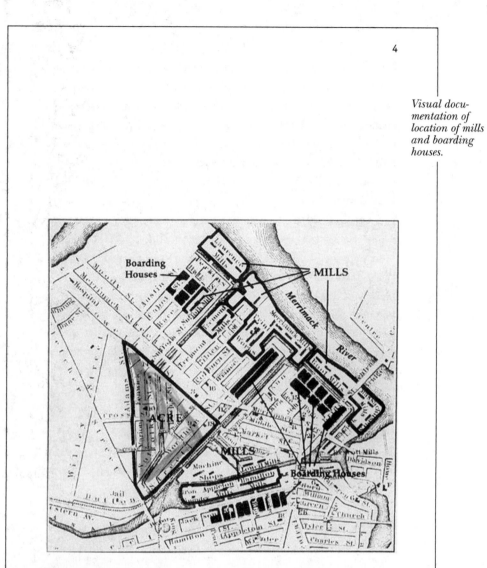

Figure 1. Adapted from Map of Lowell, Massachusetts, ca.
1845.
(Source: Barry Denenberg, *So Far from Home* (New York:
 Scholastic, 1997), 164b.)

5

The growth of Lowell between 1821 and 1840 was unprece-dented.[9] A rapidly developing textile industry like the one at Lowell needed larger and larger numbers of people to work the mechanical looms and other machines in the factories. Given the prejudice against factory work in New England, how could large numbers of natives be drawn to work in the mills? It was a question that had been carefully pondered by the wealthy men who built the big textile mills at Lowell, Massachusetts.

Recruiting women workers.

The mill owners, aware of the negative view of English mill towns, decided to confront the problem by creating a *planned* commu-nity where workers would live in solid, clean housing rather than slums. Their source of workers would also be different. The rapidly run-ning rivers that ran their mills were not near the major coastal cities. No large pool of potential laborers lived near their new town. The mill owners had to find a large group of people whose labor was not ab-solutely necessary to the farm economy. The solution to their labor problem came in the form of hundreds (later thousands) of young women who lived on the farms of the region.[10]

Several developments in the social and economic history of New England tended to make this group of workers available. Population growth was making it more and more difficult for farmers to find land close by for their sons (and their sons' families). Generations of the

Problems of the farm community.

same family had hoped to live near one another. By the 1820s, how-ever, many farms in New England, especially those on the less produc-tive land of Maine and New Hampshire, had run out of good land and had to find sources of income outside of agriculture. While some farm-ers went west to find more fertile land and a less harsh climate, others sent their sons to work on neighboring farms, or as apprentices to craftsmen (shoemakers, blacksmiths, or leather workers). Extra cash was something that most farm families were in great need of.[11]

Another factor helped set the stage for the successful industrial-ization of textile production. This one was within the structure of the family itself and worked in favor of producing a new group of workers for the mills. The position of women (wives and, especially, daughters) in the family was an inferior one. Adult, property-holding males were

6

citizens with full civil rights, but the same was not true for women *of any age.* The father of the family had the legal right to control most aspects of the lives of his wife and daughters. His wife could own no property. Her signature on a document meant nothing because only her husband could transact business. Daughters had even less independence. They were bound by social conventions to obey their fathers and rarely were able to earn money of their own. Even travel away from home was unusual. The idea that a woman's place was in the home was not merely a powerful concept, it was, with rare exceptions, a rule binding a woman's behavior. Although the work of daughters and wives was important to the family economy (it literally could not have functioned without their labor at field work, food preparation, cleaning, washing, etc.), they gained no independent income or freedom as a result. Indeed, so strong was the belief that daughters' lives would be bound by decisions made by their fathers, their older brothers, and, eventually, their husbands, that many could not imagine for themselves a life of active, public involvement of the kind expected of men. For some women, however, their inferior position in family and society gave them an incentive to take hold of any opportunity to weaken their bonds of inferiority.[12]

Subordinate status of women.

Women's motives were economic as well as social. Very few opportunities for employment outside the home existed; teaching in a local school was one of the most common, but that was very poorly paid and lasted for only a few months a year. The new mill work was steady work, and it paid more than any alternative available to women.[13] Young girls could thus contribute to their family's welfare by sending home a portion of their pay. This economic motive added to their desire to move outside the traditional sphere of the family. For many of them, the chance to live away from home and with other young women like themselves offered an independence that was otherwise impossible.[14]

Hiring young women, of course, ran up against strong Yankee resistance. As noted above, fathers rarely allowed their daughters to leave home when they were young. According to the prejudices of the period, young women were unprepared for a life among adult, male

7

Prejudice against women working outside the home. strangers. Their "innocence" and "purity" had to be protected by their family. The goal held out for these girls (almost the only respectable one) was eventual marriage. To prepare for that, they had to learn wifely duties and practical household skills. God-fearing New England fathers were very reluctant to let their daughters leave the farm to live and work among strangers in a faraway town.[15]

To confront this prejudice, the mill owners created boarding houses around the mills where groups of girls would live and take their meals under the care of a boarding housekeeper who was usually an older woman, perhaps a widow. Strict boarding-house rules were laid down by the company; rules that served the company's purposes but also reassured parents that their daughters' behavior would still be monitored even though they were away from home. For example, the young women could not have visitors in the late evening. (See Figure 2, a reproduction of boarding-house regulations.) Moreover, the girls would never grow into a permanent working class — something that no one wished to see — as it was expected that they would return to their homes for visits and after a year or two would go back to their villages. While they stayed in Lowell, their reputations (and thus their opportunity for marriage) would be protected by the town fathers.[16]

The mill owners did not advertise for help. They sent recruiters into the countryside to explain the special nature of Lowell and to soothe parents' fears. Because of the farmers' need for extra income, and the women's desire for independence, this effort was often successful.[17] Over the years, thousands of young women took the long trip by stagecoach or wagon from their rural homes to mill towns like Lowell.

Life in a mill town. Upon first arriving in Lowell, the young girls were naturally nervous. They had not lived away from home or ever worked in a factory. They were not used to the atmosphere of a city. The boarding house was new also. Living with a strange woman (and probably her family), who might or might not be a caring mother-substitute, also required adjustment. The girls shared the home with a dozen or more other girls and usually roomed with three or four of them. Most were homesick for a time. While all this was happening, of course, the girls had to make the difficult adjustment to the rigorous rules and long hours at the mill.[18]

8

Visual documentation of boarding-house life.

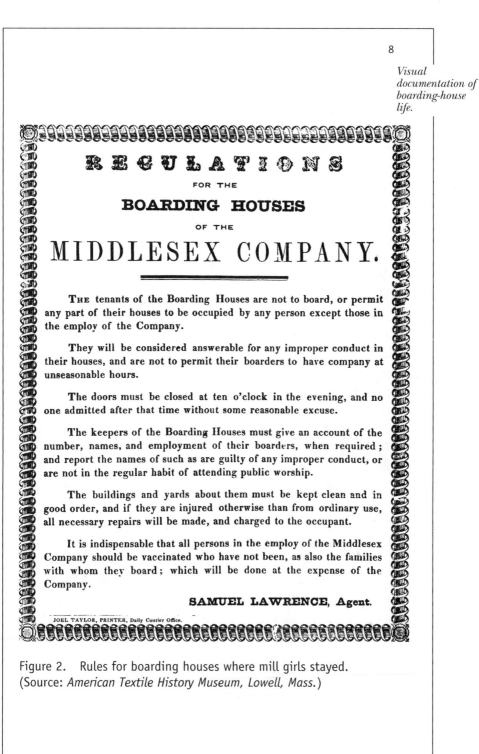

REGULATIONS

FOR THE

BOARDING HOUSES

OF THE

MIDDLESEX COMPANY.

THE tenants of the Boarding Houses are not to board, or permit any part of their houses to be occupied by any person except those in the employ of the Company.

They will be considered answerable for any improper conduct in their houses, and are not to permit their boarders to have company at unseasonable hours.

The doors must be closed at ten o'clock in the evening, and no one admitted after that time without some reasonable excuse.

The keepers of the Boarding Houses must give an account of the number, names, and employment of their boarders, when required; and report the names of such as are guilty of any improper conduct, or are not in the regular habit of attending public worship.

The buildings and yards about them must be kept clean and in good order, and if they are injured otherwise than from ordinary use, all necessary repairs will be made, and charged to the occupant.

It is indispensable that all persons in the employ of the Middlesex Company should be vaccinated who have not been, as also the families with whom they board; which will be done at the expense of the Company.

SAMUEL LAWRENCE, Agent.

JOEL TAYLOR, PRINTER, Daily Courier Office.

Figure 2. Rules for boarding houses where mill girls stayed.
(Source: *American Textile History Museum, Lowell, Mass.*)

9

Mill work and the workday.

Mill work was not only an opportunity, like so much of early factory labor, it was hard work. The typical workday began at five a.m. and did not end until seven in the evening, or later. Thus the women worked an average of twelve hours a day. They were given only thirty minutes for lunch and forty-five for dinner. Since they took their meals at the boarding house, the thirty minutes for lunch had to include a quick walk (perhaps a run) to and from the house, leaving only fifteen or twenty minutes for the meal.[19] The mills operated six days a week so that the only day off was Sunday, part of which was usually spent at church. Thus free time was confined to two or three hours in the evening (boarding-house rules required them to go to bed at ten) and to Sunday afternoon.[20] For many, however, this was still more leisure (and more freedom) than they would have had at home.

Despite a workday that, including meals, took up fourteen hours, most of the young women did not find the work very strenuous or particularly dangerous. As the mill owners had claimed, Lowell did not resemble the grimy, packed mill towns of England.[21] Still, the work was tedious and confining—doing the same operation over and over again and under the watchful eye of the overseer. In the ideal plan for Lowell, the overseer was to take the place of the absent father (just as the boarding-house widow was to be the substitute mother), someone responsible for seeing to the safety and welfare of the girls on the job. Of course, the overseer was also hired by the company to ensure that the mill ran smoothly and efficiently. He saw to it that the women worked steadily and recorded their hours of labor; any possibility of time off required his approval.[22]

The young women earned an average of three to four dollars a week from which their board of $1.25 a week was deducted.[23] At that time no other jobs open to women paid as well. As noted above, rural schoolteachers earned less than one dollar a week and taught for only three months of the year.[24] Three or four dollars a week was enough to pay their board, send badly needed money home, and still have enough left over for new clothes once in a while. Many women workers even established savings accounts, and some eventually left work with several hundred dollars, something that they could never have done at home.[25]

10

In Lowell the women became part of a growing city that had *Social life.* shops, social events, and camaraderie that were absent in their rural villages and farms. Most felt responsible to send part of their earnings home, but enough was left over to give them consumer choices un- available to their rural sisters, cousins, and friends. Also, unlike farm and family chores, mill work offered free time on Sundays and in the evenings.[26]

Even though their free time was very limited, the women en- gaged in a wide variety of activities. In the evening they wrote letters home, entertained visitors (though there was little privacy), repaired their clothing, and talked among themselves. They talked of friends and relatives and also of conditions in the mill. They could go out to the shops, especially clothing shops. The mill girls at Lowell prided themselves on a wardrobe that, at least on Sunday, was not inferior to that of the wives of prosperous citizens.[27] One of the most surprising uses of their free time was the number of meetings attended by mill girls. There were evening courses that enabled the young women to ex- tend their education beyond the few years of schooling they had re- *Leisure hours.* ceived in the countryside. They could also attend lectures by prominent speakers. It was not unusual for the audience at serious presentations to be composed mostly of mill girls. In their spare time, they also read novels and essays. So strong was the girls' interest in reading that many mills put up signs warning "No reading in the mills."[28] Perhaps the most unusual pursuit of at least some mill girls was writing. Deter- mined to challenge the idea that mill girls were mindless drones of the factory and lacked the refinement necessary to make them good wives, about seventy-five mill girls and women contributed in the 1840s to a series of publications that featured stories and essays by the workers themselves. Indeed, much of the editorial work was done by these women as well.[29]

The most well known of these publications was the *Lowell Offer-* *The* Lowell *ing.* The *Offering* stayed away from sensitive issues concerning working Offering. conditions, and the mill owners certainly benefited from the reputation for seriousness that it earned their workers. Still, the women con- trolled the content of the publication and wrote on subjects (family, courtship, fashion, morality, nature, etc.) that interested them.[30] A few of the *Offering* writers even went on to literary careers, not the kind of future that most people expected of factory workers. Charles Dickens toured the mills in 1842 and later said of the girls' writing: "Of the merits of the *Lowell Offering,* as a literary production, I will only observe . . . that it will compare advantageously with a great many English annuals."[31]

Example of a quotation with ellipsis. Short quotations are integrated into the text.

Though the *Offering* was a sign that something unusual was happening in this factory town, the women still worked in an industry that caused them hardship. In the early years, the owners had tried to keep up the image of the factory as a pleasant place. Buildings had many windows and much sunlight. The town had large green spaces and the atmosphere of a country village.[32] As time went on, however, the mill companies became more interested in profits and less concerned about their role as protectors of their young workers.

By the 1830s, tensions in the mills had begun to rise. Factory owners, observing a decline in the price of their cloth and the growth of unsold inventories, decided to lower their workers' wages.[33] When the reduction was announced in February 1834, the women workers circulated petitions among themselves pledging to stop work ("turn out") if wages were lowered.[34] When the leader of the petition drive at one mill was fired, many of the women protested. They left work and marched to the other mills to call out their workers. It is estimated that one-sixth of all women mill workers walked out as a result. The strikers wrote another petition stating that "we will not go back into the mills to work until our wages are continued . . . as they have been."[35]

Women workers' resistance to factory discipline.

Although the "turn out" was brief and did not achieve its purpose, it did demonstrate the attitude of many of the women workers. They did not accept the owners' view that they were minors under their benevolent care. The petitions prepared by the strikers indicate that they thought of themselves as the equal of their employers. The sense of independence gained by factory work and cash wages led them to reject the idea that they were mere factory hands. Petitions referred to their "unquestionable rights," and to "the spirit of our patriotic ancestors, who preferred privation to bondage. . . ." One petition ended,

12

"we are free, we would remain in possession of what kind providence has bestowed upon us, and remain *daughters of free men still.*"[36] This language indicates that the women did not think of themselves as laborers complaining about low wages. They were free citizens of a republic and deserved respect as such. Because many of the women had relatives who had fought in the Revolutionary War, they felt that they were protecting not only their jobs but also their independence.

Example of a quotation with emphasis added.

Although the strike failed and these women did not really have the "independence" they were so proud of, this issue was so important to them that many left the mills and went home when it became clear that mill work required a lessening of their status. They had accepted mill work because life away from home and good wages gave them greater freedom. When mill work came to seem more like "slavery" (a comparison that also appeared in the petitions) than independence, many changed their minds. In 1836, another effort to lower wages led to an even larger "turn out."[37] The willingness of these young women to challenge the authority of the mill owners is a sign that their new lives had given them a feeling of mutual strength.[38]

Economic recession in the late 1830s and early 1840s led to the layoff of hundreds of the women workers. Many of the mills were forced to part-time schedules. In the 1840s and 1850s, the mill owners tried to maintain profits despite increased competition and lessened demand. They did so by intensifying the work process. The speed of the machinery was increased as was the number of machines tended by each worker. Paternalism was discarded. To save money, the companies stopped building boarding houses.[39] The look of Lowell changed as well. Mill buildings took up more of the green space that had been part of the original plan.

Declining conditions of work in the Lowell mills.

By 1850, Lowell did indeed look something like an English mill town. By then, however, the desire to pacify the fears of potential workers and their families was gone. Terrible famine in Ireland in 1845 and 1846 had caused a large number of Irish to immigrate to the United States.[40] As conditions in the mills declined, more and more young Yankee women left the mills for home or other work. Their places were rapidly taken up by the very poor Irish for whom work of

The coming of Irish workers.

13

any kind in America was an opportunity, and who did not have the option of returning to their homes. Slowly, Lowell had become just another industrial city. It was dirty and overcrowded, and its mills were beginning to look run-down.

Conclusion.

By 1850, an era had passed. By then, most of the mill workers were recruited from newly arrived immigrants with backgrounds very different from those of the young New England women. During the period from the 1820s to the 1840s, however, young women from rural New England made up the majority of the textile workers in the area. At that time, an unusual era in the development of industrialization took place. Large textile mills with complex production systems were operated largely by young women who thought of themselves not as workers but as free citizens of a republic earning an independent existence for a few years before returning to their homes. These women gave the mill owners the workforce that was needed to make the U.S. textile industry large and profitable. Many fortunes were made for investors living in Boston and other major cities.[41] But the farmers'

Restatement of part of thesis.

daughters profited as well. Not only did they earn more than earlier generations of women had been able to, but they did so outside the home.

A great debate had raged during the 1830s and 1840s about the impact of industrialization on American life. Because of the general belief that women were weak, it was presumed that they would be taken advantage of as workers, especially as they were away from the protection of the male members of their families. Further, it was feared

Summary.

that mill work would "defeminize" them and that young men would not marry them because they had not been brought up in an environment of modesty, deference to their fathers and brothers, and daily practice in domestic tasks such as cleaning, sewing, and cooking.[42] (Textile mill workers were known as "spinsters," a word that came to mean a woman who never married.) Seen from a longer perspective, however, the women showed these fears to be unfounded. Even more importantly, as effective workers they undermined the stereotype of women as frail and as thriving only in a domestic environment. While these young women helped make possible the industrialization of New England, at

14

the same time they expanded their opportunities. Many women reform-   *Restatement of*
ers and radicals in later years, as they raised the banner for equal   *thesis.*
rights for women in more and more areas of life, referred back to the
example of the independent mill girls of the 1830s and 1840s who re-
sisted pressures from their employers, gained both freedom and matu-
rity by living and working on their own, and showed an intense desire
for independence and learning.[43] Great fortunes were made from the
textile mills of that era, but within those mills a generation of young
women gained something even more precious: a sense of self-respect.

15

Endnotes begin on a new page.

Endnotes

1. American attitudes toward industrialization in England and mill work in general.

1. Caroline F. Ware, *The Early New England Cotton Manufacture* (Boston: Houghton Mifflin, 1931), 4–8; Barbara M. Tucker, *Samuel Slater and the Origins of the American Textile Industry: 1790–1860* (Ithaca: Cornell University Press, 1984), 38–41; Robert F. Dalzell, *Enterprising Elite: The Boston Associates and the World They Made* (Cambridge: Harvard University Press, 1987), 12–13; Jonathan Prude, *The Coming of Industrial Order: Town and Factory Life in Rural Massachusetts, 1810–1860* (Cambridge, UK: Cambridge University Press, 1983), 6–12; Allan Kulikoff, "The Transition to Capitalism in Rural America," *William and Mary Quarterly* 46 (1989): 129–30, 141–42.

2. The rise of industrialization in England.

2. Tucker, *Slater*, 33–40.

3. The origins of industrialization in America.

3. Dalzell, 41–42; Ware, 3–8, 62.

4. Home spinning in America.

4. Thomas Dublin, *Women at Work: The Transformation of Work and Community in Lowell, Massachusetts, 1826–1860* (New York: Columbia University Press, 1979), 14; Adrienne D. Hood, "The Gender Division of Labor in the Production of Textiles in Eighteenth-Century Rural Pennsylvania," *Journal of Social History* 27 (Spring 1994),

Example of citation from the Web.

http://www.searchbank.com/infotrac/session/4/0/82904/37xrn_7.

5. Slater-type mills and family production.

5. Tucker, *Slater*, 79, 85, 99–100, 111; Barbara M. Tucker, "The Family and Industrial Discipline in Ante-Bellum New England," *Labor History* 21 (Winter 1979–80): 56–60.

6. The creation of Waltham mills.

6. Dalzell, 26–30; Tucker, *Slater*, 111–16.

7. H. C. Lowell and power loom.

7. Dalzell, 5–6.

8. The founding of Lowell.

8. Tucker, *Slater*, 116–17.

9. The growth of Lowell.

9. Dublin, 19–21, 133–35.

10. The owners' choice of a female workforce.

10. Dublin, 26, 76; Benita Eisler, ed., *The "Lowell Offering": Writings by New England Mill Women (1840–1845)* (Philadelphia: Lippincott, 1977), 15–16.

11. Problems of the farm economy.

11. Christopher Clark, "The Household Economy: Market Exchange and the Rise of Capitalism in the Connecticut Valley, 1800–1860," *Journal of Social History* 13 (Winter 1979): 175–76; Gail Fowler Mohanty, "Handloom Outwork and Outwork Weaving in Rural Rhode Island, 1810–1821," *American Studies* 30 (Fall 1989): 42–43, 48–49.

16

12. Eisler, 16, 19, 62; Barbara Welter, "The Cult of True Womanhood," *American Quarterly* 18 (1966): 155, 162–65.

13. Eisler, 16, 193; Clark, 178–79; Dalzell, 33.

14. Dublin, 40; Tucker, *Slater*, 255–56; Harriet H. Robinson, *Loom and Spindle* (1898; reprinted in *Women of Lowell*, New York: Arno Press, 1974), 194; Eisler, 61–63, 81–82.

15. On the influence of patriarchy see Tucker, *Slater*, 25–26; Robinson, 61; Welter, 152, 170–71. Also see *Sins of Our Mothers*, videocassette (Boston: WGBH/WNET/KLET/PBS, 1988).

16. Dublin, 77–79; Eisler, 19–24.

17. Eisler, 18–19. On the decline of New England agriculture see Clark, 176; Ware, 14.

18. Dublin, 80; Eisler, 73–74.

19. Dublin, 80; Robinson, 31; Lucy Larcom, "Among Lowell Mill Girls: A Reminiscence" (1881; reprinted in *Women of Lowell*), 602; Eisler, 75–77.

20. See table of mill hours printed in Eisler, 30. Boarding-house curfew is listed in "Regulations for the Boarding Houses," contained in illustration on page 9. For a very negative view of work hours and conditions, see A Citizen of Lowell, *Corporations and Operatives: Being an Exposition of the Condition [of the] Factory Operatives* . . . (1843; reprinted in *Women of Lowell*), 15–19, 21.

21. Larcom, 599–602; Eisler, 56–66.

22. "Factory Rules from the Handbook to Lowell, 1848," http://www.kentlaw.edu/ilhs/lowell.htm (accessed August 9, 1996).

23. Dublin, 66, 183, 185; Ware, 239.

24. Ware, 240–42. For teachers' pay see Eisler, 193.

25. Elisha Bartlett, *A Vindication of the Character and Condition of the Females Employed in the Lowell Mills* . . . (Lowell, MA: Leonard Huntress, Printer, 1841), 21; Dublin, 188.

26. Larcom, 599–600.

27. Eisler, 49–50.

28. Robinson, 91–93; Eisler, 113–32. For mill rules concerning reading, see Eisler, 31.

29. Robinson, 97–102.

12. The inferior position of women.
13. Limited opportunities for women in New England.
14. Women's desire for independence.
15. Early nineteenth-century rural attitudes toward women. Example of a film citation.
16. Early Lowell paternalism.
17. The method of recruiting women workers.
18. Getting used to town life and the boarding house.
19. The nature of mill work and the workday.
20. Work hours and free time.

21. Favorable comments on mill work by the Lowell mill girls.
22. The role of the overseer. (Example of a Web citation.)
23. The rate of women's pay.
24. Low alternative pay for women.
25. Savings accounts.
26. Free time.
27. Leisure time and wardrobe.
28. Reading and education.
29. Women's writing.

17

30. The Lowell Offering.	30. Eisler, 33–40; Dublin, 123–24, 129–30; Robinson, 114–20; Bertha Monica Stearns, "Early Factory Magazines in New England: The *Lowell Offering* and Its Contemporaries," *Journal of Economic and Business History* (August 1930): 690–91, 698.
31. Dickens commenting on the Lowell Offering.	
32. The early Lowell setting.	
33. The tensions of the 1830s; lowered wages.	31. Dickens is quoted in Robinson, 11. Also see Larcom, 609; Eisler, 41.
34. The 1834 "turn out."	32. Larcom, 598, 609; Eisler, 63–65.
35. Strikers' petitions.	33. Dublin, 87–90.
36. More quotes from petitions.	34. Robinson, 84; Dublin, 89–91.
37. The 1836 "turn out."	35. Dublin, 91.
	36. Dublin, 93. (Emphasis added to quotation.)
38. Mutual support.	37. Dublin, 98–99.
39. Declining working conditions.	38. Dublin, 44, 82–83, 103.
	39. Dublin, 108, 134; Robinson, 204, 208–9; Eisler, 215.
40. The workforce after 1845; Irish immigration.	40. Dublin, 140, 156, 197. On the decline of Lowell, see Dalzell, 69.
41. Profits for owners.	41. Dalzell, 60–61, 70–73.
42. The status of women.	42. Dublin 32; Welter, 151–74. For the contemporary debate about the impact of factory work on women, see these pamphlets: Bartlett, *A Vindication of the Character and Condition*, and A Citizen, *Corporations and Operatives*.
43. Lowell women activists and later movements.	43. Dublin, 127–29; Ware, 292.

18

Bibliography

Books

Bartlett, Elisha. *A Vindication of the Character and Condition of the Fe-
males Employed in the Lowell Mills.* . . . Lowell, MA: Leonard
Huntress, Printer, 1841. Reprinted in *Women of Lowell.* New York:
Arno Press, 1974.

Citizen of Lowell, A. *Corporations and Operatives: Being an Exposition of the
Condition [of the] Factory Operatives.* . . . 1843. Reprinted in *Women
of Lowell.* New York: Arno Press, 1974.

Dalzell, Robert F. *Enterprising Elite: The Boston Associates and the World
They Made.* Cambridge: Harvard University Press, 1987.

Dublin, Thomas. *Women at Work: The Transformation of Work and Community in Lowell, Massachusetts, 1826–1860.* New York: Columbia University Press, 1979.

Eisler, Benita, ed. *The "Lowell Offering": Writings by New England Mill
Women (1840–1845).* Philadelphia: Lippincott, 1977.

Prude, Jonathan. *The Coming of Industrial Order: Town and Factory Life in
Rural Massachusetts, 1810–1860.* Cambridge, UK: Cambridge University Press, 1983.

Robinson, Harriet H. *Loom and Spindle; Or, Life among the Early Mill Girls.*
1898. Reprinted in *Women of Lowell.* New York: Arno Press, 1974.

Tucker, Barbara M. *Samuel Slater and the Origins of the American Textile
Industry: 1790–1860.* Ithaca: Cornell University Press, 1984.

Ware, Caroline F. *The Early New England Cotton Manufacture.* Boston:
Houghton Mifflin, 1931.

Articles

Clark, Christopher. "The Household Economy: Market Exchange and the
Rise of Capitalism in the Connecticut Valley, 1800–1860." *Journal
of Social History* 13 (Winter 1979): 169–89.

*Bibliography be-
gins on a new
page.*

*Citations are
listed alphabeti-
cally under each
heading.*

*Second and fol-
lowing lines of
each citation are
indented.*

19

Hood, Adrienne D. "The Gender Division of Labor in the Production of
    Textiles in Eighteenth-Century Rural Pennsylvania." *Journal of So-
    cial History* 27 (Spring 1994).http://www.searchbank.com/infotrac/
    session/4/0/82904/3?xrn_7.

Kulikoff, Allan. "The Transition to Capitalism in Rural America." *William
    and Mary Quarterly* 46 (1989): 120–44.

Larcom, Lucy. "Among Lowell Mill Girls: A Reminiscence." 1881.
    Reprinted in *Women of Lowell*. New York: Arno Press, 1974.

Mohanty, Gail Fowler. "Handloom Outwork and Outwork Weaving in Rural
    Rhode Island, 1810–1821." *American Studies* 30 (Fall 1989):
    41–68.

Stearns, Bertha Monica. "Early Factory Magazines in New England: The
    Lowell Offering and Its Contemporaries." *Journal of Economic and
    Business History* (August 1930): 685–705.

Tucker, Barbara M. "The Family and Industrial Discipline in Ante-Bellum
    New England." *Labor History* 21 (Winter 1979–80): 55–74.

Welter, Barbara. "The Cult of True Womanhood." *American Quarterly* 18
    (1966): 151–74.

Documents

"Factory Rules from the Handbook to Lowell, 1848." http://www.kentlaw
    .edu/ilhs/lowell.html/.

Nonwritten Sources

"Map of Lowell, showing the location of mills and boarding houses." In
    So Far from Home, by Barry Denenberg. New York: Scholastic, Inc.,
    1997: 164b.

Middlesex Company Boarding-House Regulations, ca. 1850. The American
    Textile History Museum, Lowell, MA.

Sins of Our Mothers. Videocassette. Boston: WGBH/WNET/KCET/PBS,
    1988.

Resources for History Research

The resources in Appendix A will assist you in choosing a **topic,** narrowing a topic, and conducting research on a topic. Different kinds of resources lead you to different kinds of information. Some are most useful to you at the beginning of your research when you are choosing or refining the topic. Others are necessary later, when you are gathering the information that will support your **thesis.** Historical **dictionaries, encyclopedias,** and **atlases,** for example, will be especially useful in the early stages of your research. More specialized resources in world and U.S. history should be consulted once you have chosen your topic and become familiar with the basic information about it.

The categories of resources described in this appendix are as follows:

- Historical dictionaries, encyclopedias, and atlases (p. 186)
- Biography collections (p. 191)
- Newspaper indexes and databases (p. 193)
- Periodical indexes and databases (p. 195)
- Public documents (p. 197)
- Historical statistics (p. 199)
- General and specialized resources in world history (p. 202, 204)
- General and specialized resources in United States history (p. 223, 225)
- Electronic Discussion Lists in History (p. 243)

Each category begins with a brief description of the kinds of information the listed resources contain and at what stage of your research they are likely to be most helpful. Within each category, the individual items are listed alphabetically by title. In most cases, the title is followed by the name of the person or organization that compiled the resource and then by the publication information or the **URL.**

The resources listed in Appendix A are available in most college libraries. If a particular resource is not available to you, try another. A more complete list of resources is included in "A Student's Online Guide to History Reference Sources" at this book's Web site: bedfordstmartins.com/benjamin.

Because print sources are generally easier to find and to evaluate than online sources, this appendix emphasizes Web sites. Online material varies greatly in quality, and care must be taken when using sources from Web sites. The sites included here have been chosen because they are reliable sources of high-quality research material. As noted in Chapter 4, full-text digital resources are often available only by library subscription. If your school has not purchased access to a particular resource, you will need to search out an alternative.

Resources on **CD-ROM** or **microfiche** should be included in your library's **online catalog.** As always, the reference librarian is the best guide to your library's information resources.

DICTIONARIES, ENCYCLOPEDIAS, AND ATLASES

The resources included here will be most useful to you in choosing and refining a topic. Once you have begun research on a particular topic, they may also be helpful in explaining any unusual terms you may encounter.

A *historical dictionary* will help you define a term such as "Austro-Hungarian Empire." The brief description of this term will tell you when the empire existed, what lands it encompassed, the names of its rulers, and several of its major characteristics. This information will let you know if the term falls within the subject area of your course, and if it seems of interest to you as a possible topic. At later stages of your research, you can use a historical dictionary to obtain a brief description of a term you came across in your reading.

In most cases a *historical encyclopedia* treats a term in greater depth than a historical dictionary. It might describe how the Austro-Hungarian Empire was formed, the forces that enabled it to expand, its alliances and conflicts with neighboring states and empires, the tensions among the different peoples who were part of the empire, and the forces that worked to break up the empire. An encyclopedia article can be of assistance in choosing a topic, and in determining which aspects of the topic you wish to pursue.

A *historical atlas* contains a series of maps showing geographical changes over time or lays out in spatial form the location of different kinds of information. In the case of the Austro-Hungarian Empire, a historical atlas would likely picture the territories of the empire, when they were acquired, and what groups of people lived in those territories. A good historical atlas would include information about those peoples — for example, the population size of each group, the percentage of Catholics and Protestants in different parts of the empire, and the languages they spoke.

It is important to remember that historical dictionaries, encyclopedias, and atlases are most valuable at the beginning stages of research. They do not contain extended examinations or interpretations of historical subjects. You should not depend on them for the substance of your paper. For more highly specialized reference works, see "Specialized Resources in World History" (pp. 204–222) and "Specialized Resources in United States History" (pp. 225–242) later in this appendix. Additional reference works are included in this book's Web site: bedfordstmartins.com/benjamin.

Historical Dictionaries — World

The Blackwell Dictionary of Modern Social Thought. Ed. William Outhwaite. Malden, MA: Blackwell, 2003.

The Cambridge Historical Dictionary of Disease. Ed. Kenneth F. Kiple. New York: Cambridge University Press, 2003.

A Dictionary of Ancient History. Ed. Graham Speake. Oxford: Blackwell, 1994.

Dictionary of Contemporary History, 1945 to the Present. Ed. Duncan Townson. Oxford: Blackwell, 1999.

Dictionary of Race and Ethnic Relations. By Ernest Cashmore. London: Routledge, 1994.

A Dictionary of Twentieth-Century History, 1914–1990. Ed. Peter Teed. Oxford: Oxford University Press, 1992.

Historical Dictionary of Judaism. Ed. Norman Solomon. Lanham, MD.: Scarecrow Press, 1998.

New Dictionary of the History of Ideas. Ed. Maryanne Cline Horowitz. 6 vols. New York: Scribner, 2004. It is also online at **etext.virginia.edu/DicHist/dict.html**, available by subscription only.

The New Grove Dictionary of Music and Musicians. 2nd ed. Ed. Stanley Sadie and John Tyrrell. 29 vols. New York: Macmillan, 2001. Also see the online database *Grove Music Online.*

The New Penguin Dictionary of Modern History, 1789–1945. Ed. Duncan Townson and Alan W. Palmer. Baltimore: Penguin Books, 1994.

The Oxford Classical Dictionary. 3rd ed. Ed. Simon Hornblower and Antony Spawforth. Oxford: Oxford University Press, 1999.

The Oxford Dictionary of Byzantium. Ed. Alexander P. Kazhdan. 3 vols. New York: Oxford University Press, 1991.

The Oxford Dictionary of Philosophy. Comp. Simon Blackburn. Oxford: Oxford University Press, 1994.

The Oxford English Dictionary. 2nd ed. 20 vols. Oxford: Clarendon Press, 1989. This is the most complete English-language dictionary. If you are tracing the historical development of the meaning of a word, it is an essential reference. If, however, you wish to determine the contemporary spelling or definition of a term, other general dictionaries are better sources. If the term is colloquial or is a recent derivation, be sure to use the most recent edition. The *Oxford English Dictionary* is now on CD-ROM and online by subscription.

Historical Dictionaries—United States

Concise Dictionary of American History. Ed. David W. Voorhees. New York: Scribner, 1983. This is an abridgment of Kutler's 10-volume *Dictionary of American History.*

Dictionary of American Diplomatic History. Ed. John E. Findling. Westport, CT: Greenwood Press, 1989.

Dictionary of American History. Ed. James T. Adams and Roy V. Coleman. New York: Scribner, 1942–1961. Revised, 1976. Supplement, 1996.

Dictionary of American History. 3rd ed. Ed. Stanley I. Kutler. 10 vols. New York: Thomson Learning, 2003.

A Dictionary of American History. Ed. Thomas L. Purvis. Oxford: Blackwell, 1995.

Dictionary of United States Economic History. Ed. James S. Olson. Westport, CT: Greenwood Press, 1992.

The Penguin Dictionary of Contemporary American History, 1945 to the Present. Ed. Stanley Hochman and Eleanor Hochman. New York: Penguin Books, 1997.

Historical Encyclopedias—World

If your theme concerns recent history, or if important new facts and interpretations have arisen in recent years, be sure to use the latest edition of any historical encyclopedia that covers your topic. Online versions of some encyclopedias may be available to you.

Colonialism: An International Social, Cultural and Political Encyclopedia. Ed. Melvin E. Page. 3 vols. Santa Barbara, CA: ABC-CLIO, 2003.

Companion Encyclopedia of the History of Medicine. New York: Routledge, 1997.

Encyclopaedia Britannica. 15th ed. 32 vols. Chicago: Encyclopaedia Britannica Educational Corp., 2001. This is one of the best encyclopedias. It is also available on the Web at www.britannica.com, but only by subscription.

Encyclopedia Judaica. Ed. Cecil Rovhand and Geoffrey Wigoder. 16 vols. Jerusalem: Keter Publishing, 1972. Reprint, New York: Coronet Books, 1994.

The Encyclopedia of Ancient Civilizations of the Near East and Mediterranean. Ed. John Heywood. New York: M. E. Sharpe, 1997.

Encyclopedia of Bioethics. Rev. ed. Ed. Warren Thomas Reich. 5 vols. New York: Macmillan Library Reference, 1995.

Encyclopedia of Early Cinema. Ed. Richard Abel. New York: Routledge, 2005.

Encyclopedia of Nationalism. Ed. Alexander Motyl. New York: Academic Press, 2000.

Encyclopedia of Religion. Ed. Mircea Eliade. 16 vols. New York: Macmillan, 1993.

Encyclopedia of Religion. 2nd ed. Ed. Lindsay James. Detroit: Macmillan Reference USA, 2005.

Encyclopedia of Social History. Ed. Peter N. Stearns. New York: Garland, 1994.

Encyclopedia of Western Colonialism since 1450. Ed. Thomas Benjamin. Farmington Hills, MI: Macmillan Reference USA, 2007.

Encyclopedia of World Environmental History. Ed. Shepard Krech, John R. McNeill, and Carolyn Merchant. 3 vols. New York: Routledge, 2004.

Encyclopedia of World History. 6th ed. Ed. Peter N. Stearns. Boston: Houghton Mifflin, 2001. An open, online version (with advertisements) is available at **www.bartleby.com/67/**.

Film Encyclopedia. 4th ed. Ed. Ephraim Katz. New York: HarperCollins, 2001.

The Harper Encyclopedia of Military History: From 3500 B.C. to the Present. Ed. Ernest R. Dupuy and Trevor N. Dupuy. New York: Harper & Row, 1993.

The Harper Encyclopedia of the Modern World [1760 to present]. Ed. Richard B. Morris and Graham W. Irwin. New York: Harper & Row, 1970.

The Historical Encyclopedia of World Slavery. Ed. Junius P. Rodriguez. 2 vols. Santa Barbara, CA: ABC-CLIO, 1997.

New Catholic Encyclopedia. 2nd ed. Detroit: Gale, 2003.

New Encyclopedia of Islam. Ed. Cyril Glasse. Walnut Creek, CA: Alta Mira Press, 2001.

The Oxford Companion to the History of Modern Science. Ed. J. L. Heilbron. Oxford: Oxford University Press, 2003.

Routledge Encyclopedia of Philosophy. Ed. Edward Craig. 10 vols. New York: Routledge, 1998.

Women's Studies Encyclopedia: History, Philosophy, and Religion. Ed. Helen Tierney. 2 vols. Westport, CT: Greenwood Press, 1999.

Historical Encyclopedias—Europe

Ancient Europe, 8000 B.C. to A.D. 1000: An Encyclopedia of the Barbarian World. Ed. Peter Bogucki and Pam Crabtree. New York: Scribner, 2003.

Encyclopedia of Barbarian Europe: Society in Transformation. By Michael Frassetto. Santa Barbara, CA: ABC-CLIO, 2003.

Encyclopedia of European Social History [1350–2000]. Ed. Peter N. Stearns. 6 vols. New York: Scribner, 2005. Print and e-book versions.

Encyclopedia of the Enlightenment [eighteenth-century French intellectual history]. Ed. Alan C. Kors. Oxford: Oxford University Press, 2003.

Encyclopedia of the Holocaust. Ed. Israel Gutman. 4 vols. New York: Macmillan, 1995.

The Encyclopedia of the Middle Ages. Ed. Norman F. Cantor. New York: Viking, 1999.

Encyclopedia of the Renaissance. Ed. Paul F. Grendler. New York: Scribner, 1999.

Europe 1450–1789: Encyclopedia of the Early Modern World. Ed. Jonathan Dewald. New York: Scribner, 2003.

Europe 1789–1914: Encyclopedia of the Age of Industry and Empire. New York: Scribner, 2006.

Europe since 1945: An Encyclopedia. Ed. Bernard A. Cook. 2 vols. New York: Garland, 2001.

The Longman Handbook of Modern European History, 1763–1997. Ed. Chris Cook and John Stevenson. New York: Longman, 1998.

Modern European History: 1789 to the Present. Ed. John Santore. 2 vols. New York: M. Wiener, 1983.

The Oxford Encyclopedia of the Reformation. Ed. Hans J. Hillerbrand. 4 vols. New York: Oxford University Press, 1996.

Historical Encyclopedias — United States

Encyclopedia of American Agricultural History. By Edwin I. Schapsmeier and Frederick H. Schapsmeier. Westport, CT: Greenwood Press, 1975.

Encyclopedia of American Economic History. Ed. Glen Porter. 3 vols. New York: Scribner, 1980.

Encyclopedia of American History. 7th ed. Ed. Richard B. Morris. New York: HarperCollins, 1996.

Encyclopedia of American History. Ed. Gary B. Nash. 11 vols. New York: Facts on File, 2003.

The Encyclopedia of American Political History. Ed. Paul Finkleman and Peter Wallenstein. Washington, DC: CQ Press, 2001.

Encyclopedia of American Religious History. 6th ed. J. Gordon Mellon. Detroit: Gale, 1999.

Encyclopedia of American Social History. Ed. Mary K. Cayton, Elliott J. Gorn, and Peter W. Williams. 3 vols. New York: Scribner, 1993.

Encyclopedia of the American Military. Ed. John E. Jessup. 3 vols. New York: Scribner, 1994.

Encyclopedia of the United States in the Nineteenth Century. Ed. Paul Finkelman. 3 vols. New York: Scribner, 2001.

Encyclopedia of the United States in the Twentieth Century. Ed. Stanley Kutler. 4 vols. New York: Scribner, 1996.

Encyclopedia of United States Foreign Relations. Ed. Bruce Jentleson and Thomas Patterson. Oxford: Oxford University Press, 1997.

Encyclopedia of Urban America. Ed. Neil L. Shumsky. Santa Barbara, CA: ABC-CLIO, 1998.

Encyclopedia of Women in American History. Ed. Joyce Appleby et al. 3 vols. New York: M. E. Sharpe, 2002.

Historical Atlases — World

Atlas of the Roman World. Comp. Tim Cornell and John Matthews. New York: Facts on File, 1982.

Atlas of World History. Rev. ed. Ed. Robert R. Palmer et al. Chicago: Rand McNally, 1995.

The Complete Atlas of World History. 3 vols. New York: M. E. Sharpe, 1997.

David Rumsey Map Collection. **www.davidrumsey.com/collections/cartography.html**. A large online collection of maps and related materials. Emphasis is on North and South America in the eighteenth and nineteenth centuries.

Harper Atlas of World History. New York: HarperCollins, 1992.

Historical Atlas of the Islamic World. Cartographica, 2004.

National Geographic Atlas of the World. 7th ed. Washington, DC: National Geographic Society, 1999.

The Penguin Historical Atlas of Ancient Civilizations. Ed. Andrew Jotischky and Caroline Hull. London: Penguin Books, 2005.

The Penguin Historical Atlas of the Medieval World. Ed. John Haywood. London: Penguin Books, 2005.

The Perry-Castañeda Library Map Collection. University of Texas. www.lib.utexas .edu/maps/index.html. An extensive collection of historical maps covering many areas of the world.

The Routledge Atlas of Jewish History. 6th ed. Ed. Martin Gilbert. London: Routledge, 2003.

The Times Atlas of the World: Comprehensive Edition. 10th ed. London: Times Publishing, 1999.

Historical Atlases — United States

Atlas of American History. Rev. ed. By Robert H. Ferrell and Richard Natkiel. New York: Facts on File, 1995.

Digital Sanborn Maps. See below, *Map Collections of the Library of Congress, 1500–2003.*

Historical Atlas of the United States. Ed. Wilbur E. Garrett. Washington, DC: National Geographic Society, 1988.

Map Collections of the Library of Congress, 1500–2003. Library of Congress, American Memory. **memory.loc.gov/ammem/gmdhtml/gmdhome.html**. A large collection from many eras and areas.

Mapping America's Past. By Mark C. Carnes. New York: Henry Holt, 1996. Emphasis on social and cultural maps.

Omni Gazetteer of the United States of America. Ed. Frank R. Abate. 11 vols. Detroit: Omnigraphics, 1991. A gazetteer is a list of place-names, including insignificant ones. This volume organizes places by region and state.

Osher Map Library. Smith Center for Cartographic Education, University of Southern Maine. **www.usm.maine.edu/maps/web_exhibit.html**. Over 600 maps and related documents, essays, and annotated bibliographies.

BIOGRAPHY COLLECTIONS

The resources in this section will provide you with background information about a particular individual whose name you have come across in your research. An article in a biography collection will give you a brief (or in some cases a fairly comprehensive) description of an individual's life and will usually end with a list of sources to consult for further information. Each biography collection has its own criteria for determining which individuals to include. Take care to select the one most likely to include the individuals on whom you are seeking information. More highly specialized biography collections for some countries are listed in the "Specialized Resources in World History" section of this appendix.

International Biography Collections

International biography collections list persons of all national origins.

Biography and Genealogy Master Index. Ed. Miranda C. Herbert and Barbara McNeil. 8 vols. Detroit: Gale, 1980–. Supplements issued annually. Also available on CD-ROM and online.

Biography and Genealogy Master Index. Thomson Gale. A database containing multiple indexes to a wide range of biographical resources. By subscription only.

Biography Index: A Cumulative Guide to Biographical Material in Books and Magazines. New York: H. W. Wilson, 1949–. Now in database form as *Biography Index: Past and Present.*

Biography Index: Past and Present. H. W. Wilson. An updated, searchable database of the yearly *Index* since its initial edition. By subscription only.

Biography Resource Center. Thomson Gale. Combines a large number of Marquis *Who's Who* publications with other biographical databases. Some biographies include related articles, images, and links. Fully searchable. By subscription only.

The Continuum Dictionary of Women's Biography. Expanded ed. Ed. Jennifer S. Uglow. New York: Continuum, 1989.

Current Biography. New York: H. W. Wilson, 1940–. A cumulative index was published in 2000. Also see above, *Biography Index: Past and Present.*

Dictionary of International Biography. Cambridge: England International Biographical Centre, 1985.

Dictionary of Scientific Biography. Ed. Charles C. Gillispie. 16 vols. New York: Scribner, 1970–1980.

International Who's Who. London: Europa, 1935–. Now part of the Thomson Gale online database *Biography Resource Center,* available by subscription.

New York Times Obituary Index, 1858–1968, 1969–1980. New York: New York Times, 1970, 1980. Current volumes are published by Meckler, 1990–.

Who's Who in the World. Chicago: Marquis, 1971–. Now part of the Thomson Gale online database *Biography Resource Center,* available by subscription.

Who Was Who. Vol. 1, 1897–1915; vol. 2, 1916–1928; vol. 3, 1929–1940; vol. 4, 1941–1950; vol. 5, 1951–1960; vol. 6, 1961–1970; vol. 7, 1971–1980; vol. 8, 1981–1990; vol. 9, 1991–1995; vol. 10, 1996–2000. A cumulative index for 1897–1990 was published in 1991. These collections of biographies are now part of the Thomson Gale online database *Biography Resource Center,* available by subscription.

United States Biography Collections

American Men and Women of Science. New York: Bowker, 1906–. The twenty-third edition is now online from Thomson Gale. By subscription only.

American National Biography. Ed. John A. Garraty and Mark C. Carnes. 24 vols. New York: Oxford University Press and American Council of Learned Societies, 1999. Supplement, 2002. The newest and most extensive print collection of U.S. biographies. Also available online by subscription only.

American Reform and Reformers: A Biographical Dictionary. Ed. Randall M. Miller and Paul A. Cimbala. Westport, CT: Greenwood Press, 1996.

Biographical Dictionary of American Business Leaders. Ed. John Ingham. 4 vols. Westport, CT: Greenwood Press, 1983.

Biographical Dictionary of American Journalism. Ed. Joseph P. McKerns. Westport, CT: Greenwood Press, 1989.

Biographical Dictionary of American Labor. Rev. ed. Ed. Gary Fink. Westport, CT: Greenwood Press, 1984.

Biographical Dictionary of American Sports. Ed. David L. Porter. Westport, CT: Greenwood Press, 1998.

Biographical Directory of the United States Executive Branch, 1774–1989. Westport, CT: Greenwood Press, 1990.

Biographical Directory of the United States Congress, 1774–2005. U.S. Congress. **bioguide.congress.gov/biosearch/biosearch.asp**. Print and Web editions. Member biographies and information concerning the papers of U.S. senators and representatives.

Dictionary of American Biography. New York: Scribner, 1928–1996, including supplements. When using older editions or volumes of a print biography collection, note the date of publication because it will indicate which individuals might be included. A one-volume work containing shortened versions of these biographies is published under the title *Concise Dictionary of American Biography*, 5th ed., 1997. An index to the multivolume collection was published in 1996.

Dictionary of American Negro Biography. Ed. Rayford W. Logan and Michael Winston. New York: Norton, 1982.

The Encyclopedia of American Biography. Ed. John Garraty and Jerome Sternstein. New York: HarperCollins, 1996.

Notable American Women, 1607–1950: A Biographical Dictionary. Ed. Edward T. James. 3 vols. Cambridge, MA: Harvard University Press, 1971. Supplemented by *Notable American Women: The Modern Period*. 1980. The supplement covers women who died between 1951 and 1975.

Research Guide to American Historical Biography. Ed. Suzanne Niemeyer. New York: Beacham, 1990.

Who Was Who in America: Historical Volume, 1607–1896. Chicago: Marquis, 1967. If you are uncertain about your subject's death date, check *Who Was Who in America: Index* (2002). These volumes are now part of the Thomson Gale online database *Biography Resource Center*, available by subscription.

Who Was Who in America, with World Notables, 1897–2002. 14 vols. Chicago: Marquis, 2002. The years covered in each volume indicate the dates of death of those included in it.

NEWSPAPER INDEXES AND DATABASES

If you need to find newspaper articles from the time period you are writing about, a newspaper **index** will tell you where copies of a particular newspaper can be found. Newspaper **databases** contain the full text of newspaper articles but only for certain newspapers and only for a particular span of years. Most full-text newspaper databases are searchable, but they are usually available only by subscription. If your library does not have access to the online database that you want, check the **library catalog** for newspapers on **microfilm, microfiche,** or **CD-ROM.** Only English-language newspapers are included here.

Newspaper Indexes and Databases — General

Canadian Online Historical Newspapers. Chadwyk-Healey. Fully searchable collections of the *Toronto Star* and the *Globe and Mail.* Coverage begins in the mid-to-late nineteenth century. By subscription only.

LexisNexis Academic Universe. **www.lexisnexis.com/academic/**. Full text of articles in newspapers and magazines from the late 1980s on. Emphasis is on current developments in law, business, and government.

Newspapers on Microfilm: A Union Check List. Ed. George Schwegman Jr. Washington, DC: Library of Congress, 1963. This volume is supplemented by *Newspapers in Microform: United States, 1948–1984.*

Official Index to The Times [of London]. London: 1907–. See next item.

Palmer's Index to the Times [of London], *1790–1905.* Succeeded by the CD-ROM *Official Index to the Times, 1906–1980* (Chadwyk-Healey). Chadwyk-Healey also has an *Index Online* from 1790 to 1905 and the full text from 1800 to 1870. Both are searchable. By subscription only.

Newspaper Indexes and Databases — United States

American Newspapers, 1821–1936: A Union List of Files Available in the United States and Canada. Ed. Winifred Gerould. New York: H. W. Wilson, 1937. Also available on microfilm. Ann Arbor: University Microfilms, 1966.

Early American Newspapers, Series I, 1690–1876. NewsBank. **www.readex.com/readex/?content=96**. A searchable archive of over 600 newspapers, most from the eighteenth century. By subscription only.

New York Times Index. New York: New York Times, 1913–. This is usually the best source for beginning students. Most libraries have files of the *New York Times,* and the index has been extended back to 1851. Some libraries have Internet access to all of the articles themselves. In this case you can search by keyword. Also see below, *ProQuest Historical Newspapers.*

Nineteenth Century Masterfile. ProQuest. A large online database featuring a wide range of media on a variety of subjects, including history. Also contains a large newspaper database. By subscription only.

ProQuest Historical Newspapers. Available are the *New York Times,* 1851–2001, the *Wall Street Journal,* 1889–1987, the *Washington Post,* 1877–1988, the *Christian Science Monitor,* 1908–1991, and the *Los Angeles Times,* 1881–1984, among others. Fully searchable. By subscription only.

PERIODICAL INDEXES AND DATABASES

Once you have chosen a topic and a theme, you will be looking for books and **primary documents** that give you an understanding of them and support the thesis of your paper. An important source of information is articles in **periodicals.** These are of two types: *magazine articles* written at the time of the events being discussed (usually primary documents) and *articles in scholarly journals* analyzing a variety of historical themes (**secondary sources**). Resources for finding articles of each type are in the next two lists.

Magazine indexes and databases help you to find contemporary articles in popular magazines concerning events, persons, or issues that are part of your topic. Some print indexes to magazine articles are in the reference section of your library. Most searchable magazine databases are online, and those available to you will be included in the library's online catalog under a heading such as "electronic," "digital," or "online" resources. Be sure that the database you are searching includes the kind of magazines most likely to have articles related to your topic.

Journal indexes and databases help you to find articles in scholarly journals. Most databases of scholarly journal articles are online and by subscription only. The history journal databases available to you will be listed in your library's online catalog. Such databases allow you to search for articles in a large number of journals, and some provide full-text access. If your library does not subscribe to the most promising journal database listed below, try another database.

Magazine Indexes and Databases

Index to Early American Periodicals. Computer Indexed Systems. This database features articles written in American periodicals during the eighteenth, nineteenth, and early twentieth centuries. Large collection on microfilm.

LexisNexis Academic. This database covers journals, magazines, news providers, and legal materials. It is particularly useful for researching current events. Online by subscription only.

Nineteenth Century Masterfile. ProQuest. A large online database featuring a wide range of media on a variety of subjects, including history. Also contains a large newspaper database. By subscription only.

Nineteenth-Century Periodicals: 1815–1900. Library of Congress, American Memory. **memory.loc.gov/ammem/ndlpcoop/moahtml/snchome.html.** A searchable collection of periodicals. Years of coverage of each periodical are indicated. Many articles are full text.

Poole's Index to Periodical Literature, 1802–1881. Boston: Houghton Mifflin, 1891. Now available online. See above, *Nineteenth Century Masterfile.*

Readers' Guide Full Text, Mega Edition. Wilson Web. Searchable full text of magazines but only for articles published since 1994.

Readers' Guide Retrospective: 1890–1982. H. W. Wilson. This database allows you to search for articles among several hundred popular magazines going back to 1890. Note that many of the periodicals included were written for a popular rather than a scholarly audience. These magazines are valuable as records of popular opinions and interests.

Readers' Guide to Periodical Literature. New York: H. W. Wilson, 1900–. Annual updates still available in print. Beginning with articles published in 1983, this *Guide* began to appear in online form by subscription only. The annual volumes for the period before 1983 are now in digital form in *Readers' Guide Retrospective: 1890–1982*.

Ulrich's International Periodicals Directory. 41st ed. New York: Bowker, 2003.

Journal Indexes and Databases

Academic Search Premier. EBSCOhost EJS. A large multidisciplinary database. By subscription only.

America: History and Life [United States and Canada]. A large database with abstracts of articles in 2,000 scholarly journals published since 1964. All topics in U.S. and Canadian history are covered. The print edition has been published since 1965 by ABC-CLIO. The latest print edition is 1995. Online by subscription.

American Periodical Series. Chadwyk-Healey. A searchable full-text database of American magazines from the mid-eighteenth to the mid-twentieth century. Microfilm. By subscription only.

C.R.I.S.: The Combined Retrospective Index Set to Journals in History, 1838–1974. Ed. Annadel N. Wile. Arlington, VA: Carrollton Press, 1977.

Directory of Scholarly Electronic Journals and Academic Discussion Lists. Washington, DC: Association of Research Libraries, 2000. Also online at **www.arl.org/ scomm/edir/**. A searchable database of online journals. Neither the print nor online version is updated after 2000.

Historical Abstracts. Ed. Eric H. Boehm. Part A, *Modern History (1450–1914)*. Part B, *The Twentieth Century (1914–Present)*. Santa Barbara, CA: ABC-CLIO, 1955–. Most commonly found now on CD-ROM and online. See below, *Historical Abstracts: World History since 1450*.

Historical Abstracts: World History since 1450. This database offers abstracts of articles from a great number of scholarly journals on all areas except the United States and Canada. Those two areas are covered by *America: History and Life*. By subscription only.

Historical Periodicals Directory. Ed. Eric H. Boehm, Barbara H. Pope, and Marie Ensign. Vol. 1, *United States and Canada*. Vol. 2, *Europe (West)*. Vol. 3, *Europe (East)*. Vol. 4, *Latin America*. Vol. 5, *Australia and New Zealand*. Santa Barbara, CA: ABC-CLIO, 1981–1986.

History Cooperative. Full text of recent articles in twelve major history journals. Complements *JSTOR* (see next page). By subscription only.

Humanities Index. New York: H. W. Wilson, 1974–. Covers a wide range of journals in the humanities. Annual volumes. Now available in online form.

Humanities Index Retrospective, 1907–1894. H. W. Wilson. Available online by subscription only.

JSTOR. Fully searchable database includes the full text of articles in over 200 academic journals, including many prominent historical journals. The most current articles are not available in *JSTOR.* For more current articles in scholarly journals see *Project Muse* (below) and *History Cooperative.* (previous page). All by subscription only.

Periodicals Archive Online. ProQuest. Full-text articles from a large number of international journals in history and social science. Database articles run from 1802 to 1995. By subscription only.

Project Muse. Searchable database of full text of recent articles in over 200 journals across many academic disciplines, including history. Some of the journals in this database are interlinked with the *JSTOR* database, so searching the full **date range** is possible. By subscription only.

Book Review Indexes and Databases

If you wish to know more about a particular book before deciding to use it in your research, seek out book reviews written by scholars. These reviews usually appear in scholarly journals. The following indexes and databases enable you to find reviews of a particular book.

Book Review Digest: Author/Title Index, 1905–1974. Ed. Leslie Dunmore-Lieber. 4 vols. New York: H. W. Wilson, 1976.

Book Review Digest Retrospective: 1905–1982. Wilson Web. A large database of book reviews. Note that many of these books were written quite a few years ago. Note also that these "reviews" consist of excerpts from reviews that appeared at the time the books were written. Brief descriptive summaries of the books are included. By subscription only.

Book Review Index: Master Cumulation, 1965–1984. Ed. Gary C. Tarbert and Barbara Beach. 10 vols. Detroit: Gale, 1985.

Combined Retrospective Index to Book Reviews in Scholarly Journals, 1886–1974. 15 vols. Arlington, VA: Carrollton Press, 1982.

H-Reviews. www.h-net.org/reviews. A searchable online collection of full-text book reviews in all fields of history.

Index to Book Reviews in the Humanities. Detroit: Gale, 1960–1990. Annual.

New York Times Book Review Index, 1896–1970. 5 vols. New York: New York Times, 1973.

Reviews in American History. Johns Hopkins University Press. Full-text longer reviews of recent books. Back issues through *JSTOR* (see above). Also available in print.

PUBLIC DOCUMENTS

These resources lead you to documents created by official bodies such as national governments. Only English-language documents are included here.

Public Documents — Britain and Canada

Ancestry Library Edition. ProQuest. Searchable genealogical information from the United States and the United Kingdom taken from census, church, court, immigration, and other records. Online, by subscription only.

British History Online. Institute of Historical Research. **www.british-history .acuk/subject.asp**. Documents relating to British history concerning local, national, and international affairs. Searchable by subject or place.

British Official Publications Collaborative Reader Information Service. **www.bopcris .ac.uk/browse/subjindex.html**. A search facility for a wide range of British government documents, 1688–1995. Access to abstracts but not to documents themselves.

Government of Canada — Digital History Collections. **collections.ic.gc.ca/E/Subject .asp**. A large number of searchable topics on Canadian history.

U.K. National Archives. **www.nationalarchives.gov.uk/documentsonline**. Click "Documents Online" for digitized records. There is a download fee for most documents. Major categories of documents are "Family History" (military records, wills), "Society and Law," "Home and Foreign Affairs," and "Military and Defense."

United Nations: Official Documents of the United Nations. **documents.un.org/ welcome.asp?language=E**. Only a small portion of pre-1993 UN documents are online. The UN search engines are complex and contain some non-English documents.

Public Documents — United States

American State Papers, 1789–1838. Readex — Newsbank. **www.readex.com/ readex/product.cfm?product=6**. A searchable database of printed material from the legislative and executive branches of government. By subscription only.

ARC. Archival Research Catalog. **www.archives.gov/research/arc/**. This site allows users to search for U.S. government documents housed in regional archives. Only a small fraction of these documents are online.

CQ Supreme Court Collection. CQ Electronic Library. Historical analysis and commentary on U.S. Supreme Court decisions, biographies of justices, and links to additional resources. By subscription only.

Foreign Relations of the United States. U.S. Department of State. Washington, DC: Government Printing Office, 1861–. These volumes are issued regularly and contain actual diplomatic correspondence. These are **primary sources.**

House and Senate Journals, 1789–1817. Readex–Newsbank. Records of the sessions of the U.S. Congress. By subscription only.

LexisNexis Congressional. An online archive of congressional hearings, legislation, and background to legislation. By subscription only.

LexisNexis U.S. Serial Set Digital Collection. An online archive of congressional publications covering the period 1789–1969. Searchable. By subscription only.

List of National Archives Microfilm Publications, 1947–1974. Washington, DC: National Archives and Records Administration, 1974. Supplemented by

Supplementary List of National Archives Publications, 1974–1982. Washington, DC: National Archives and Records Administration, 1982.

National Archives and Records Administration. **www.archives.gov/research/topics .html**. A portal to an enormous collection of U.S. government documents. It contains an extensive searchable catalog. Only a small fraction of this huge collection of materials is available online.

Oyez: U.S. Supreme Court Multimedia. Jerry Goldman, Northwestern University. **www.oyez.org/oyez/frontpage**. Audio files, abstracts, transcriptions, oral arguments, and written opinions. Covers 3,300 Supreme Court cases; selected cases starting in 1955, and all cases since 1995. Keyword searching of fourteen broad categories.

Presidential Libraries and Museums. **www.archives.gov/presidential-libraries/**. Every president since Herbert Hoover has his own library of presidential papers. This site contains links to each of the libraries. As yet, few presidential papers have been placed online.

Public Documents Masterfile. Paratext. A large database of U.S. government documents covering 1774 to the present. By subscription only.

Subject Guide to Major United States Government Publications. Comp. William J. Wiley. Chicago: American Library Association, 1987.

U.S. Citizenship and Immigration Services. **uscis.gov/graphics/aboutus/history/ tools.html**. A large number of links to government records especially concerning immigration and naturalization. These records go back to about 1890. Actual records are not online.

U.S. Supreme Court Opinions. **www.findlaw.com/10fedgov/judicial/supreme _court/opinions.html**. This site allows you to search Supreme Court opinions.

United States Congressional Committee Hearings Index, 1833–1969. Washington, DC: Congressional Information Service, 1981. Also available as part of *Lexis-Nexis Congressional* (see previous page).

United States Congressional Committee Prints Index from Earliest Publications through 1969. 5 vols. Washington, DC: Congressional Information Service, 1980. Now available on microfilm and online from LexisNexis. By subscription only.

United States Serial Set Indexes: American State Papers . . . 1789–1969. Washington, DC: Congressional Information Service, 1975. Now available online. See (on previous page) *LexisNexis U.S. Serial Set Digital Collection*.

University of Michigan Documents Center. **www.lib.umich.edu/govdocs/index .html**. Information, statistics, legislation, and news relating to each level of government.

HISTORICAL STATISTICS

These resources lead you to a wide range of numerical data useful to research in such areas as political, economic, and social history.

Historical Statistics — General

Demography and Population Studies. **demography.anu.edu.au/VirtualLibrary**. This site links to census figures, journals, and demography conferences.

Historical Tables, 58 B.C.–A.D. 1990. By Sigfrid H. Steinberg. New York: Tuttle, 1991.

Index to International Statistics. Part of *LexisNexis Statistical.* By subscription only.

League of Nations Statistical Yearbook. Northwestern University: **www.library .northwestern.edu/govinfo/collections/league/stat.html**. Full text of the yearbook from 1926 to 1944.

Statistical Resources on the Web. University of Michigan. **www.lib.umich.edu/ govdocs/stats.html**. Statistics from the United States and from around the world. Links to many of the most important compilers of statistical information. Some sources are free; others are by subscription only.

Statistical Yearbook. New York: United Nations Statistical Office, 1949–.

United Nations: Demographic Yearbook. A large collection of population statistics covering the years 1948–1997. Available on CD-ROM.

Historical Statistics — National and Regional

Annual Abstract of Statistics. London: Office of National Statistics. Available in print and online. Earlier statistics are accessed through the link "Time Series" and are free to search and download.

The Arab World, Turkey and the Balkans, 1878–1914: A Handbook of Historical Statistics. Ed. Justin McCarthy. Boston: G. K. Hall, 1982.

British Historical Statistics. Ed. B. R. Mitchell. Cambridge: Cambridge University Press, 1988.

British Labour Statistics: Historical Abstract, 1886–1968. London: Great Britain Department of Employment and Productivity, 1971.

The British Voter: An Atlas and Survey since 1885. By Michael Kinnear. London: Batsford, 1981.

Census Finder. U.S. Census Bureau. Links to census records for the United Kingdom, Canada, Sweden, and Norway available at **www.censusfinder.com/**. For United States data see the section "Historical Statistics — U.S." (next page).

The Gallup International Public Opinion Polls: Great Britain, 1937–1975; France, 1939, 1944–1975. By George H. Gallup. Westport, CT: Greenwood Press, 1976–1977.

Heritage Quest Online. ProQuest. A large database of nineteenth- and twentieth-century census statistics, most from the United States but also from the United Kingdom and Canada. By subscription only.

Historical Statistics of Canada. By M. C. Urquhart. Ottawa: Statistics Canada, 1983. Available on the Web.

Historical Statistics of Canada. Statistics Canada. Ed. F. H. Leacy. **www.statcan.ca/ english/freepub/11-516-XIE/sectiona/toc.htm**. Searchable online version of printed volume. Over 1,000 tables drawn from historical data for the period 1867 to 1970s.

International Historical Statistics: The Americas: 1750–1988. Ed. B. R. Mitchell. New York: Stockton Press, 1998.

International Historical Statistics: Europe, 1750–2000. Ed. B. R. Mitchell. New York: Palgrave Macmillan, 2003.

Oxford Latin American Economic History Database. **oxlad.qeh.ox.ac.uk/**. Statistical information on the economies and societies of Latin America in the twentieth century.

Statistical Abstract of Latin America. Ed. James W. Wilkie. Los Angeles: UCLA Center of Latin American Studies, 1955–.

Twentieth-Century British Political Facts, 1900–2000. By David Butler and Gareth Butler. New York: Palgrave Macmillan, 2000.

Historical Statistics — United States

American Statistics Index: A Complete Guide and Index to the Statistical Publications of the United States Government. Washington, DC: Congressional Information Service, 1973–. Now part of *LexisNexis Statistical.* By subscription only.

Election Statistics. U.S. House of Representatives. **clerk.house.gov/members/ electionInfo/elections.html**. Federal election returns since 1920.

Federal Population Censuses 1790–1890: A Catalogue of Microfilm Copies of the Schedules. Washington, DC: National Archives and Records Administration. Catalogs of the 1900, 1910, 1920, and 1930 census have also been created. Note that these catalogs contain no online data; they are to assist researchers who go to the sites where the records are kept.

The Gallup Poll. By George H. Gallup. New York: Random House and Scholarly Resources, 1935–.

The Gallup Poll Cumulative Index: Public Opinion, 1935–1997. Wilmington, DE: Scholarly Resources, 1999. Also available online, by subscription, at brain.gallup.com.

Gallup Polls. Gallup Organization. **brain.gallup.com/**. Gallup polls beginning in the 1930s. By subscription only.

Heritage Quest Online. ProQuest. A large database of nineteenth- and twentieth-century census statistics, most from the United States but also some from the United Kingdom and Canada. By subscription only.

Historical Statistics of the United States, Colonial Times to 1970. Washington, DC: Bureau of the Census, 1976, and Government Printing Office, 1989. Also available on CD-ROM and online.

National Archives Publications. **www.archives.gov/publications/microfilm-catalogs/ census/1790-1890/part-01.html**. These are *descriptions* of census data. The actual census information is in the National Archives. Some federal census data has been digitized by volunteers and is online at *The USGenWeb Census Project,* described in Appendix B (p. 249).

Roper Center for Public Opinion Research. University of Connecticut. **www.ropercenter .uconn.edu**. This site offers access to data gathered from Roper opinion polls, archived collections, and the Roper magazine.

Statistical Abstract of the United States. Washington, DC: Government Printing Office, 1878–. Annual. Also available on the Web.

Statistical Abstract of the United States. U.S. Census Bureau. **www.census.gov/ prod/www/abs/statab1878-1900.htm**. Yearly collection of statistics. Files for most years are downloadable but are very large. Files are available for the years 1878 to the present.

Statistical Resources on the Web. University of Michigan. **www.lib.umich.edu/ govdocs/stats.html**. Statistics from the United States and from around the world. Links to many of the most important compilers of statistical information. Some sources are free; others are by subscription only.

U.S. Census Bureau. **www.census.gov/compendia/statab/**. This site contains a limited number of historical statistics gathered by the Census Bureau since the mid-nineteenth century. Some individual census data online is available at *The USGenWeb Census Project* (see p. 249 in Appendix B).

United States Historical Census Data Browser. University of Virginia. **fisher.lib .virginia.edu/collections/stats/histcensus/**. Allows searching of census data statistics from 1790 to 1960, with links to more recent population statistics and census information. Does not include individuals by name. Online use only; cannot be downloaded.

U.S. Presidential Election Maps: 1860–1996. University of Virginia Library. **fisher.lib.virginia.edu/collections/stats/elections/maps/**. Popular and electoral vote totals mapped by state for each presidential election since 1860.

GENERAL RESOURCES IN WORLD HISTORY

Before examining the general resources in world history listed in this section and the specialized resources described on pp. 204–22, you should consult the historical dictionaries, encyclopedias, and atlases listed at the beginning of this appendix (pp. 186–91). They will enable you to choose a topic and narrow it to a theme.

The general resources in this section consist of bibliographies and Web sites that cover large areas and many periods of world history. The specialized resources described later will be useful once you have chosen a topic and have a clear understanding of the kind of research you will need to do to develop and support your thesis. Even if you have already narrowed your topic, you should not ignore the following general resources, because many of them include sections on or links to specialized topics.

Reference Works and Bibliographies

Academic Info: World History Gateway. **www.academicinfo.net/hist.html**. This site categorizes and annotates links to history Web sites and allows you to search by keyword.

Best of History Web Sites. **www.besthistorysites.net**. This annotated site uses a ranking system to guide users through Internet resources in history.

Bibliography of the History of Art. RLG. A database of article abstracts, books, and exhibition catalogs. By subscription only.

A Bibliography of Modern History. Ed. John Roach. Cambridge: Cambridge University Press, 1968. This bibliography was created to accompany *The New Cambridge Modern History.*

The Cambridge Modern History. 13 vols. Ed. A. W. Ward, G. W. Prothero, and Stanley Leather. Cambridge: Cambridge University Press, 1902–1912. These volumes have large bibliographies. *The New Cambridge Modern History* (14 vols., 1957–1979) has no bibliography.

Reference Sources in History: An Introductory Guide. 2nd ed. Ed. Ronald H. Fritze. Santa Barbara, CA: ABC-CLIO, 2003.

Slavery and Slaving in World History: A Bibliography, 1900–1991. Ed. Joseph C. Miller. New York: M. E. Sharpe, 1997–1998.

Web Sites

Berkeley Digital Library SunSITE. **sunsite.berkeley.edu/.** Texts and images, including classical and medieval works, the Emma Goldman papers, and a strong collection relating to California.

Dead Sea Scrolls. **www.ibiblio.org/expo/deadsea.scrolls.exhibit/intro.html.** Essays and brief translations.

Directory of Historical Resources. History Database, Los Angeles. **www.history .la.ca.us/hddirect.htm.** An extensive database of Web sites relating to history and historical research.

Dissertation Abstracts International. See next page, *ProQuest Dissertations and Theses Database.*

Film Index International. Chadwyk-Healey. A searchable database of information on 115,000 films from 170 countries. By subscription only.

Historical Text Archive. historicaltextarchive.com. A searchable database of articles, books, and links.

History E-Book Program. American Council of Learned Societies. **ets.umdl .umich.edu/a/acls/subject/A.html.** Collection of digitized history books.

History Resource Center: Modern World. Gale Group. **www.galegroup.com/ modernworld/.** A digital library. By subscription only.

History Studies Centre. Chadwyk-Healey. A large collection of print and image resources. Nine separate collections. By subscription only.

Humbul Humanities Hub—History. Oxford University. **www.humbul.ac.uk/ history/.** A large number of links to a wide range of history Web sites. A nonsubscription database.

InfoMine. University of California, Riverside. **infomine.ucr.edu/.** A large database of links to history and other Web sites. A nonsubscription database.

Internet History Sourcebooks. Paul Halsall, Fordham University. **www.fordham .edu/halsall.** Features full text of scholarly works organized by period, area, and, in a few cases, subject. Works appear without annotation. Some offsite links are no longer live.

Internet Public Library. **www.ipl.org/div/subject/browse/hum30.00.00/.** This site offers free access to magazines, newspapers, and over 20,000 books through the Web.

Librarians' Index to the Internet. **www.lii.org/pub/topic/reference**. Organized by California librarians. Annotates Web sites of interest to historians.

Paratext Reference Universe. A large collection of databases including this one of reference works. By subscription only.

Project Gutenberg. **www.gutenberg.org/info/**. A large, searchable database of books. Access to most of the books is unrestricted.

ProQuest Dissertations and Theses Database. Citations to all U.S. dissertations (since 1861). Abstracted after 1980. Full text available on microfilm from UMI.

ProQuest Research Library. A group of several databases including "History Studies Center" and "Reference Works." By subscription only.

Questia. Questia Media America, Inc. **www.questia.com/library/history**. A large database of books and articles on many areas and aspects of history. Fully searchable. By subscription only.

SAGE. Selected Archives at Georgia Tech and Emory Digital Archive Project. **sage.library.emory.edu/**. This site displays online multimedia exhibits.

Swarthmore Peace Collection. Swarthmore College. **www.swarthmore.edu/library/peace**. A large library of links on the topic of peace.

Tennessee Tech History Web Site. **www2.tntech.edu/history/**. A great number of history links on most subjects and areas.

University of Pennsylvania Digital Library. **onlinebooks.library.upenn.edu/**. This site's Online Books page features over 25,000 books. It highlights banned books, female writers, and foreign-language texts.

Voice of the Shuttle History Page. **vos.ucsb.edu/**. Organizes a great number of links in an easily searchable format.

World History Archives. **www.hartford-hwp.com/archives/**. Organizes links geographically and topically, presenting a balance to Western-centered history.

World History Compass. **www.worldhistorycompass.com/**. Organizes annotated links geographically and by subject, and includes countries often underrepresented on such sites.

World History Matters. **chnm.gmu.edu/worldhistorysources/whmfinding.php**. A large index that evaluates Web sites in many areas and eras of history except for the United States. U.S. Web sites are evaluated at *History Matters:* **historymatters.gmu.edu/browse/wwwhistory/**.

WWW Virtual Library. **vlib.iue.it/history/index.html**. A large collection of links to history Web sites organized by topic, area, and era. Some materials not in English.

SPECIALIZED RESOURCES IN WORLD HISTORY

Once you have chosen your topic with the aid of the historical dictionaries, encyclopedias, and atlases listed at the beginning of this appendix (pp. 186–91), you are ready to seek out primary and secondary sources that you will use to develop and support your thesis.

The world history resources in this section are organized by time period ("Ancient") and by region ("Africa"). The sources for each specialized period or region are separated into two groups. The first group contains reference works and bibliographies available in print form. The second group contains a list of Web sites organized alphabetically by the name of the site.

Additional specialized print and digital resources in world history are available on this book's Web site: bedfordstmartins.com/benjamin.

Ancient History

Ancient Europe 8000 B.C. – A.D. 1000: Encyclopedia of the Barbarian World. Ed. Peter I. Bogucki and Pam J. Crabtree. 2 vols. New York: Thomson Gale, 2004.

The Cambridge Ancient History. Cambridge: Cambridge University Press. First edition, 12 vols., 1924–1939. Second edition, 14 vols., 1970–2005. A multivolume work with extensive bibliographies.

Civilizations of the Ancient Near East. Ed. Jack S. Sasson. New York: Scribner, 1995.

Encyclopedia of Early Christianity. Ed. Everett Ferguson et al. New York: Garland, 1998.

Encyclopedia of the Crusades. Ed. Alfred J. Andrea. Westport, CT: Greenwood Press, 2003.

Encyclopedia of the Roman Empire. Rev. ed. Ed. Matthew Bunson. New York: Facts on File, 2002.

The Oxford Encyclopedia of Ancient Egypt. Ed. Donald B. Redford. Oxford: Oxford University Press, 2001.

The Oxford History of the Classical World. Ed. John Boardman et al. Oxford: Oxford University Press, 1988–. An excellent bibliography is included.

ABZU: Guide to Resources for the Study of the Ancient Near East. **www.etana.org/abzu/**. A searchable catalog with links to Internet resources relating to the ancient Near East.

Academic Info: Ancient History. **www.academicinfo.net/histanc.html**. Annotated links to materials on ancient Greece, Rome, India, Mesopotamia, China, and Egypt, as well as information on archaeology.

Academic Info: Classical Studies. **www.academicinfo.net/classics.html**. Annotated links to materials on the languages, literatures, art, cultures, and histories of ancient Greece and Rome.

The Ancient Greek World. University of Pennsylvania Museum of Archaeology and Anthropology. **www.museum.upenn.edu/Greek_World/Index.html**. Text and images that explore the history and culture of ancient Greece.

Centre for the Study of Ancient Documents Oxford University. **www.csad.ox.ac.uk/index.html**. Presents information on and links to the materials and scripts of ancient writing.

Duke Papyrus Archive. Duke University. **scriptorium.lib.duke.edu/papyrus/**. Texts and images of 1,300 papyri. These are summarized but not translated.

Egyptology Resources. Cambridge University. **www.newton.cam.ac.uk/egypt/**. Texts, images, and links to organizations, publications, archaeological digs, and museums about Egypt.

Electronic Antiquity: Communicating the Classics. **scholar.lib.vt.edu/ejournals/ElAnt/**. Articles and book reviews relating to ancient Greece and Rome.

Encyclopedia Coptica. Coptic Network. **www.coptic.net/EncyclopediaCoptica/**. A scripture-based history of the Christian Church.

Exploring Ancient World Cultures. University of Evansville. **eawc.evansville.edu/**. Primary sources about and links to the ancient Near East, India, Egypt, China, Greece, Rome, Islam, and Europe.

Illustrated History of the Roman Empire. **www.roman-empire.net/**. An extensive text with chronologies, forums, and maps.

Oriental Institute of Oxford University — Electronic Text Corpus of Sumerian Literature. **www-etcs/.orient.ox.ac.uk/edition2/etcs/bycat.php**. Translations of portions of 400 Sumerian texts from ancient Mesopotamia.

Perseus Project. www.perseus.tufts.edu. Primary source material mostly from classical era, but also relating to the English Renaissance, history of science, and regional United States.

Worlds of Late Antiquity. University of Pennsylvania. **ccat.sas.upenn.edu/jod/wola.html**. Covers several areas between 200 and 700 CE.

Europe — General

Bibliography of European Economic and Social History. By Derek Howard Aldcroft. Manchester, UK: Manchester University Press, 1984.

Celtic Culture: A Historical Encyclopedia. Ed. John T. Koch. 5 vols. Santa Barbara, CA: ABC-CLIO, 2005.

Dictionary of Scandinavian History. Ed. Byron J. Nordstrom. Westport, CT: Greenwood Press, 1986.

Encyclopedia of European Social History [1350–2000]. Ed. Peter N. Stearns. 6 vols. New York: Scribner, 2005. Print and e-book versions.

Encyclopedia of the Industrial Revolution. Ed. Thomas Heinrich. 3 vols. New York: M. E. Sharpe, 2002.

Historical Dictionary of Germany. Ed. Wayne C. Thompson, Susan L. Thompson, and Juliet S. Thompson. Metuchen, NJ: Scarecrow Press, 1994.

Scandinavian History: 1520–1970. Comp. Stewart P. Oakley. London: Historical Association of London, 1984.

Times Atlas of European History. Ed. Thomas Cussans. New York: Times/Harper-Collins, 1994.

Women in Western European History: A Select Chronological, Geographical and Topical Bibliography from Antiquity to the French Revolution. Ed. Linda Frey, Marsha Frey, and Joanne Schneider. Westport, CT: Greenwood Press, 1982. Supplement, 1986.

AdHoc [history of Christianity]. Yale University, Yale Divinity School. **research.yale.edu:8084/divdl/adhoc/**. Images from all eras of the history of Christianity.

Eurodocs: Primary Historical Documents from Western Europe. **eudocs.lib.byu.edu/index.php/Main_Page**. An extensive collection of documents from European history, beginning with the Middle Ages and continuing to the present day. Translations of primary and secondary sources. Each collection has both internal and external links. Find documents for individual countries under the country headings.

History Guide. **www.historyguide.de/**. Links, bibliographies, journals, and materials relating primarily to American and European history.

Library of Iberian Resources Online. **libro.uca.edu/**. Several hundred digitized works in English on the histories of Spain and Portugal.

United States Holocaust Memorial Museum. **www.ushmm.org/**. Multimedia exhibits and historical information relating to the Holocaust, World War II, and genocide.

Web Gallery of Art. **www.wga.hu/index.html**. Images and information about the history of European art from 1100 to 1850. The database is searchable. Extensive annotation of artists and eras.

Europe—Medieval

Atlas of Medieval Europe. Ed. Angus Konstern and Roger Kean. New York: Facts on File, 2000.

Dictionary of the Middle Ages. Ed. Joseph R. Strayer. 13 vols. New York: Scribner, 1998.

Encyclopedia of the Crusades. By Alfred J. Andrea. Westport, CT: Greenwood Press, 2003.

Literature of Medieval History, 1930–1975. Ed. Gray C. Boyce. 5 vols. Millwood, NY: Kraus International, 1981.

Medieval France: An Encyclopedia. Ed. William W. Kibler et al. New York: Garland, 1995.

Medieval Germany: An Encyclopedia. Ed. John M. Jeep. New York: Garland, 2001.

Medieval Jewish Civilization: An Encyclopedia. Ed. Norman Roth. New York: Routledge, 2002.

The New Cambridge Medieval History. Ed. Rosamond McKitterick. 7 vols. New York: Cambridge University Press, 1995–2000.

Dumbarton Oaks Electronic Texts. **www.doaks.org/etexts.html**. A collection of digitized, full-text documents in Byzantine studies.

ITER: Gateway to the Middle Ages and Renaissance. University of Toronto. **www.itergateway.org/**. A large, searchable database of journal articles on topics relating to Europe from 400 to 1700. By subscription only.

The Labyrinth: Resources for Medieval Studies. Georgetown University. **www .georgetown.edu/labyrinth/**. This site allows you to search bibliographies, discussion groups, images, and primary and secondary works by category.

Libro: Medieval Spain. **libro.uca.edu/**. A modest archive of full-text scholarly works in (or translated into) English. Covers the Iberian Peninsula from the fifth to the seventeenth centuries.

NetSERF: The Internet Connection for Medieval Resources. **www.netserf.org/**. An extensive and well-organized collection of annotated links to research sites.

ORB: The Online Reference Book for Medieval Studies. **the-orb.net**. Translations of medieval texts.

Europe — Early Modern

Encyclopedia of Witchcraft: The Western Tradition. Ed. Richard M. Golden. 4 vols. Santa Barbara, CA: ABC-CLIO, 2006.

The Oxford Encyclopedia of the Reformation. Ed. Hans J. Hillerbrand. New York: Oxford University Press, 1996.

Reformation Europe: A Guide to Research. Ed. Steven Ozment. St. Louis: Center for Reformation Research, 1982.

Renaissance and Reformation: Reference Library Cumulative Index. Detroit: U.X.L., 2002.

Renaissance Humanism, 1300–1550: A Bibliography of Materials in English. Ed. Benjamin Kohl. New York: Garland, 1985.

CERES. Cambridge English Renaissance Electronic Service. **www.english.cam.ac.uk/ceres/links.htm**. A large database of links to Renaissance documents online.

Columbus and the Age of Discovery. Millersville University. **www.millersville.edu/~columbus/**. Over 1,100 articles about Columbus and cross-cultural encounters.

European Voyages of Exploration. University of Calgary. **www.ucalgary.ca/applied_history/tutor/eurvoya**. A tutorial with maps and documents describing these sea voyages.

ITER: Gateway to the Middle Ages and Renaissance. University of Toronto. **www.itergateway.org/**. A large, searchable database of journal articles on topics relating to Europe from 400 to 1700. By subscription only.

Renaissance Forum: An Electronic Journal of Early-Modern Literary and Historical Studies. **www.hull.ac.uk/Hull/EL_Web/renforum**. This directory features historical and literary articles and book reviews relating to early modern Europe.

Renascence Editions [Renaissance]. **darkwing.uoregon.edu/~rbear/ren.htm**. Provides online access to texts printed in English between the late fifteenth century and the end of the eighteenth century.

Witchcraft Collection. Cornell University. **historical.library.cornell.edu/witchcraft/browse.html**. A collection of digitized books on witchcraft, principally in Europe.

Europe — Modern

Dictionary of Modern Italian History. Ed. Frank J. Coppa. Westport, CT: Greenwood Press, 1985.

Encyclopedia of European Social History [1350–2000]. Ed. Peter N. Stearns. 6 vols. New York: Scribner, 2005. Print and e-book versions.

Encyclopedia of the Industrial Revolution. Ed. Thomas Heinrich. 3 vols. New York: M. E. Sharpe, 2002.

European Political Facts, 1900–1996. 4th ed. By Christopher Cook and John Paxton. New York: St. Martin's Press, 1998.

The European Powers in the First World War: An Encyclopedia. Ed. Spencer C. Tucker. New York: Garland, 1999.

Europe since 1945: An Encyclopedia. Ed. Bernard A. Cook. 2 vols. New York: Garland, 2001.

French Culture, 1900–1975. Ed. Catharine Savage Brosman and Tom Conley. Detroit: Gale Research, 1995.

German Women in the Nineteenth Century: A Social History. Ed. John Fout. New York. Holmes & Meier, 1984.

Historical Dictionary of European Imperialism. Ed. James S. Olson. Westport, CT: Greenwood Press, 1991.

Historical Dictionary of France from the 1815 Restoration to the Second Empire. Ed. Edgar Leon Newman and Robert Lawrence Simpson. 2 vols. Westport, CT: Greenwood Press, 1987.

A Historical Dictionary of Germany's Weimar Republic, 1918–1933. Ed. C. Paul Vincent. Westport, CT: Greenwood Press, 1997.

Historical Dictionary of Modern Spain, 1700–1988. Ed. Robert W. Kern. Westport, CT: Greenwood Press, 1990.

Historical Dictionary of the French Fourth and Fifth Republics, 1946–1991. Ed. Wayne Northcutt. Westport, CT: Greenwood Press, 1992.

Historical Dictionary of the Spanish Civil War, 1936–1939. Ed. James W. Cortada. Westport, CT: Greenwood Press, 1982.

Historical Dictionary of the Third French Republic, 1870–1940. Ed. Patrick H. Hutton, Amanda S. Bourque, and Amy J. Staples. 2 vols. Westport, CT: Greenwood Press, 1986.

The Longman Handbook of Modern European History, 1763–1997. Ed. Chris Cook and John Stevenson. New York: Longman, 1998.

Modern European History: 1789 to the Present. Ed. John Santore. 2 vols. New York: M. Wiener, 1983.

Modern Germany: An Encyclopedia of History, People and Culture, 1871–1900. Ed. Dieter K. Buse. New York: Garland, 1998.

Modern Italian History: An Annotated Bibliography. Comp. Frank J. Coppa and William Roberts. Westport, CT: Greenwood Press, 1990. A companion to *Dictionary of Modern Italian History* (see previous page).

Nazism, Resistance, and the Holocaust in World War II: A Bibliography. Ed. Vera Laska. Metuchen, NJ: Scarecrow Press, 1985.

Women in Western European History: A Select Chronological, Geographical, and Topical Bibliography; The Nineteenth and Twentieth Centuries. Ed. Linda Frey and Marsha Frey. Westport, CT: Greenwood Press, 1984.

Anarchism Pamphlets. Labadie Collection of the University of Michigan. **www.hti.umich.edu/l/labadie/**. A searchable database of several hundred anarchist books and pamphlets.

Cold War International History Project. Woodrow Wilson International Center for Scholars. **www.wilsoncenter.org/index.cfm?topic_id=1409&fuseaction=topics .home**. Publications and documents relating to the study of international relations during the Cold War. Many documents from former Soviet archives.

Einstein Archives Online. Hebrew University of Jerusalem. **www.alberteinstein .info/**. A large collection of Einstein's nonscientific writings, many in German, some in English.

Encyclopedia of the Revolutions of 1848. **www.cats.ohiou.edu/~chastain**. Online encyclopedia with the author of each article noted.

Exploring the French Revolution. Center for New Media, George Mason University History Project, CUNY. **chnm.gmu.edu/revolution/searchfr.php**. A collection of texts and other kinds of resources on various aspects of the Revolution.

German History in Documents and Images. German Historical Institute. **germanhistorydocs.ghi-dc.org/home.cfm**. Documents covering 1815–1866, 1866–1890, 1890–1918, and 1961–1989. Historical overviews included. Expects to have selected and translated documents (and images, maps, etc.) covering all periods of German history.

Italian Life under Fascism. University of Wisconsin, Madison. **www.library .wisc.edu/libraries/dpf/Fascism/Home.html**. This online exhibit features materials from the Fry Collection, organized thematically.

The Nuremburg War Crimes Trials. Avalon Project at Yale Law School. **www.yale .edu/lawweb/avalon/imt/imt.htm**. A large number of online documents from the official records of the trials.

The Siege and Commune of Paris, 1870–71. Northwestern University. **www.library .northwestern.edu/spec/siege/index.html**. A database of a wide range of documents and images from besieged Paris.

Southworth Spanish Civil War Collection. University of California, San Diego. **orpheus.ucsd.edu/speccoll/southwcoll.html**. Propaganda posters, children's drawings, newspapers, poems, and other primary resources.

Spartacus Educational. **www.spartacus.schoolnet.co.uk/**. Short hyperlinked essays focusing mostly on modern European political history. Degree of documentation for essays varies. Separate collections for many aspects of modern European history and also for some non-European topics.

World War II Links on the Internet. University of California, San Diego. **history.acusd.edu/gen/ww2_links.html**. Annotated links relating to the Second World War.

WWI: The World War I Document Archive. Brigham Young University. **www.lib .byu.edu/~rdh/wwi/**. Government documents, maps, photographs, and biographies.

Britain

General

Historical Atlas of Britain. Ed. Malcolm Falkus and John Gillingham. New York: Crescent Books, 1987.

British History Online. Institute of Historical Research. **www.british-history .ac.uk/subject.asp**. Documents relating to British history concerning local, national, and international affairs. Searchable by subject or place.

British Trials, 1660–1900. Chadwyk-Healey. Index of thousands of trials. Descriptions range from brief outlines to verbatim transcripts. Microfilm. By subscription only.

Dictionary of National Biography [United Kingdom]. Ed. Leslie Stephen and Sidney Lee. Oxford: Oxford University Press, 1908–. A summary of this large multivolume collection can be found in *A Concise Dictionary of National Biography, from Earliest Times to 1985.* The book is now online. See below, *Oxford Dictionary of National Biography.*

English Poor Laws, 1639–1890. UMI. A collection of contemporary books, pamphlets, and public papers from England, Scotland, and Ireland focusing on the poor and the unemployed as public issues. Microfiche. By subscription only.

Oxford Dictionary of National Biography. Oxford University Press. **www.oup.com/oxforddnb/info/online/**. Fully searchable, regularly updated United Kingdom online biography collection. By subscription only.

Royal Historical Society. **www.rhs.ac.uk/bibl/bibwel.asp**. A large, searchable database of books and articles related to British history. Articles on British history are drawn from 570 journals.

U.K. National Archives. **www.nationalarchives.gov.uk/documentsonline**. Click "Documents Online" for digitized records. There is a download fee for most documents. Major categories of documents are "Family History" (military records, wills), "Society and Law," "Home and Foreign Affairs," and "Military and Defense."

Britain before 1800

A Bibliography of British History, Stuart Period, 1603–1714. Ed. Mary Keeler. Oxford: Clarendon Press, 1970.

The Blackwell Encyclopedia of Anglo-Saxon England. Ed. Michael Lapidge. New York: Blackwell, 2000.

Early Modern British History, 1485–1760. Comp. Helen Miller and Aubrey Newman. London: Historical Association of London, 1970.

The Kings of Medieval England, c. 560–1485: A Survey and Research Guide. Ed. Larry W. Usilton. Lanham, MD: Scarecrow Press, 1996.

Medieval England: An Encyclopedia. Ed. Paul E. Szarmch et al. New York: Garland, 1998.

The Oxford History of England: Consolidated Index. Comp. Roger Raper. Oxford: Clarendon/Oxford University Press, 1995.

Tudor England: An Encyclopedia. Ed. Arthur F. Kinney et al. New York: Garland, 2000.

Women in Early Modern England, 1500–1700. Ed. Jacqueline Eales. New York: Garland, 1998.

Britannia History Index: The Age of Empire. **www.britannia.com/history/h80.html**. Documents, chronologies, articles, biographies, and links relating to Great Britain during the Age of Empire (1689–1901).

Britannia History Index: Reformation and Restoration [England, 1486–1689]. **www.britannia.com/history/h70.html**. Documents, chronologies, articles, biographies, and links relating to England during the Reformation, Civil War, and Restoration.

The British Library. **www.bl.uk**. This site offers online access to historical newspapers, special exhibits, Magna Carta, and the Gutenberg Bible, available at the British Library in London.

CERES. Cambridge English Renaissance Electronic Service. **www.english.cam .ac.uk/ceres/links.htm**. A large database of links to Renaissance documents online.

Eighteenth Century Collections Online [1701–1800]. Thomson Gale. A large full-text database of eighteenth-century materials printed in Britain. By subscription only.

Eighteenth-Century Resources — History. Rutgers, Newark. **andromeda.rutgers .edu/~jlynch/18th/history.html**. A large number of annotated links; particularly strong in American and British history but covers related areas as well.

The Norman Conquest and Its Aftermath. **www.bbc.co.uk/history/war/normans/ after_01.shtml**. A series of essays and linked images by British scholars.

Proceedings of the Old Bailey, London, 1674 to 1834. **www.oldbaileyonline.org/**. A searchable collection of 100,000 criminal trials at London's central criminal court.

Tudor History. **tudorhistory.org/files/texts.html**. A small archive of texts and documents from the Tudor period as well as commentaries on it.

Britain since 1800

A Bibliography of British History, 1789–1851. Ed. Lucy Brown and Ian R. Christie. Oxford: Clarendon Press, 1977.

A Bibliography of British History, 1851–1914. Ed. Henry J. Hanham. Oxford: Oxford University Press, 1989.

A Bibliography of British History, 1914–1989. Ed. Keith Robbins. Oxford: Clarendon Press, 1996.

British Economic and Social History: A Bibliographical Guide. 3rd ed. Ed. W. H. Chaloner and R. C. Richardson. Manchester, UK: Manchester University Press, 1995.

The Cambridge Historical Encyclopedia of Great Britain and Ireland. Ed. Christopher Haigh. Cambridge: Cambridge University Press, 1990.

Cambridge History of the British Empire. Comps. John Rose, Arthur Newton, and Ernest Benians. Cambridge: Cambridge University Press, 1929–1988.

Modern England, 1901–1984: A Bibliographical Handbook. Comp. Alfred F. Havighurst. Cambridge: Cambridge University Press, 2002.

The Oxford History of England: Consolidated Index. Comp. Roger Raper. Oxford: Clarendon/Oxford University Press, 1995.

Victorian Britain: An Encyclopedia. Ed. Sally Mitchell. New York: Garland, 1988.

Britannia History Index: The Age of Empire. **www.britannia.com/history/h80 .html**. Documents, chronologies, articles, biographies, and links relating to Great Britain during the Age of Empire (1689–1901).

British and Irish Women's Letters and Diaries. Alexander Street Press. A large collection of personal writings from the sixteenth to the twentieth centuries. By subscription only.

British Empire. BBC—History. **www.bbc.co.uk/history/state/empire**. A series of essays (with linked images) written by named British scholars. Many aspects of the subject, covering several periods.

Church and Reformation. BBC—History. **www.bbc.co.uk/history/state/ church_reformation/**. A series of essays (with linked images) written by named British scholars. Many aspects of the subject are covered.

Industrialization. BBC—History. **www.bbc.co.uk/history/society-culture/ industrialization**. A series of essays and linked commentary on the causes and impact of industrialization in Britain.

Nineteenth Century Parliamentary Papers. Chadwyk-Healey. Covers 1801 to 1900. Searchable. Will eventually be extended up to the present. By subscription only.

Society and Culture. BBC—History. **www.bbc.co.uk/history/society_culture/ society**. A series of essays (with linked images) written by named British scholars. Covers many aspects of social history from the seventeenth to twentieth centuries.

Spartacus Educational. **www.spartacus.schoolnet.co.uk**. Short hyperlinked essays focusing mostly on modern European political history. The degree of documentation for the essays varies. Several deal with the modern United Kingdom.

Victoria Research Web. Patrick Leary. **victorianresearch.org**. A wide-ranging research-oriented site.

Victorian Census Project. University of Staffordshire. **www.staffs.ac.uk/schools/ humanities_and_soc_sciences/census/downcen.htm**. Databases from the 1831 and 1861 censuses.

The Victorian Web. **www.victorianweb.org/**. Links relating to Victorian culture, history, and politics in Great Britain.

The Workhouse. Oxford University. **users.ox.ac.uk/%7Epeter/workhouse/ index.html**. An archive of linked resources examining the legal and actual treatment of the poor in England, Ireland, Scotland, and Wales in the eighteenth, nineteenth, and twentieth centuries. A small but excellent site.

Ireland and Scotland

A Bibliography of Works Relating to Scotland, 1916–1950. Ed. P. D. Hancock. Edinburgh: Edinburgh University Press, 1959–1960.

A Chronicle of Irish History since 1500. Ed. J. E. Doherty and D. J. Hickey. Savage, MD: Rowman and Littlefield, 1990.

A Dictionary of Irish History since 1800. Ed. D. J. Hickey and J. E. Doherty. Totowa, NJ: Barnes & Noble, 1980.

British and Irish Women's Letters and Diaries. Alexander Street Press. A large collection of personal writings from the sixteenth to the twentieth centuries. By subscription only.

CELT: Corpus of Electronic Texts [Irish studies]. University College Cork. **www.ucc.ie/celt/links.html**. Links to journals, bibliographies, and archives for research in Irish studies.

Great Hunger Collection Online [Ireland]. Quinnipiac University. **www.quinnipiac .edu/x6779.xml**. A modest collection of full-text documents.

The Highland Clearances [nineteenth-century Scotland]. **www.theclearances .org/clearances/main.php**. A large number of well-organized, annotated documents concerning the nineteenth-century displacement of Scots farmers and the emigration of many.

Ireland and Scotland: British Invasions. **www.bbc.co.uk/history/state/nations/ireland_invasion_01.shtml**. A series of essays and linked images by British scholars. Covers the twelfth to the fourteenth centuries and the legacy of the invasions.

Irish Resources in the Humanities [history]. **www.irith.org/irith.service?request =search&subject=history**. A collection of links to archives and other academic resources in Irish history.

National Archives of Ireland. **www.nationalarchives.ie/research/databases.htm**. A description of each collection of documents is available. Some documents are online but not a great number.

Scotland and the Four Nations. BBC. **www.bbc.co.uk/history/state/nations/four_nations_01.shtml**. An extensive scholarly essay linked to articles, biographies, timelines, etc.

Views of the [Irish] Famine. Vassar College. **vassun.vassar.edu/~sttaylor/FAMINE**. A large number of drawings from contemporary newspapers.

The Word on the Street: Broadsides at the National Library of Scotland. **www.nls.uk/broadsides**. A searchable database of broadsides from 1650 to 1910. Many are transcribed and downloadable.

Writings on Irish History. Royal Historical Society. **www.irishhistoryonline.ie/projhist.php**. A project to place online the very large bibliography published in print since the 1930s. The material since 1995 is now going online.

East Europe

The American Bibliography of Slavic and East European Studies. Stanford, CA: American Association for the Advancement of Slavic and East European Studies, 1956–1994. Now available online. See below, *ABSEES Online*.

Dictionary of East European History since 1945. Ed. Joseph Held. Westport CT: Greenwood Press, 1994.

Encyclopedia of Eastern Europe. Ed. Richard Frucht. New York: Garland, 2000.

Historical Atlas of East Central Europe. Ed. Paul R. Magocsi and Geoffrey J. Matthews. Seattle: University of Washington Press, 1993.

Ukraine: A Bibliographic Guide to English Language Publications. Ed. Bohdan Wynar. Englewood, CO: Ukrainian Academic Press, 1990.

Yugoslavia: A Comprehensive English-Language Bibliography. Ed. Francine Friedman. Wilmington, DE: Scholarly Resources, 1993.

ABSEES Online. EBSCO, American Association for the Advancement of Slavic and East European Studies. A bibliography of books, journal articles, online resources, etc. It covers many disciplines and is now available by subscription only.

Bulgaria's History. Aumda Gallery. **www.omda.bg/engl/common/history.htm**. A series of short hypertext essays on a variety of historical topics.

Czech and Slovak History: An American Bibliography. Ed. George J. Kovtun. **www.loc.gov/rr/european/cash/cash1.html**. An extensive bibliography of books and articles in English. Contains works written before 1994.

Radio Prague's History Online Virtual Exhibit. Radio Prague. **archiv.radio.cz/ history/history00.html**. A short essay on Czech history with images.

Russia and the Soviet Union

The American Bibliography of Slavic and East European Studies. Stanford, CA: American Association for the Advancement of Slavic and East European Studies, 1956–1994. Now available online. See below, *ABSEES Online.*

The Blackwell Encyclopedia of the Russian Revolution. Ed. Harold Shukman. Cambridge, MA.: Blackwell Reference, 1994.

Dictionary of the Russian Revolution. Ed. George Jackson. Westport, CT: Greenwood Press, 1989. Also available as an e-book from Thomson Gale.

Encyclopedia of Russian History. Ed. James R. Milar. 4 vols. New York: Macmillan Reference USA, 2004.

The Rise and Fall of the Soviet Union: A Selected Bibliography of Sources in English. Ed. Abraham J. Edelheit and Hershel Edelheit. Westport, CT: Greenwood Press, 1992.

Russia and the Former Soviet Union: A Bibliographic Guide to English Publications, 1986–1991. Ed. Helen F. Sullivan and Robert H. Burger. Englewood, CO: Libraries Unlimited, 1994.

The Russian Revolution, 1905–1921: A Bibliographic Guide to the Works in English. Ed. Murray Frame. Westport, CT: Greenwood Press, 1995.

Soviet Foreign Policy, 1918–1945: A Guide to Research and Research Materials. Ed. Robert H. Johnston. Wilmington, DE: Scholarly Resources, 1997.

The Soviet Union: A Biographical Dictionary. Ed. Archie Brown. New York: Macmillan, 1991.

ABSEES Online. EBSCO; American Association for the Advancement of Slavic and East European Studies. A bibliography of books, journal articles, online resources, etc. It covers many disciplines and is now available by subscription only.

Alexander II and His Times. Eastern Michigan University. **www.emich.edu/public/ history/moss/index.htm**. A documented narrative on the era.

Revelations from the Russian Archives. **www.loc.gov/exhibits/archives/intro.html**. Documents from the Soviet era focusing on repression and espionage.

Russia Engages the World: 1453–1825. New York Public Library. **russia.nypl.org/**. A collection of documents on Russia and the West (and also Asia) in the fifteenth to nineteenth centuries.

Africa

Africa and the World: An Introduction to the History of Sub-Saharan Africa from Antiquity to 1840. By Lewis H. Gann and Peter Duignan. 1972. Reprint, Lanham, MD: University Press of America, 1999.

Africana: The Encyclopedia of the African and the African American Experience. 2nd ed. Ed. Kwame Anthony Appiah and Henry Louis Gates Jr. 5 vols. New York: Oxford University Press, 2005.

The Cambridge History of Africa. 8 vols. Cambridge: Cambridge University Press, 1975–1986.

Dictionary of African Biography. New York: Reference Publications, 1977–1995.

Dictionary of African Historical Biography. Ed. Mark R. Lipschultz and R. Kent Rasmusson. Berkeley: University of California Press, 1986.

Encyclopedia of African Nations and Civilizations. Ed. Keith Lye. New York: Facts on File, 2002.

Encyclopedia of Africa South of the Sahara. Ed. John Middleton. 4 vols. New York: Scribner, 1997.

The Encyclopedia of Pre-Colonial Africa. Ed. Joseph O. Vogel. Walnut Creek, CA: Alta Mira Press, 1997.

Encyclopedia of Twentieth-Century African History. Ed. Tiyambe Zeleza. New York: Routledge, 2002.

Historical Dictionary of Pre-Colonial Africa. Ed. Robert O. Collins. Lanham, MD: Scarecrow Press, 2001.

South African History: A Bibliographic Guide with Special Reference to Territorial Expansion and Colonization. Ed. Naomi Musiker. New York: Garland, 1984.

African National Congress: Historical Documents. **www.anc.org.za/ancdocs/ history**. A collection of documents by and about the ANC and about organizations that supported their struggle.

African Studies. Columbia University Libraries. **www.columbia.edu/cu/lweb/ indiv/africa/cuvl/index.html**. A collection of links to sources of research on Africa including its "History and Culture."

Africa South of the Sahara: Selected Internet Resources. Stanford University. **library .stanford.edu/africa**. Links relevant to African cultures and history by country and topic.

Digital Image Project of South Africa: South African Freedom Struggle. University of Natal. **disa.nu.ac.za**. Digital images of forty-four South African publications, 1950–1994.

National Archives of the Republic of South Africa. **www.national.archives.gov.za/ index_content.htm**. Search facilities only.

National Museum of African Art. Smithsonian Institution. **africa.si.edu/collections/ index.htm**. An online permanent exhibit. A large number of annotated images organized by three categories: "diversity," "use," and "imagery."

The Story of Africa. **www.bbc.co.uk/worldservice/africa/features/storyofafrica**. Essays on numerous aspects of African history. Interviews with African scholars. A project of the BBC.

Middle East and North Africa

The Cambridge Encyclopedia of the Middle East and North Africa. Ed. Trevor Mostyn. Cambridge: Cambridge University Press, 1988.

Encyclopedia of the Modern Middle East and North Africa. 2nd ed. Ed. Philip Hatter et al. 4 vols. Detroit: Macmillan Reference USA, 2004.

Middle East and Islam: A Bibliographical Introduction. Geneva: Inter Documentation, 1979. Supplement, 1986.

The Oxford Encyclopedia of the Modern Islamic World. New York: Oxford University Press, 1995. Covers the eighteenth century to the present.

Index Islamicus: Index to the Literature on Islam. Cambridge University Library. A large database of literature on Islam, the Middle East, and the Muslim World. By subscription only.

The Islamic World of 1600. University of Calgary. **www.ucalgary.ca/applied _history/tutor/islam**. A well-crafted tutorial examining many aspects of Islamic societies.

Middle East Studies Internet Resources. Columbia University Libraries. **www .columbia.edu/cu/lweb/indiv/mideast/cuvlm/index.html**. This site organizes resources by subject.

Question of Palestine: History. United Nations. **www.un.org/Depts/dpa/ngo/ history.html**. This UN multimedia document discusses the history of Palestine since 1917.

Asia

General

Bibliography of Asian Studies. Ann Arbor: Association for Asian Studies, 1956–1991. Succeeded by *BAS Online* (Association for Asian Studies). A fully searchable database of journal articles and other scholarly resources on Asia. By subscription only.

Encyclopedia of Asian History. Ed. Ainslie T. Embree. 4 vols. New York: Scribner, 1988.

Southeast Asia: A Historical Encyclopedia. Ed. Ooi Keat Gin. 3 vols. Santa Barbara, CA: ABC-CLIO, 2004.

Vietnam Studies: An Annotated Bibliography. Ed. Carl Singleton. Lanham, MD: Scarecrow Press, 1997.

The Wars in Vietnam, Cambodia, and Laos, 1945–1982: A Bibliographic Guide. Ed. Richard Dean Burns and Milton Leitenberg. Santa Barbara, CA: ABC-CLIO, 1992.

Asian Division, Area Studies. Library of Congress. **www.lcweb.loc.gov/rr/asian**. Information on the Library of Congress's Asian studies collections, as well as a Korean bibliography and a Japanese Documentation Center with a searchable database.

Asian Studies Search Engines. T. Matthew Ciolek. **www.ciolek.com/Search Engines.html**. Onsite access to a series of offsite search engines including H-Nets. Also a database of images.

East Asian Library. University of Pittsburgh. **www.library.pitt.edu/libraries/ eal/**. This site is a prominent specialist library.

Formosa. Reed College. **academic.reed.edu/formosa/formosa_index_page/ Formosa_index.html**. An archive of U.S. writings on "Formosa" in the nineteenth century. Also maps, art, photographs, etc.

Huntington Archive of Buddhist and Related Art. Ohio State University. **kaladarshan .arts.ohio-state.edu**. A searchable database of photographed images of art from Asia and South Asia.

Indonesia: Society and Culture, World Wide Web Virtual Library. Australian National University. **coombs.anu.edu.au/WWWVLPages/IndonPages/WWWVL-Indonesia .html**. Annotated links to resources in Indonesian studies, including information on Islam in Indonesia.

Philippine Bibliography. Library of Congress. **lcweb2.loc.gov/asian/philhtml/ bib9.html**. An online bibliography of the Library of Congress's Philippine history collection.

Portal to Asian Internet Resources. University of Wisconsin Library. **digicoll .library.wisc.edu/PAIR/directory/history.html**. An annotated list of sites on Asian studies. This URL brings you to resources in Asian history.

Southeast Asian Archive. University of California, Irvine. **www.lib.uci.edu/ libraries/collections/sea/sasian.html**. Virtual exhibits and annotated links to Southeast Asian resources.

Viettouch. **www.viettouch.com**. Essays covering Vietnamese history with internal links to art, chronology, etc. Especially strong in ancient Vietnam.

South Asia — India, Pakistan, and Sri Lanka

The Cambridge Encyclopedia of India, Pakistan, Sri Lanka, Nepal, Bhutan and the Maldives. Ed. Francis Robinson. Cambridge: Cambridge University Press, 1989.

Encyclopedia of India. Ed. Stanley A. Wolpert. 4 vols. New York: Scribner, 2005.

A Historical Atlas of South Asia. Ed. Joseph E. Schwartzberg. New York: Oxford University Press, 1992.

India: A Critical Bibliography. Ed. J. Michael Mahar. Tucson: University of Arizona Press, 1980.

South Asian Civilizations: A Bibliographical Synthesis. Ed. Maureen Patterson. Chicago: University of Chicago Press, 1981.

Digital South Asia Library. University of Chicago. **dsal.uchicago.edu**. Categorizes resources useful in South Asian research, including documents, books, newspapers, references, journals, bibliographies, and maps.

Harappa: Glimpses of South Asia before 1947. **www.harappa.com/index.html**. Text and images from early Indus Valley civilizations. Also, images, sound, and film from the decades prior to independence and partition.

Mahatma Gandhi Research and Media Service. Gandhi Serve Foundation. **www.gandhiserve.org/**. A searchable archive of Gandhi's correspondence, published writings, etc.

Primary Documents for the Study of Indian History, c. 1890–2000. **www.sscnet.ucla .edu/southasia/History/Independent/Histbiblio_indepindia.html**. A series of linked essays and annotated documents. Part of a larger site on the history of India.

South Asia Resource Access on the Internet [SARAI]. Columbia University. **www .columbia.edu/cu/libraries/indiv/area/sarai/**. Links to journals, organizations, and topical guides on South Asian history.

China

China: A Historical and Cultural Dictionary. Ed. Michael Dillon. Richmond, Surrey, UK: Curzon, 1998.

China Bibliography: A Research Guide to Reference Works about China Past and Present. Ed. Harriet T. Zurndorfer. Honolulu: University of Hawaii Press, 1999.

Modern China: An Encyclopedia of History, Culture, and Nationalism. Ed. Wang Kewen. New York: Garland, 1998.

Academic Info: Chinese History. **www.academicinfo.net/chinahist.html**. Selected, annotated links to chronologies, databases, bibliographies, journals, and dictionaries. Site has some advertisements.

Chinese History Research Site. University of California, San Diego. **orpheus.ucsd .edu/chinesehistory/**. A primary-source guide, archives, links, book reviews, and a bibliography (after the Qing period), as well as information on contemporary research by scholars worldwide.

Chinese Propaganda Posters. Leiden University. **www.iisg.nl/~landsberger/**. Hundreds of Chinese propaganda posters covering 1949 to 2000. Organized by theme.

The Gate of Heavenly Peace. Long Bow Group. **www.pbs.org/wgbh/pages/frontline/ gate/**. Digital material organized around a PBS documentary on the Tienanmen Massacre of June 4, 1989. Includes background material and a variety of perspectives on the event. Articles, essays, audio, video, and artwork.

John Fairbank Memorial Chinese History Virtual Library. CND. **www.cnd.org/ fairbank/**. Information about the Qing period, the Republican era, and the People's Republic of China.

Japan and Korea

The Cambridge History of Japan. Ed. John Whitney Hall. 6 vols. Cambridge: Cambridge University Press, 1988–.

Concise Dictionary of Modern Japanese History. Ed. Janet Hunter. Berkeley: University of California Press, 1984.

Japan and Korea: A Critical Bibliography. Ed. Bernard Silberman. Westport, CT: Greenwood Press, 1982.

Japanese History and Culture from Ancient to Modern Times: Seven Basic Bibliographies. Ed. John Dower and Timothy George. New York: M. Wiener, 1997.

Japanese Studies from Pre-History to 1990: A Bibliographical Guide. Ed. Richard Perren. Manchester, UK: Manchester University Press, 1992.

Modern Japan: An Encyclopedia of History, Culture and Nationalism. Ed. James Huffman. New York: Garland, 1998.

Studies on Korea: A Scholar's Guide. Ed. Han-kyo Kim. Honolulu: University of Hawaii Press, 1980.

Asian Division, Area Studies. Library of Congress. **www.loc.gov/rr/asian/**. Information on the Library of Congress's Asian studies collections.

Harvard Korean Studies Bibliography. **www.fas.harvard.edu/~korbib/**. This site, which covers the late sixteenth century to the present in a searchable on-line database, features over 80,000 references.

Japanese Studies Resources. East Asian Collection, Duke University Libraries. **www.lib.duke.edu/ias/eac/japan/japanesestudies.html**. An extensive compilation of bibliographies, journals, dictionaries, reference works, materials, and listservs useful to the study of Japan.

J Guide: Stanford Guide to Japan Information Resources. **jguide.stanford.edu/**. Covers all aspects of Japanese culture and history, with extensive links.

Korean Bibliography. Library of Congress. **lcweb2.loc.gov/misc/korhtml/ korbibhome.html**. A searchable database of books on Korea in English.

Korean History: A Bibliography. University of Hawaii. **www.hawaii.edu/korea/ bibliography/bibliotable.htm**. An online bibliography organized by period.

Kyoto National Museum. **www.kyohaku.go.jp/eng/syuzou/index.html**. An extensive online collection of pre-1800 Japanese art.

Australia and New Zealand

Australian Dictionary of Biography. Ed. Douglas Pike et al. 16 vols. Carlton, Victoria: Melbourne University Press, 1966–.

Australian Federation Full Text Database. University of Sydney. **setis.library .usyd.edu.au/oztexts/fed.html**. Transcribed debates and related writings on the Federation movement.

Australian Studies Resources. University of Sydney. **setis.library.usyd.edu.au/ oztexts/index.html**. A large digital collection of Australian literary and historical texts and journals.

National Library of New Zealand: Papers Past. **paperspast.natlib.govt.nz/**. A digital collection of nineteenth-century New Zealand newspapers and periodicals.

Latin America and the Caribbean

Encyclopedia of Latin American History and Culture. Ed. Barbara A. Tenenbaum. 5 vols. New York: Scribner, 1995.

A Guide to the History of Brazil, 1500–1822: The Literature in English. Ed. Francis A. Dutra. Santa Barbara, CA: ABC-CLIO, 1980.

Handbook of Latin American Studies. Cambridge, MA: Harvard University Press, 1936–1947; and Gainesville: University of Florida Press, 1948–. Annual volume. Also a searchable database on the Web site of the Library of Congress at rs6.loc.gov/hlas.

Hispanic Culture of South America. Ed. Peter Standish. Detroit: Gale Research, 1995.

Historical Dictionary of the Spanish Empire, 1402–1975. Ed. Sam L. Slick. Westport, CT: Greenwood Press, 1991.

The History Atlas of South America. Ed. Edwin Early. New York: Macmillan, 1998.

Latin America and the Caribbean: A Critical Guide to Research Sources. Ed. Paula H. Covington et al. Westport, CT: Greenwood Press, 1992.

Latin American Politics: A Historical Bibliography. Santa Barbara, CA: ABC-CLIO, 1986.

The Oxford Encyclopedia of Mesoamerican Cultures: The Civilizations of Mexico and Central America. Ed. David Carrasco. Oxford: Oxford University Press, 2001.

A Reference Guide to Latin American History. Ed. James D. Henderson et al. New York: M. E. Sharpe, 2000.

Ancient Mesoamerican Civilizations. University of Minnesota. **www.angelfire.com/ ca/humanorigins/**. Ancient Mesoamerican politics, culture, writing, government, and astronomy, with links to other sites of interest.

Castro Speech Database. University of Texas. **www.lanic.utexas.edu/la/cb/ cuba/castro.html**. English translations of Fidel Castro's speeches.

Central American Archives. ProQuest. Primary documents from the national archives of several Central American nations. Mostly in Spanish, for the period 1519 to 1898. By subscription only.

CHC: Cuban History Collection. University of Miami. **digital.library.miami.edu/ chcdigital/collections.shtml**. Mostly twentieth-century documents in Spanish, some with English summaries.

Columbus and the Age of Discovery. Millersville University. **www.millersville.edu/ ~columbus/**. Over 1,100 articles about Columbus and cross-cultural encounters.

Dumbarton Oaks Electronic Texts. **www.doaks.org/etexts.html**. A collection of digitized, full-text documents in pre-Columbian studies.

Internet Resources for Latin America. **lib.nmsu.edu/subject/bord/laguia/#pub**. Open databases on Latin American studies.

Latin American Network Information Center. University of Texas. **lanic.utexas .edu/la/region/history/**. This site organizes online history resources on Latin America.

Mexico: From Empire to Revolution. Getty Research Institute. **www.getty.edu/ research/conducting_research/digitized_collections/mexico/**. A photographic archive of Mexico covering the years 1857–1923.

Mystery of the Maya. Canadian Museum of Civilization. **www.civilization.ca/ civil/maya/mminteng.html**. A multimedia exhibit on the culture and civilization of the Maya.

The Perry-Castañeda Library Map Collection. University of Texus. **www.lib.utexas .edu/maps/index.html**. An extensive collection of maps covering many areas of the world.

Realms of the Sacred: Early Written Records of Mesoamerica. University of California, Riverside. **www.lib.uci.edu/libraries/exhibits/meso/sacred.html**. An annotated collection of "Codices" — documents in the native "languages" of the Aztec, Maya, and Mixtec people of Mexico and Central America.

Templo Mayor Museum. **archaeology.asu.edu/tm/index2.htm**. This site guides you through the halls of the museum, dedicated to ancient Mexican history and artifacts.

Canada

Bibliography of Ontario History, 1867–1976: Cultural, Economic, Political and Social. By Olga B. Bishop. 2 vols. Toronto: University of Toronto Press, 1980. Supplement, 1976–1986. Toronto: Dunburn Press, 1989.

The Canadian Encyclopedia, 2000. Ed. James H. March. Toronto: McClelland and Stewart, 2000.

Canadian Reference Sources. Ed. Mary E. Bond and Martine M. Caron. Vancouver: University of British Columbia Press, 1996.

Canadian Who's Who. 37 vols. Toronto: University of Toronto Press, 2002.

Dictionary of Canadian Biography. Toronto: University of Toronto Press, 1966–. For an index to this multivolume work, see *Dictionary of Canadian Biography: Index, Volumes I to XII, 1000 to 1900.*

Economic History of Canada: A Guide to Information Sources. Ed. Trevor J. O. Dick. Detroit: Gale, 1978.

Historical Atlas of Canada. Ed. R. Cole Harris and Donald Kerr. Toronto: University of Toronto Press, 1987.

Canada's Digital Collections. Government of Canada. **collections.ic.gc.ca/E/SL _CandianHistory.asp**. An alphabetical index to a large number of online sites concerning many aspects of Canadian history.

Canadian Archival Resources on the Internet. University of Saskatchewan. **www.archivescanada.ca/car/menu.html**. This site allows you to search archives and historical Internet resources relating to Canada.

The Canadian Encyclopedia. **www.thecanadianencyclopedia.com/**. This site allows you to search information relating to Canadian history. Created for beginning researchers.

Canadian Native Law Cases, 1763–1978. University of Saskatchewan. **library .usask.ca/native/cnlc/index.html**. Documents for the study of these kinds of cases.

The Canadian West. Library and Archives Canada. **www.collectionscanada.ca/ 05/0529/052901_e.html**. A broad-ranging essay with links and images concerning the experience of Natives and Europeans on the Canadian "frontier."

Civilization Canada: The Last Best West, Advertising for Immigrants to Western Canada, 1870–1930. Canadian Museum of Civilization. **www.civilization.ca/ hist/advertis/ads1-01e.html**. Text and images concerning the effort to attract European immigrants to western Canada.

Dictionary of Canadian Biography Online. **www.biographi.ca/EN/index.html/**. A searchable database that covers Canadians who lived or were well known by 1930. This date will move forward as the database is updated.

Early Canadiana Online. **www.canadiana.org/eco/english/collect.html**. A centralized, rapidly growing collection of documents relating to Canadian history through the early twentieth century. Some collections available to subscribers only.

Government of Canada — Digital History Collections. **collections.ic.gc.ca/E/ Subject.asp**. A large number of searchable topics on Canadian history.

Library and Archives Canada. Canadian Government. **www.collectionscanada .ca/topics/index-e.html**. Wide-ranging collections of primary-source materials and research guides.

The Urban Past [urban history]. University of Guelph. **www.uoguelph.ca/ history/urban/citybibV04.html**. A series of bibliographies on urban history emphasizing Canadian cities from the eighteenth to the twentieth centuries. Other urban history links. Based on a course in urban history.

GENERAL RESOURCES IN UNITED STATES HISTORY

Before examining the general resources in U.S. history listed in this section and the specialized resources described on pp. 225–42, you should consult the historical dictionaries, encyclopedias, and atlases listed at the beginning of this appendix (pp. 186–91). They will enable you to choose a topic and narrow it to a theme.

The general resources in this section consist of bibliographies and Web sites that cover large areas and many periods of U.S. history. The specialized resources described later will be useful once you have chosen a topic and have a clear understanding of the kind of research you will need to do to develop and support your thesis. Even if you have already narrowed your topic, you should not ignore the following general resources, because many of them include sections on or links to more specialized topics.

Reference Works and Bibliographies

The American Historical Association's Guide to Historical Literature. 3rd ed. Ed. Mary Beth Norton. 2 vols. Ithaca: Cornell University Press, 1995. This guide contains a large section on U.S. history.

Directory of Oral History Collections. Ed. Allen Smith. Phoenix: Oryx, 1988.

Encyclopedia of American Cultural and Intellectual History. Ed. Mary Kupiec Cayton and Peter W. Williams. New York: Scribner, 2001.

Encyclopedia of American History. 7th ed. Ed. Richard B. Morris. New York: HarperCollins, 1996.

Encyclopedia of American History. Ed. Gary B. Nash. 11 vols. New York: Facts on File, 2003.

Encyclopedia of the American Constitution. 2nd ed. Ed. Leonard Levy. 6 vols. New York: Macmillan, 2000.

Encyclopedia of the American Judicial System. Ed. Robert J. Janosik. New York: Scribner, 1987.

Guides to Archives and Manuscript Collections in the United States: An Annotated Bibliography. Comp. Donald L. DeWitt. Westport, CT: Greenwood Press, 1994.

Handbook for Research in American History: A Guide to Bibliographies and Other Reference Works. 2nd ed. Ed. Francis Paul Prucha. Lincoln: University of Nebraska Press, 1994.

Harvard Guide to American History. Rev. ed. Ed. Oscar Handlin et al. Cambridge, MA: Harvard University Press, 1979. Chapters 6 through 30 contain detailed reading lists for many periods and topics in U.S. history.

The Literature of American Legal History. Ed. William E. Nelson and John P. Reid. New York: Oceana, 1985.

Pamphlets in American History: A Bibliographical Guide to the Microfilm Collections. 4 vols. Sanford, NC: Microfilming Corp. of America, 1979–1983.

The Reader's Companion to American History. Ed. Eric Foner and John A. Garraty. Boston: Houghton Mifflin, 1991.

Web Sites

Academic Info: United States History Resources. **www.academicinfo.net/histus.html**. This site includes gateways, reference materials, and topical sites with annotated links.

American Memory: Historical Collections for the National Digital Library. **memory .loc.gov/ammem/index.html**. This site is run by the Library of Congress and features more than 7 million documents relating to American history.

American Studies at the University of Virginia. **xroads.virginia.edu**. A variety of multimedia and hypertext sources, exhibits, timelines, and other resources of use for studying American history, with a special section on the 1930s.

Archives USA. Chadwyk-Healey. **archives.chadwyck.com**. A searchable directory of over 5,000 archives of primary-source material. By subscription only. Updates and supersedes *Directory of Archives and Manuscript Repositories in the United States* (Phoenix: Oryx, 1988).

Avalon Project: Documents in Law, History and Diplomacy. Yale Law School. **www.yale.edu/lawweb/avalon/avalon.htm**. Documents in law, history, and diplomacy from many periods in American history, organized by century.

Berkeley Digital Library SunSITE. **sunsite.berkeley.edu/**. Texts and images, including classical and medieval works, the Emma Goldman papers, and a strong collection relating to California.

Broadsides and Printed Ephemera: 1600–2000. Library of Congress, American Memory. **memory.loc.gov/ammem/rbpehtml/pehome.html**. A searchable collection of 10,000 posters, advertisements, leaflets, propaganda pieces, and business cards.

Core Historical Literature of Agriculture. Cornell University. **chla.library.cornell .edu/**. A collection of primary and secondary documents on agriculture in the nineteenth and twentieth centuries, including over 800 monographs.

Duke University Rare Book, Manuscript, and Special Collections Library. **scriptorium .lib.duke.edu/scriptorium/**. Highly specialized and in-depth collections of digital materials on a variety of subjects but especially in the areas of advertising, the history of women, African American history, and Native American history.

The Great Chicago Fire. **www.chicagohs.org/fire/intro/gcf-index.html**. Essays, images, and primary documents about the fire of 1871.

History Matters. George Mason University. **historymatters.gmu.edu**. An annotated list of over 700 sites for serious research in U.S. history on the Web.

History Resource Center: U.S. Gale Group. **www.galegroup.com/HistoryRC/ index.htm**. This site requires a subscription to use its integrated text and commentary.

In the First Person. Alexander Street Press. A searchable index to a large database of oral history collections in English.

Library of American Civilization: Titles Available Online. Quinnipiac University. **www.quinnipiac.edu/x6781.xml**. Free online works drawn from the Library of American Civilization.

Making of America. University of Michigan. **www.hti.umich.edu/m/moajrnl/** for searching journals; **www.hti.umich.edu/m/moa/** for searching books. Scanned images of books and magazine articles (over 9,000 books and

50,000 journal articles) from nineteenth-century America, particularly focused on social history. Full-text access. See also the Cornell University site, next.

Making of America. Cornell University Library. **library8.library.cornell.edu/ moa/**. Complements coverage by the University of Michigan site with its own collection of nineteenth-century books and articles. Full-text access.

National Gallery of the Spoken Word. Michigan State University. **www .historicalvoices.org/**. A searchable database of oral history archives throughout the United States.

The National Union Catalog of Manuscript Collections. Washington, DC: Library of Congress, 1959–1993. **www.loc.gov/coll/nucmc/**. A searchable catalog, with complex search rules, of manuscript materials held by universities, libraries, archives, historical associations, etc.

The Nineteenth Century in Print. Library of Congress, American Memory. **memory .loc.gov/ammem/ndlpcoop/moahtml/mnchome.html/**. A large, searchable collection of nineteenth-century books.

ProQuest Dissertations and Theses Database. Citations to all U.S. dissertations (since 1861). Abstracted after 1980. Full text available on microfilm from UMI.

ProQuest History Studies Center. A large database of reference works, media, journals, etc. All by subscription. Find out which of the individual information collections can be accessed from your library.

Questia Net Library. Questia. **www.questia.com/library/history/united-stateshistory**. A large database of digitized research sources on all eras and aspects of U.S. history. By subscription only.

WestWeb: Western History. CUNY. **scholar.library.csi.cuny.edu/westweb/**. Primary sources, links, timelines, and bibliographies relating to the history of the American West.

WWW-VL History: United States. **vlib.iue.it/history/USA/**. This site categorizes links and materials by media, topic, and era.

SPECIALIZED RESOURCES IN UNITED STATES HISTORY

Once you have chosen your topic with the aid of the historical dictionaries, encyclopedias, and atlases listed at the beginning of this appendix (pp. 186–91), you are ready to seek out primary and secondary sources that you will use to develop and support your thesis. The U.S. history resources in this section are organized by subject, and the resources listed for each subject are divided into two groups. The first group contains reference works and bibliographies available in print form. The second group contains a list of Web sites organized alphabetically by the name of the site. Additional specialized print and digital resources in U.S. history are available on this book's Web site: bedfordstmartins.com/benjamin.

Regional, State, and Local

A Bibliography of American County Histories. Comp. P. William Filby. Baltimore: Genealogical Publishing, 1985.

Directory of Historical Organizations in the United States and Canada, 2002. 15th ed. Comp. Mary Bray Wheeler. Nashville: American Association for State and Local History, 2002.

Encyclopedia of the American West. 4 vols. New York: Simon and Schuster/ Macmillan, 1996.

Encyclopedia of Local History. Ed. Carol Kammen. Walnut Creek, CA: Alta Mira Press, 2000.

Encyclopedia of Southern Culture. Ed. Charles Reagan Wilson and William Ferris. Chapel Hill: University of North Carolina Press, 1989.

Genealogical and Local History Books in Print. 5th ed. 4 vols. Washington, DC: Genealogical Books in Print, 1996–1997.

United States Local Histories in the Library of Congress: A Bibliography. 5 vols. Ed. Marion J. Kaminkow. Baltimore: Magna Carta, 1975.

Center for the Study of Southern Culture. University of Mississippi. **www.olemiss .edu/depts/south**. This site offers publications and a media archive.

Colorado Digitalization Project. **www.cdpheritage.org**. A variety of media, including maps, letters, and government documents, relating to the history of Colorado.

Directory of State Archives and Records Programs. **www.statearchivists.org/ states.htm**. A linked list of state archives throughout the United States.

Documenting the American South. University of North Carolina. **docsouth.unc .edu/**. A wide array of primary sources relating to the American South before 1940, especially North Carolina.

Everglades Digital Library. **www.fiu.edu/~glades/library/**. This site is dedicated to the study of the environment of southern Florida and offers historical and scientific information relating to the Everglades.

The Handbook of Texas Online. University of Texas, Austin. **www.tsha.utexas .edu/handbook/online/search.html**. Thousands of full-text journal articles. Many of these deal with the Spanish and Mexican periods of Texas history.

History of the American West, 1860–1920. Library of Congress, American Memory; Denver Public Library. **memory.loc.gov/ammem/award97/codhtml/ hawphome.html**. About 30,000 photos taken between 1860 and 1920 of Colorado towns; mining industry; Indian communities; World War II–era photos. Keyword searchable.

Maritime Westward Expansion: 1820–1890. Library of Congress, American Memory. **memory.loc.gov/ammem/award99/mymhihtml/mymhihome.html**. A searchable collection of documents, images, and other resources in a multimedia format.

Ohio River Valley: 1750–1820. Library of Congress, American Memory. **memory .loc.gov/ammem/award99/icuhtml/fawhome.html**. A searchable collection of documents, images, and other resources in a multimedia format.

Online Archive of California. California Digital Libraries. **www.oac.cdlib.org/ about/oacprojects.html**. Digital resources relating to the history of California. Several collections are more broad in scope.

State Archives Collections Online. Archives Resource Center. **www.statearchivists .org/arc/education/online_coll.htm**. A linked list of online materials on state archive Web sites.

Texas Tides. **tides.sfasu.edu/**. Timelines and documents of the five major ethnic groups in Texas history.

Colonial, Revolutionary, and Early National, 1607–1800

The American Revolution, 1775–1783: An Encyclopedia. New York: Garland, 1993.

The Blackwell Encyclopedia of the American Revolution. Ed. Jack P. Greene. Cambridge, MA: Blackwell, 1994.

Colonial Wars of North America, 1512–1763: An Encyclopedia. Ed. Alan Gallay. New York: Garland, 1995.

Encyclopedia of the North American Colonies. Ed. Jacob E. Cooke. 3 vols. New York: Scribner, 1993.

James Madison and the American Nation, 1751–1836: An Encyclopedia. Ed. Robert A. Rutland. New York: Scribner, 1994.

American Journeys: Eyewitness Accounts of Early American Exploration and Settlement. Wisconsin Historical Society. **www.americanjourneys.org/index.asp**. A collection of documents drawn from the library and archives of the Wisconsin Historical Society.

Classics of American Colonial History. Dinsmore Documentation. **dinsdoc.com/ colonial-3.htm**. A full-text collection of journal articles and book chapters. About twenty different aspects of life during the colonial era are covered.

Continental Congress and Constitutional Convention: 1774–1789. Library of Congress, American Memory. **memory.loc.gov/ammem/collections/continental/**. A searchable collection of documents.

Doing History: Martha Ballard's Diary Online. Film Study Center, Harvard University. **DoHistory.org**. The diary of an eighteenth-century midwife.

Early American Newspapers, Series I, 1690–1876. NewsBank. **www.readex.com/ readex/product.cfm?product=10**. A searchable archive of over 600 newspapers, most from the eighteenth century. By subscription only.

Early Encounters in North America. Alexander Street Press. A large collection of primary materials by and about the Native and European American peoples in the early years of their contact. By subscription only.

Eighteenth-Century Resources — History. Rutgers, Newark. **newark.rutgers.edu/ ~jlynch/18th/history.html**. Annotated links; particularly strong in American and British history.

Electronic Text Center. University of Virginia. **etext.lib.virginia.edu/**. Searchable e-books and collections, including the writings of George Washington, information relating to the Plymouth Colony and to the Salem witchcraft trials, as well as materials in a variety of languages.

George Washington Papers at the Library of Congress, 1741–1799. Library of Congress, American Memory. **memory.loc.gov/ammem/gwhtml/gwhome.html**. Allows you to search and browse digitized versions of George Washington's manuscript papers.

James Madison: 1723–1836. Library of Congress, American Memory. **memory .loc.gov/ammem/collections/madison_papers/index.html**. A searchable collection of papers.

Omohundro Institute for Early American History and Culture. **www.wm.edu/ oieahc/**. Access to the papers of John Marshall and links to other resources relating to early American history.

Pennsylvania Gazette. Accessible Archives. This database on CD-ROM includes the full range of the publication — 1728 to the early 1800s. A wide range of search options is available.

Plimoth-on-Web: Plimoth Plantation's Web Page [colonial America, 1620–1692]. **www.plimoth.org**. Multimedia educational materials about colonial America and the Plymouth Colony.

Plymouth Colony Archive Project. Patricia Scott Deetz, Christopher Fennell, and J. Eric Deetz, University of Virginia. **etext.lib.virginia.edu/users/deetz**. Documents and analytical essays; social history of Plymouth Colony from 1620 to 1691.

Religion and the Founding of the American Republic. Library of Congress. **lcweb.loc.gov/exhibits/religion/religion.html**. Documents and visual images; significance of religion for early American history; manuscripts, letters, books, prints, paintings, artifacts, and music.

Salem Witch Trials. University of Virginia. **etext.virginia.edu/salem/witchcraft/ home.html**. Trial transcripts, contemporary narratives, pamphlets, and sermons. Also a historical overview and links to relevant organizations and archives.

Thomas Jefferson Digital Archive. University of Virginia. **etext.virginia.edu/ jefferson**. About 2,000 texts by or about Jefferson. These include correspondence, books, speeches, and published papers. Excerpts from Jefferson's writings are searchable as is a large Jefferson bibliography.

Thomas Jefferson Papers. Library of Congress, American Memory. **memory .loc.gov/ammem/collections/jefferson_papers/**. About 27,000 documents including Jefferson's letters, notes, and official writings. Reading the handwriting can be slow going.

Native American

American Indian Religious Tradition: An Encyclopedia. Ed. Suzanne J. Crawford and Ennis F. Kelly. Santa Barbara, CA: ABC-CLIO, 2005.

Atlas of American Indian Affairs. Ed. Francis Paul Prucha. Lincoln: University of Nebraska Press, 1990.

A Bibliographical Guide to the History of Indian-White Relations in the United States. Ed. Francis Paul Prucha. Chicago: University of Chicago Press, 1977. Continued in *Indian-White Relations in the United States: A Bibliography of Works Published 1975–1980.* Ed. Francis Paul Prucha. Lincoln: University of Nebraska Press, 1982.

Cambridge History of the Native Peoples of the Americas. Vol. 1. Ed. Bruce Triggas and Wilcomb Washburn. New York: Cambridge University Press, 1997.

Encyclopedia of Native American Religions: An Introduction. Ed. Arlene B. Hirschfelder and Paulette Fairbanks Molin. New York: Facts on File, 2000.

Encyclopedia of Native American Tribes. Ed. Carl Waldman. New York: Checkmark Books, 1999.

Ethnographic Bibliography of North America. Ed. George P. Murdock and Timothy J. O'Leary. 5 vols. New Haven: HRAF Press, 1990. Updated on CD-ROM.

The Gale Encyclopedia of Native American Tribes. Ed. Sharon Malinowski. 4 vols. Detroit: Gale, 1998.

Handbook of American Indians North of Mexico. Ed. Frederick W. Hodge et al. 1910. Reprint, New York: Rowman and Littlefield, 1979.

Handbook of North American Indians. Ed. William C. Sturtevant. 17 vols. Washington, DC: Smithsonian Institution, 1978–2001.

Native American Periodicals and Newspapers, 1828–1982: Bibliography, Publishing Record, and Holdings. Comp. Maureen Hardy. Westport, CT: Greenwood Press, 1984.

Native Americans: An Encyclopedia of History, Culture and Peoples. 2 vols. Santa Barbara, CA: ABC-CLIO, 1998.

Early Encounters in North America. Alexander Street Press. Primary sources describing the relationship between Native and European Americans from 1534 to 1850. By subscription only.

NativeWeb. **www.nativeweb.org**. This site, which is updated and expanded regularly, features information about Native American studies.

Oneida Indian Nation: Culture and History. Oneida Indian Nation. **oneida-nation .net/historical.html**. Includes Oneida documents and studies focusing on the Revolutionary War period and recent efforts to pursue land claims, six essays by Oneida Nation historians, and excerpts from an oral history project in which thirteen tribal elders discuss various topics.

Slavery and the Civil War

American Civil War Reference Library. Gale Reference Library. Detroit: U.X.L, 2003. A searchable e-book.

Dictionary of Afro-American Slavery. Ed. Randall M. Miller and John David Smith. Westport, CT: Greenwood Press, 1997.

Encyclopedia of the Confederacy. Ed. Richard N. Current. 4 vols. New York: Scribner, 1998.

Reconstruction Era Reference Library. 3 vols. Detroit: U.X.L, 2005.

Abolition and Reconstruction. Rutgers University. **www.libraries.rutgers.edu/rul/ rr_gateway/research_guides/history/civwar.shtml**. Many full-text documents from the period of the 1830s to the 1890s. Site includes many links to serious Civil War sites.

The Abolition Movement. Library of Congress. **www.loc.gov/exhibits/african/ afam005.html**. A multimedia exhibit guiding users through African American history, particularly the abolition movement.

Abraham Lincoln: 1850–1865. Library of Congress, American Memory. **memory .loc.gov/ammem/alhtml/malhome.html**. A searchable collection of papers.

American Civil War Letters and Diaries. Alexander Street Press. A 100,000-page collection, indexed and searchable. By subscription only.

American Civil War Resources. **spec.lib.vt.edu/civwar**. Links to manuscript collections, dissertation information, print collections, and a guide to manuscript resources.

Born in Slavery: Slave Narratives from the Federal Writer's Project, 1936–1938. Library of Congress, American Memory. **lcweb2.loc.gov/ammem/snhtml/ snhome.html**. Over 2,000 firsthand accounts of slavery; introductory essay discusses the significance of slave narratives.

Civil War Resources on the Internet: Abolitionism to Reconstruction, 1830's–1890's. Rutgers University. **www.libraries.rutgers.edu/rul/rr_gateway/research_guides/ history/civwar.shtml/**. Selected and partially annotated links to documents, bibliographies, studies, images, and other sites relating to the Civil War.

The Dred Scott Case. Washington University Libraries. **www.library.wustl.edu/ vlib/dredscott**. This site features the papers of the Dred Scott case, as well as a chronology and information about the papers.

Freedmen's Bureau Online. **www.freedmensbureau.com**. Freedmen's Bureau records: supervision of relief and education activities for refugees and freedmen; issuing rations, clothing, medicine; issues concerning confiscated land; labor contracts; a variety of other records and reports.

Geography of Slavery in America. Virginia Center for Digital History and University of Virginia. **www.vcdh.virginia.edu/gos**. Several thousand runaway slave newspaper advertisements between 1736 and 1777.

Museum of African Slavery. Johns Hopkins University. **jhunix.hcf.jhu.edu/ ~plarson/smuseum/welcome.htm**. A scholarly investigation into and resources about the atrocities of African slavery.

North American Slave Narratives, Beginnings to 1920. William Andrews, University of North Carolina, Chapel Hill. **docsouth.unc.edu/neh/neh.html**. Over 200 full-text documents; all known published slave narratives; many published biographies of slaves.

Samuel J. May Anti Slavery Collection. Cornell University Library. **www.library .cornell.edu/mayantislavery**. A rich collection of antislavery and Civil War materials. Over 10,000 pamphlets, leaflets, broadsides, local antislavery society newsletters, sermons, and essays. Slave trade and emancipation; 300,000 full-text pages. Searchable. Many links to other collections.

Slaves and the Courts, 1740–1860. Library of Congress, American Memory. **memory.loc.gov/ammem/sthtml/sthome.html/**. Pamphlets, books, and primary documents illustrate the treatment of slaves and slavery by the U.S. courts prior to emancipation.

The Trans-Atlantic Slave Trade. Ed. David Eltis, Cambridge University Press. A database on CD-ROM. Records of slave ship voyages between 1595 and 1866. Interactive multimedia capabilities.

Uncle Tom's Cabin and American Culture. University of Virginia. **www.iath .virginia.edu/utc**. An excellent multimedia archive created around Harriet Beecher Stowe's famous novel. Draws on a wide range of documents to trace the origins of the book, its reception, and the evolution of the debate about slavery and race in America.

Valley of the Shadow: Two Communities in the American Civil War. Edward Ayers et al., University of Virginia. **www.iath.virginia.edu/vshadow2**. Documents from a northern county and a southern county throughout the Civil War, offering primary sources and secondary narrative and analysis.

African American

Africana: The Encyclopedia of the African and the African American Experience. 2nd ed. Ed. Kwame Anthony Appiah and Henry Lewis Gates Jr. 5 vols. New York: Oxford University Press, 2005.

Black/White Relations in American History: An Annotated Bibliography. Ed. Leslie V. Tischauser. Lanham, MD: Scarecrow Press, 1998.

Black Women in America: An Historical Encyclopedia. Bloomington: Indiana University Press, 1994.

Encyclopedia of African-American Culture and History. Ed. Jack Salzman, David L. Smith, and Cornel West. 5 vols. New York: Simon and Schuster/Macmillan, 1996. Supplement, 2000.

Encyclopedia of African-American Religions. Ed. Larry G. Murphy et al. New York: Garland, 1993.

Encyclopedia of the Harlem Renaissance. Ed. Cary D. Wintz and Paul Finkelman. 2 vols. New York: Routledge, 2004. E-book, Taylor & Francis, 2004.

The African-American Mosaic. Library of Congress. **www.loc.gov/exhibits/african/afam001.html**. This online multimedia exhibit guides the reader through annotated images of many aspects of African American history.

African American Newspapers: Nineteenth Century. Accessible Archives. Full text of articles from major nineteenth-century African American newspapers. Searchable online. By subscription only.

African-American Perspective, 1818–1907. Library of Congress, American Memory. **memory.loc.gov/ammem/aap/aaphome.html**. The database of the Daniel A. P. Murray Pamphlet Collection, which focuses on the late nineteenth and early twentieth centuries in America.

African-American Religion: A Documentary History Project. Amherst College. **www.amherst.edu/~aardoc/menu.html**. Materials span 1441 to the present. Includes limited information and sample documents. The project eventually will be published in print form.

African-American Women. Duke University, Special Collections Library. **scriptorium.lib.duke.edu/collections/african-american-women.html**. Published and unpublished writings, most from the nineteenth century.

African American Women Writers of the 19th Century. Digital Schomburg. **digital.nypl.org/schomburg/writers_aa19**. Full text of poetry, essays, novels, and other writings by African American women during the nineteenth century.

Africans in America. PBS Online. **www.pbs.org/wgbh/aia**. Complements a four-part television series covering the seventeenth to the nineteenth centuries. Contains several hundred documents, images, and maps, as well as comments by a large number of historians.

Afro-Louisiana History and Genealogy, 1717–1820. **www.ibiblio.org/laslave/**. A searchable database of the genealogy and life of slaves in the Gulf of Mexico region.

Black Thought and Culture. Alexander Street Press. A large database of publications and documents written by leaders of the black community. Covers the eighteenth to the twentieth centuries. By subscription only.

In Motion: The African-American Migration Experience. New York Public Library. **www.inmotionaame.org/home.cfm**. An excellent collection of texts, maps, and images examining the many migrations of Africans and African Americans from the era of the slave trade to the late twentieth century.

Schomburg Center for Research in Black Culture. New York Public Library. **www.nypl.org/research/sc/sc.html**. Oral histories and online exhibits.

W. E. B. Du Bois Institute for Afro-American Research. Harvard University. **dubois .fas.harvard.edu/index.html**. Links to recent projects and research, including databases, bibliographies, and other materials.

Women's

The Female Experience in Eighteenth- and Nineteenth-Century America: A Guide to the History of American Women. Ed. Jill K. Conway. New York: Garland, 1982.

The Female Experience in Twentieth-Century America: A Guide to the History of American Women. Ed. Jill K. Conway. New York: Garland, 1991.

Handbook of American Women's History. 2nd ed. Ed. Angela M. Howard and Frances M. Kavenik. Thousand Oaks, CA: Sage, 2000.

Women's Studies Encyclopedia: History, Philosophy, and Religion. Vol. 3. Ed. Helen Tierney. Westport, CT: Greenwood Press, 1999.

American Women's History: A Research Guide. **www.mtsu.edu/~kmiddlet/ history/women.html**. A large collection of links to sites related to the study of women.

Civil War Women. Duke University, Special Collections Library. **scriptorium.lib .duke.edu/collections/civil-war-women.html**. Diaries, letters, and other writing by women during the Civil War.

Documents from the Women's Liberation Movement. Duke University, Digital Scriptorium. **scriptorium.lib.duke.edu/wlm**. A searchable database of primary texts from the 1960s and 1970s.

Marriage, Women, and the Law. RLG. **www.rlg.org/en/page.php?Page_ID=493**. A primary-source archive of nineteenth-century family law, focusing on the legal treatment of women in America from 1815 to 1914. Now by subscription only.

North American Women's Letters and Diaries. Alexander Street Press. A large collection of primary sources by women from a variety of backgrounds and circumstances. Excellent searching facilities. By subscription only.

Trails of Hope: Overland Diaries, 1846–1869. Brigham Young University. **overlandtrails.lib.byu.edu/**. Background essays and about sixty full-text diaries of the westward migration.

Woman Suffrage: 1848–1921. Library of Congress, American Memory. **memory .loc.gov/ammem/naw/nawshome.html**. A searchable collection of books and pamphlets.

Women and Social Movements in the United States, 1775–2000. SUNY, Binghamton. **womhist.binghamton.edu/**. Bibliographies, links, and hundreds of primary-source documents. Includes interpretive essays and images. Parts of the collection are by subscription only through Alexander Street Press.

Women Working, 1800–1930. Harvard University Library. **ocp.hul.harvard.edu/ ww/**. A large archive of manuscripts, pamphlets, and photographs on the role of women in the U.S. economy. Several of the subcollections examine social, cultural, "racial," and gender issues.

Immigrant and Ethnic

American Immigrant Cultures. Ed. David Levinson and Melvin Ember. 2 vols. New York: Macmillan, 1997.

Asian American Studies: An Annotated Bibliography and Research Guide. Ed. Hyung-Chan Kim. Westport, CT: Greenwood Press, 1989.

Asians in America: A Selected, Annotated Bibliography. Ed. Isao Fujimoto. Davis: University of California Press, 1983.

Bibliography of Mexican-American History. Comp. Matt S. Meier. Westport, CT: Greenwood Press, 1984.

Dictionary of Asian American History. Ed. Hyung-Chan Kim. Westport, CT: Greenwood Press, 1986.

Dictionary of Mexican American History. Ed. Matt S. Meier and Feliciano Rivera. Westport, CT: Greenwood Press, 1981.

Encyclopedia of American Immigration. Ed. James Ciment. 4 vols. New York: M. E. Sharpe, 2001.

European Immigration and Ethnicity in the United States and Canada: A Historical Bibliography. Ed. David L. Brye. Santa Barbara, CA: ABC-CLIO, 1983.

Harvard Encyclopedia of American Ethnic Groups. Ed. Stephen Thernstrom et al. Cambridge, MA: Harvard University Press, 1980.

The Italian-American Experience: An Encyclopedia. Ed. Salvatore J. LaGumina et al. New York: Garland, 1999.

American Family Immigration History Center. **ellisisland.org/**. Much useful advice about conducting family history. Search of passenger lists beginning in 1892. Full access requires "membership."

California History Online. California Historical Society. **www.californiahistory .net/**. Texts and images dealing with the Spanish and Mexican eras of California history.

The Chinese in California: 1850–1925. Library of Congress, American Memory. **memory.loc.gov/ammem/award99/cubhtml/cichome.html**. A searchable collection of documents, images, and other resources in a multimedia format.

Columbia River Basin Ethnic History Archive. Washington State University. **www .vancouver.wsu.edu/crbeha/browse.htm**. A searchable multimedia database of materials relating to each of the many ethnic groups that live in the portions of Oregon, Washington, and British Columbia (in Canada) surrounding the Columbia River.

Immigration History Research Center. **www.ihrc.umn.edu/research/index.htm**. A searchable archive of personal papers and images of immigrants, with a brief abstract for each collection. No full text online.

Immigration: The Changing Face of America. Library of Congress, American Memory. **memory.loc.gov/ammem/ndlpedu/features/immig/oldflash.html**. A multimedia exhibit of immigration to America from many different parts of the world.

Japanese American Relocation Digital Archive. JARDA. **jarda.cdlib.org**. A large collection of primary sources and images concerning the World War II internment of Japanese Americans.

Japanese American Relocation Digital Archive. University of Southern California. **digarc.usc.edu:8089/cispubsearch/collectionlist.jsp**. Over 200 newspaper photos and captions from the period 1941–1946.

Korean American Digital Archives. University of Southern California. **digarc.usc .edu:8089/cispubsearch/collectionlist.jsp**. Primary materials related to Koreans living in the United States from 1903 to 1965. Difficult to navigate; collections not well organized.

North American Immigrant Letters and Diaries. Alexander Street Press. A large collection of primary sources by immigrants covering the period from 1840 to the present.

Puerto Rico and the Dawn of the Modern Age. Library of Congress, American Memory. **memory.loc.gov/ammem/prhtml/prhome.html**.

Puerto Rico Books and Pamphlets: 1831–1929. Library of Congress, American Memory. **memory.loc.gov/ammem/collections/puertorico/**. A searchable collection of books and pamphlets.

Social and Cultural

American Family History: A Historical Bibliography. Santa Barbara, CA: ABC-CLIO, 1984.

Biographical Dictionary of American Sports. Ed. David L. Porter. Westport, CT: Greenwood Press, 1995.

The Cambridge History of American Theater. Ed. Don B. Wilmeth. 3 vols. Cambridge: Cambridge University Press, 1998–2000.

A Dictionary of American Social Change. By Louis Filler. Malabar, FL: Kreiger, 1982.

Dickinson's American Historical Fiction. 5th ed. Ed. Virginia B. Gerhardstein. Metuchen, NJ: Scarecrow Press, 1986.

Encyclopedia of American Social History. Ed. Mary K. Cayton, Elliott J. Gorn, and Peter W. Williams. 3 vols. New York: Scribner, 1993.

Encyclopedia of Early Cinema. Ed. Richard Abel. New York: Routledge, 2005.

Encyclopedia of Lesbian and Gay Histories and Cultures. New York: Garland, 1999.

Historical Dictionary of American Education. Ed. Richard J. Altenbaugh. Westport, CT: Greenwood Press, 1999.

History of the Mass Media in the United States: An Encyclopedia. Ed. Margaret A. Blanchard. Chicago: Fitzroy Dearborn, 1998.

The New Grove Dictionary of Jazz. Ed. Barry Kornfeld. New York: Oxford University Press, 2001.

Social Reform and Reaction in America: An Annotated Bibliography. Santa Barbara, CA: ABC-CLIO, 1984.

A Subject Bibliography of the History of American Higher Education. Comp. Mark Beach. Westport, CT: Greenwood Press, 1984.

United States Cultural History: A Guide to Information Sources. By Philip I. Mitterling. Detroit: Gale, 1980.

Ad*Access. Duke University, Special Collections Library. **scriptorium.lib.duke .edu/adaccess**. Newspaper advertisements between 1911 and 1955; 7,000 examples in fields: beauty, hygiene, radio, television, transportation, and World War II.

American Cultural History: 1920–1929. Kingwood College Library. **kclibrary .nhmccd.edu/decades.html**. A hypertext narrative explaining the primary cultural and political events of the 1920s.

American Film Institute Catalog. Chadwyk-Healey. A catalog of (almost) every American film from 1893 to 1970; 45,000 films, plot summaries, director and actor entries, etc. By subscription only.

Americans' First Look into the Camera: Daguerreotype Portraits and Views, 1839–1864. Library of Congress, American Memory. **memory.loc.gov/ammem/ daghtml/daghome.html**. Over 700 early photographs, primarily daguerreotypes. A short introduction to the daguerreotype medium.

American Variety Stage: Vaudeville and Popular Entertainment, 1870–1920. Library of Congress, American Memory. **memory.loc.gov/ammem/vshtml/vshome .html**. Scripts, theater programs, playbills, motion pictures, ten sound recordings, 143 photos.

Clash of Cultures in the 1910s and 1920s. Ohio State University. **history.osu.edu/ projects/clash/**. Explains the cultural turmoil of the early twentieth century by focusing on the Scopes trial, Prohibition, immigration restriction, the Ku Klux Klan, and the "New Woman."

Dime Novels and Penny Dreadfuls. Stanford University. **www-sul.stanford.edu/ depts/dp/pennies**. Over 2,000 images of covers, nine full-text selections, weekly story papers, and essays. Searchable by subject.

Emergence of Advertising in America, 1850–1920. Duke University, Digital Scriptorium. **scriptorium.lib.duke.edu/eaa**. Over 9,000 advertising items and publications from the period 1850–1920. Advertising ephemera, trade cards, calendars, almanacs, postcards, broadsides, and advertising cookbooks. Searchable by keyword or ad content.

Federal Theatre Project: 1935–1939. Library of Congress, American Memory. **memory.loc.gov/ammem/fedtp/fthome.html**. A searchable collection of documents, images, and other resources in a multimedia format.

The Fifties Web. **www.fiftiesweb.com/fifties.htm**. This site focuses on American popular culture in the 1950s, particularly music, film, and television, with a bibliography of other sources.

Film Literature Index Online. **webapp1.dlib.indiana.edu/fli/index.jsp**. A collection of links.

Helios: The Smithsonian American Art Museum Photography Collection. Smithsonian American Art Museum. **AmericanArt.si.edu/helios**. Three hundred photos;

175 daguerreotypes. Scholars discuss images, landscape photos, and the history of daguerreotypes, among other topics.

Historical American Sheet Music. Duke University, Special Collections Library. **scriptorium.lib.duke.edu/sheetmusic**. Digital images of 3,000 examples of sheet music from the period 1850–1920. Background essays.

Medicine and Madison Avenue. National Humanities Center; Duke University, Digital Scriptorium. **odyssey.lib.duke.edu/mma**. Traces the evolution and complexity of twentieth-century health-related marketing. Over 600 health-related ads from 1910 to 1960. Also, transcripts of 1,930 radio commercials, plus medical journal articles.

New Deal Stage: Selections from the Federal Theater Project, 1935–1939. Library of Congress, American Memory. **memory.loc.gov/ammem/fedtp/fthome .html**. Over 13,000 images; 71 play scripts; 168 documents from Federal Theater Project records.

Performing Arts in America, 1875–1923. New York Public Library for the Performing Arts. **digital.nypl.org/lpa/nypl/sitemap/sitemap.cfm**. Over 16,000 items relating to the performing arts in the late nineteenth and early twentieth centuries: documents, photographs, clippings, films, theater programs, and sheet music.

Radio Program Archive. University of Memphis. **umdrive.memphis.edu/mbensman/ public/**. Transcripts of several thousand radio programs, most from the 1930s to the 1950s.

Red Hot Jazz Archive: A History of Jazz before 1930. Scott Alexander. **www .redhotjazz.com**. Biographical information, photos, and audio and video files for more than 200 jazz bands and musicians active from 1895 to 1929; biographical essays, discographies, and short jazz films.

September 11 Digital Archive. Center for History and New Media, George Mason University; American Social History Project, City University of New York. **www.911digitalarchive.org/**. Annotated resources connected with 9/11: firsthand accounts, e-mails, digital images, posters, press releases, brochures, and newsletters.

Social Welfare and Visual Politics: The Story of the Survey Graphic. **newdeal.feri.org/ sg/**. A series of articles from this journal. Includes a collection of online resources in U.S. social history.

Southern Mosaic: The John and Ruby Lomax 1939 Southern States Records Trip. Library of Congress, American Memory. **memory.loc.gov/ammem/lohtml/ lohome.html**. In 1939, John Lomax, curator of the Library of Congress Archive of American Folk Songs, and his wife Ruby took a 6,500-mile journey and recorded 700 folk tunes, available in these audio files.

Southern Oral History Project. University of North Carolina, Chapel Hill. **sohp.org/**. Index to a large collection of interviews. A small selection online.

Temperance and Prohibition. K. Austin Kerr, Ohio State University. **prohibition .osu.edu/**. A collection of images, speeches, newspaper and journal articles, advertisements, reports, and statistics.

TV News Archive. **tvnews.vanderbilt.edu/**. Major network news programs since 1968. By subscription only.

Vaudeville and Popular Entertainment [1870–1920]. Library of Congress, American Memory. **lcweb2.loc.gov/ammem/vshtml/vshome.html**. Library of Congress digital multimedia holdings about vaudeville in America.

Political

The American Presidency: A Historical Bibliography. Santa Barbara, CA: ABC-CLIO, 1984.

Dwight D. Eisenhower: A Bibliography of His Times and Presidency. Comp. R. Alton Lee. Wilmington, DE: Scholarly Resources, 1991.

Encyclopedia of American Political History: Studies of the Principal Movements and Ideas. Ed. Jack P. Greene. 3 vols. New York: Scribner, 1984.

Encyclopedia of the American Left. Ed. Mari J. Buhle. Oxford: Oxford University Press, 1998.

Encyclopedia of the American Presidency. New York: Simon and Schuster, 1994.

Guide to the Presidency. 3rd ed. Ed. Michael Nelson. Washington, DC: Congressional Quarterly, 2002.

Guide to United States Elections. 3rd ed. Ed. John L. Moore. Washington, DC: Congressional Quarterly, 1994.

Herbert Hoover: A Bibliography of His Times and Presidency. Comp. Richard D. Burns. Wilmington, DE: Scholarly Resources, 1991.

Historical Dictionary of the Gilded Age. Ed. Leonard Schlup. Armonk, NY: M. Sharpe, 2003.

Historical Dictionary of the Progressive Era, 1890–1920. Ed. John D. Buenker. Westport, CT: Greenwood Press, 1988.

Political Parties and Elections in the United States: An Encyclopedia. Ed. L. Sandy Maisel. 2 vols. New York: Garland, 1991.

Protest, Power and Change: An Encyclopedia of Non-Violent Action. New York: Garland, 1997.

Abraham Lincoln Historical Digitization Project. Drew VandeCreek, Northern Illinois University. **lincoln.lib.niu.edu**. Illinois history focusing on Lincoln's years there (1831–1860).

Abraham Lincoln Papers. Library of Congress, American Memory; Lincoln Studies Center, Knox College. **memory.loc.gov/ammem/alhtml/malhome .html**. Twenty thousand documents relating to Lincoln's life and career.

America in the 1930's. American Studies Program, University of Virginia. **xroads.virginia.edu/~1930s/DISPLAY/displayframe.html**. Offers audio, visual, and textual sources to survey the culture and politics of the time.

Civil Rights Documentation Project: A Bibliography of Oral History Interviews. University of Southern Mississippi. **www.usm.edu/crdp/**. This site features an oral history bibliography, oral history transcripts, and a civil rights timetable. Organized by topic, by holding institution, and by name of person interviewed.

Franklin D. Roosevelt Presidential Library and Digital Archives. Franklin D. Roosevelt Library and Museum, Marist College. **www.fdrlibrary.marist.edu**. Ten thousand documents from FDR's presidency: correspondence, reports, memoranda, etc.

Free Speech Movement. University of California, Berkeley. **www.fsm-a.org/**. An archive of documents concerning student activism at the university in the early 1960s.

The Gilded Age. Alexander Street Press. A large archive of primary and secondary works on this period. By subscription only.

The Gilded Page. **srnels.people.wm.edu/gildage/giltext.html**. Documents and links to materials relating to the American Gilded Age (1870–1898).

Living Room Candidate: A History of Presidential Campaign Commercials, 1952–2004. American Museum of the Moving Image. **www.ammi.org/livingroomcandidate**. Over 188 political TV commercials.

Martin Luther King Jr. Papers Project. Stanford University. **www.stanford.edu/group/King**. This site features materials relating to the life and works of Dr. King and includes his writings, speeches, and sermons, audio files, chronologies, and analysis.

The New Deal Network. Franklin and Eleanor Roosevelt Institute/Columbia University. **newdeal.feri.org**. Over 900 documents and 5,000 images, as well as bibliographies and information about the era.

Populism. Missouri State University. **history.missouristate.edu/wrmiller/Populism/Texts/populism.htm**. A modest but useful site containing a text by the site's author along with a group of related documents and links.

Posters, WPA: 1936–1943. Library of Congress American Memory. **memory.loc.gov/ammem/wpaposters/wpahome.html**. A searchable collection of posters.

Presidential Elections, 1860–1912. Harpweek LLC. **elections.harpweek.com/**. Annotated political cartoons, campaign overviews, and biographical sketches.

The President John F. Kennedy Assassination Records Collection. National Archives. **www.archives.gov/research_room/jfk/index.html**. Documentation of the assassination and its investigation.

Prosperity and Thrift: The Coolidge Era and the Consumer Economy, 1921–1929. Library of Congress, American Memory. **memory.loc.gov/ammem/coolhtml/coolhome.html/**. A collection of documents illustrating the economic and political forces at work in the 1920s.

Red Scare, 1918–1921. Baruch College, CUNY. **newman.baruch.cuny.edu/digital/redscare/default.htm**. A searchable image database.

Rutgers Oral History Archive of World War Two. **history.rutgers.edu/oralhistory/orlinf.htm**. Interviews with survivors of World War II and links to other resources.

Senate Executive Journals, 1789–1866. Readex —Newsbank. **www.readex.com/readex/product.cfm?product=8**. Records of the nonlegislative sessions of the U.S. Senate. By subscription only.

Truman Presidential Museum and Library. Harry S. Truman Library. **www.trumanlibrary.org/library.htm**. An archive of hundreds of government documents from Truman's presidency.

Woman Suffrage and the 19th Amendment. National Archives. **www.archives.gov/digital_classroom/lessons/woman_suffrage/woman_suffrage.html**.This site offers primary documents relating to the woman suffrage movement.

Foreign Relations and International

America and the Indo-China Wars, 1945–1990: A Bibliographic Guide. Ed. Lester Brune. Claremont, CA: Regina Books, 1991.

The Cambridge History of American Foreign Relations. Ed. Bradford Perkins et al. 4 vols. New York: Cambridge University Press, 1995. Also available on CD-ROM.

The Encyclopedia of United States Foreign Relations. Ed. Bruce Jentleson and Thomas Patterson. Oxford: Oxford University Press, 1997.

Encyclopedia of the Vietnam War: A Political, Social, and Military History. Ed. Spencer Tucker. New York: Oxford University Press, 2001.

Guide to American Foreign Relations since 1700. 2nd ed. Ed. Robert Beisner. Santa Barbara, CA: ABC-CLIO, 2001.

The United States in the First World War: An Encyclopedia. New York: Garland 1999.

Writing about Vietnam: A Bibliography of the Literature of the Vietnam Conflict. Ed. Sandra M. Wittman. Boston: G. K. Hall, 1989.

The Age of Imperialism. **www.smplanet.com/imperialism/toc.html/**. A brief but detailed narrative and links about American imperialism in the late nineteenth and early twentieth centuries.

Anti-Imperialism in the United States, 1898–1935. Jim Zwick. **www.boondocksnet.com/ ai/index.html**. Important texts on American imperialism and its opponents; 800 essays, speeches, pamphlets, political platforms, editorial cartoons, and petitions. Unfortunately many ads also.

CIA Electronic Reading Room. Central Intelligence Agency. **www.foia.cia.gov/.** The CIA has digitized thousands of formerly secret documents. These documents were declassified to comply with requests made under the Freedom of Information Act. Keyword searchable.

Cold War International History Project. Woodrow Wilson International Center for Scholars. **wilsoncenter.org/index.cfm?fuseaction=topics.home&topic_id=1409**. Lists publications and information relating to the study of international relations during the Cold War.

Documents Relating to American Foreign Policy [World War I]. Mount Holyoke College. **www.mtholyoke.edu/acad/intrel/ww1.htm**. A large collection of primary documents. Some onsite, some off. Some dead links. Onsite documents not annotated.

Documents Relating to American Foreign Policy, pre-1898. Mount Holyoke College. **www.mtholyoke.edu/acad/intrel/pre1898.htm/**. A large collection of primary documents. Some onsite, some off. Some dead links. Onsite documents not annotated.

Documents Relating to American Foreign Policy, 1898–1914. Mount Holyoke College. **www.mtholyoke.edu/acad/intrel/to1914.htm/**. A large collection of primary documents, some onsite, some off. Some dead links. Onsite documents not annotated.

Documents Relating to American Foreign Policy in Vietnam. Mount Holyoke College. **www.mtholyoke.edu/acad/intrel/vietnam.htm**. A large collection of primary documents. Some onsite, some off. Some dead links. Onsite documents not annotated.

Iraqgate: Saddam Hussein, U.S. Policy and the Prelude to the Persian Gulf War, 1980–1994. Digital National Security Archive. Declassified U.S. government documents concerning U.S. relations with Iraq. By subscription only.

Korean War. Project Whistlestop. **www.trumanlibrary.org/whistlestop/study _collections/korea/large/**. A history of the war, official documents, links, and teaching materials.

The Mexican-American War and the Media. **www.history.vt.edu/MexAmWar/ INDEX.HTM**. A digital archive of newspaper articles related to the war.

National Security Archive. George Washington University. **www.gwu.edu/ ~nsarchiv/**. Declassified U.S. government documents relating to many countries and to many aspects of U.S. foreign policy since 1945. Contains several different collections of documents, some open and others by subscription through Chadwyk-Healey at nsarchive.chadwyck.com.

Terrorism and U.S. Policy, 1968–2002. Digital National Security Archive. A collection of declassified U.S. government documents, with introductory essay and bibliography. Searchable. By subscription only.

U.S. Nuclear Nonproliferation Policy, 1945–1991. Digital National Security Archive. Declassified U.S. government documents along with annotations and a bibliography. By subscription only.

Vietnam War Bibliography. Clemson University. **www.clemson.edu/caah/history/ FacultyPages/EdMoise/bibliography.html**. A list of books and articles relevant to the study of the Vietnam War.

Vietnam War Internet Project. **www.vwip.org/**. Documents about, images of, newsgroups on, and links to the events and debates surrounding the Vietnam War.

The Wars for Vietnam: 1945 to 1975. Vassar College. **vassun.vassar.edu/~vietnam/**. Overview of the Vietnam War, documents for study, and links.

World War II Links on the Internet. University of San Diego. **history.acusd.edu/ gen/ww2_links.html**. Annotated links relating to World War II.

WWI: The World War I Document Archive. Brigham Young University. **www.lib .byu.edu/~rdh/wwi/**. Government documents, maps, photographs, and biographies.

Science, Technology, Environment, and Medicine

Encyclopedia of Environmental Issues. Ed. Craig Allin. Pasadena, CA: Salem Press, 2000.

The History of Science and Technology in the United States: A Critical and Selective Bibliography. Ed. Marc Rothenberg. New York: Garland, 1993.

The History of Science in the United States: An Encyclopedia. Ed. Marc Rothenberg. New York: Garland, 2001.

ECHO: Exploring and Collecting History Online — Science and Technology. Center for History and New Media, George Mason University. **echo.gmu.edu/**. History of science and technology; 800 firsthand accounts from Memory Bank. A directory of history of science Web sites; has 2,700 entries.

Environmental History. Tennessee Technological University. **www2.tntech.edu/ history/envir.html**. Links relating to environmental history.

Evolution of the Conservation Movement: 1850–1920. Library of Congress, American Memory. **memory.loc.gov/ammem/amrvhtml/conshome.html**. A searchable collection of documents, images, and other resources in a multimedia format.

National Library of Medicine: History of Medicine Division. **www.nlm.nih.gov/hmd/index.html**. Images, texts, and exhibits relating to all aspects of the history of medicine.

Seeing Is Believing: 700 Years of Scientific and Medical Illustration. New York Public Library. **seeing.nypl.org**. Traces the impact of illustrative technique on progress in medicine.

Whole Cloth: Discovering Science and Technology through American History. Smithsonian Institution. **invention.smithsonian.org/centerpieces/whole_cloth/**. Information relating to the history of American textiles in a multimedia format.

Labor, Business, Economic, and Urban

American Economic History: An Annotated Bibliography. Ed. John Braeman. Englewood Cliffs, NJ: Salem Press, 1994.

American Working Class History: A Representative Bibliography. By Maurice F. Neufeld, Daniel J. Leab, and Dorothy Swanson. New York: Bowker, 1983.

A Financial History of the United States [to 1900]. Ed. Jerry W. Markham. New York: M. E. Sharpe, 2002.

Gale Encyclopedia of United States Economic History. 2nd ed. Ed. Thomas Carson. Detroit: Gale, 2005. Also available in e-Book format as part of *Gale Virtual Reference Library.*

Labor in America: A Historical Bibliography. Santa Barbara, CA: ABC-CLIO, 1985.

Labor Unions. Ed. Gary Fink. Westport, CT: Greenwood Press, 1977. Contains a brief history and bibliography for each major union.

Urban History. Ed. John D. Buenker. Detroit: Gale, 1981.

Advertising: 1850–1920. Library of Congress, American Memory. **memory.loc .gov/ammem/collections/advertising/**. A searchable collection of documents, images, and other resources in a multimedia format.

Haymarket Affair: 1886–1887. Library of Congress, American Memory. **memory .loc.gov/ammem/award98/ichihtml/hayhome.html**. A searchable collection of documents, images, and other resources in a multimedia format.

Like a Family: The Making of a Southern Cotton Mill World. University of North Carolina, Chapel Hill. **www.ibiblio.org/sohp/laf**. A selection of oral histories. Life in southern textile mill towns from 1880s to 1930s. Mill work, company towns, labor protests, and audio clips.

The Triangle Factory Fire. Cornell University—ILR. **www.ilr.cornell.edu/trianglefire/**. A collection of essays connect documents and images relating to immigrant, sweatshop labor in the early twentieth century.

Who Built America? From the Centennial Celebration of 1876 to the Great War of 1914—The Voyager Company. (Disk I). *Who Built America? From the Great War of 1914 to the Dawn of the Atomic Age in 1946.* (Disk II). A large collection of primary documents (and a variety of media) relating to many aspects of American history in the period covered. On CD-ROM.

Religious

Atlas of American Religion: The Denominational Era, 1776–1990. Ed. William Newman. Walnut Creek, CA: Alta Mira Press, 2000.

Encyclopedia of the American Religious Experience. Ed. Charles H. Lippy. New York: Scribner, 1988.

Encyclopedia of American Religious History. Ed. Edward L. Queen, Stephen R. Prothero, and Gardiner H. Shattuck. 2 vols. New York: Facts on File, 2001.

Encyclopedia of Fundamentalism. Ed. Brenda E. Brashau. New York: Routledge, 2001.

New Historical Atlas of Religion in America. Ed. Edwin Scott Gaustad. New York: Oxford University Press, 2001.

Adhoc [history of Christianity]. Yale University, Yale Divinity School. **research .yale.edu:8084/divdl/adhoc/subjects.jsp**. A large collection of images and a few texts drawn from the history of Christianity.

ATLA-CDRI. American Theological Library Association and Cooperative Digital Resource Initiative. **www.atla.com/digitalresources/browsecoll.asp**. An extensive online archive of texts and images concerning many religious topics, including the history of Christian missionary work.

ATLA Religious Database. EBSCO Publishing. A large index of journal articles, book reviews, and essays. Includes an online collection of religion and theology journals. By subscription only.

Divining America. National Humanities Center. **www.nhc.rtp.nc.us:8080/ tserve/siteguide.htm**. A site for teachers but also useful for student researchers. Essays and a series of links on religion and U.S. culture.

Military

American Naval History: A Guide. Ed. Paolo E. Coletta. Lanham, MD: Scarecrow Press, 1998.

Guide to the Sources of United States Military History. By Robin Higham. Hamden, CT: Archon Books, 1975. Supplements, 1981, 1986, 1993, 1998.

Reference Guide to United States Military History, 1607–1815. Ed. Charles R. Shrader. New York: Replica Books, 1999.

Experiencing War: Stories from the Veterans History Project Library. Library of Congress, American Folklife Center. **www.loc.gov/folklife/vets/stories/ ex-war-home.html**. Oral histories from American veterans of twentieth-century wars; memoirs, letters, diaries, photo albums, scrapbooks, poetry, artwork, and official documents.

Korean War. Project Whistlestop. **www.trumanlibrary.org/whistlestop/study _collections/korea/large/**. A history of the war, official documents, links, and teaching materials.

Vietnam Center. Vietnam Center, Texas Tech University. **archive.vietnam.ttu .edu/vietnamcenter/**. Over 200 recorded oral histories. More than 63,000 documents.

ELECTRONIC DISCUSSION LISTS IN HISTORY

Discussion Lists by Category

If you want to talk online about history to other students or faculty—or to anybody else who is interested—you should join a discussion list—that is, a **listserv**. To join one of the many lists at H-Net, visit www.h-net.org/lists/, select a specific discussion network of interest, and then click on "Subscribe!" After entering your name, your e-mail address, and the name of your school, you will receive an e-mail confirmation with further information. The home site for history discussion lists is www.h-net.org/. Here are the names and topics of some of the larger discussion groups:

H-Africa [African history and culture]
H-Afro-Am [African American studies]
H-AHC [Association for History and Computing]
H-Albion [British and Irish history]
H-AmIndian [American Indian history and culture]
H-AmRel [American religious history]
H-Amstdy [American studies]
H-Asia [Asian studies and history]
H-Business [History of business and commerce]
H-Canada [Canadian history and studies]
H-Caribbean [Caribbean studies]
H-Childhood [History of childhood and youth]
H-CivWar [U.S. Civil War history]
H-Demog [Demographic history]
H-Diplo [Diplomatic history, international affairs]
H-Education [History of education]
H-Environment [Environmental history]
H-Ethnic [Ethnic and immigration history]
H-Film [Cinema history and the uses of media]
H-History-and-Theory [Philosophy of history]

H-Holocaust [Holocaust studies]
H-Ideas [Intellectual history]
H-Labor [Labor history]
H-LatAm [Latin American history]
H-Law [Legal and constitutional history]
H-Local [State and local history]
H-Mediterranean [Mediterranean history]
H-Minerva [Women and the military]
H-Nationalism [History of nationalism]
H-OIEAHC [Colonial and early American history]
H-Pol [U.S. political history]
H-Public [Public history]
H-Rural [Rural and agricultural history]
H-Sci-Med-Tech [Science, medicine, and technology]
H-Slavery [History of slavery]
H-South [History of the U.S. South]
H-USA [International study of the United States]
H-Urban [Urban history]
H-War [Military history]
H-Women [Women's history]
H-World [World history]

APPENDIX

B

Historical Sources in Your Own Backyard

The history that surrounds you is local history. Wherever you live, that place has its own historical record and can be researched like any other historical research project. Such a project has the advantage of being something that you can, literally, reach out and touch. The documents and artifacts recording local history are easily within reach. Every town (or city, county, or region) has its own historical repository. It usually has a name such as "Anytown Historical Society." Whatever the official name, it will contain old books, documents, illustrations, artifacts, and photographs, among other historical items. You do your research by simply walking in the door. Unless the items you want to see are very rare or delicate, you can often hold them in your hands. These are the primary sources for the history of this particular place. The research skills set out in this book will enable you to make sense of these primary sources and to connect them to what you have learned about "anytown" from traditional historical resources.

Wherever you live, or wherever your school is located, you are probably not more than a short drive from one of these local history archives. Find the address and make a visit. Ask the archivist to see, say, a hundred-year-old photograph of the town or the deed to the very building you have walked into. You can hold in your hand a "token" used to pay "car fare" on the trolleys that took people around the town before anyone took a bus. You can look at a box filled with letters written by a mother to her son fighting in France in World War I. If you know something about the town and about the era in which the deed, the "token," and the letter were parts of daily life, you can begin to draw in your mind a picture of "anytown" that is a hundred years old. These primary documents could become part of a research project just as valid and just as serious as a study of town transportation in 1900 or of the impact of World War I on people's lives. In fact, the "token" and the letter would be vital evidence in supporting a thesis on either of these topics.

Some of the most rewarding kinds of historical research concern people, events, and places that have formed the basis for your own life. The experiences of your parents and grandparents are pieces of history that have touched you more than any other aspect of the past — even if you are not aware of it. As you discover more about the history of your family, you learn more about yourself. The primary documents of your family's history (even if yours is not a "traditional" family) do exist. They may be in an old trunk in "grandma's" attic or stuffed into a shoe box at the back of a closet. Family papers may consist of old photograph albums, birth, marriage, and death records, letters, old newspaper articles, report cards, or anything else that a member of the family purposely kept or didn't have the heart to throw out. You might discover a dozen neat boxes with clear labels, or you might find only a worn envelope with faded directions to a cemetery. Most likely, you will find a range of clues to your family's past: a dress that your grandmother told your mother had belonged to her own mother; a postcard in Chinese mailed to someone in your family and dated "Hong Kong, October, 24, 1938"; a photograph of a house in Cincinnati, Ohio, with a note on the back saying "Uncle Boris's house." Not much to go on. Still, you have more than you may think. Armed with nothing more than your family's name, a place where family members once lived (in this or another country), the postcard from Hong Kong, and the photo of the house in Cincinnati, you can search the public records (held by governments, towns, organizations, and businesses, among others) to find evidence of your ancestors' existence. Even if family members from "anytown" kept no records, that town kept records of them.

HOW TO RESEARCH YOUR FAMILY HISTORY

The effort to reconstruct your family's history is very personal and each discovery an exciting event. Each discovery is also evidence of the connection between the members of your family and the world around them. Your ancestors' lives were touched— perhaps deeply— by the events of their day. The postcard from Hong Kong, when translated, says that your great uncle was desperate to leave China for America because of the growing civil conflict there. Uncovering the history of your family makes you aware of the ways, however indirect, in which your own life has been touched by large historical events. Knowledge of your family's history and its meaning can give you a sense of your social and cultural roots — something that will strengthen you throughout your lifetime.

The private evidence of your family's past (however slight) and the public records of its existence can be fleshed out by the most important kind of evidence: the memories of your living relatives. Once you are as familiar as you can be about the relationships, places, and events of your family's history, you are ready to interview as many of your older relatives as you can find.

The interview is the core of a family history because, in most instances, it is the only way of uncovering the day-to-day nature of your family's life. Without the recollections of your relatives, you would not be able to discover more than a handful of names, dates, and places — only the barest outline of your family's history.

In preparing for this crucial aspect of family research, you must familiarize yourself with the basic history of your family so that you can place in proper context the information you obtain from the people you interview. You will need to prepare your questions beforehand, focusing on important aspects of family life and of the larger social and political life surrounding your family. Be sure that your questions establish the basics: the names, relationships, and principal home and workplace activities of each member of the family in each generation, going as far down the trunk and out on the limbs of the family tree as possible given the scope of your project and the memories of your relatives. Look for information that will enable you to make comparisons between generations of your family and between it and other families. Investigate such topics as the type of dwelling and neighborhood, parent-child and husband-wife relationships, authority and status patterns, income and social mobility. When you come across major family events— immigration, military service, job and residence changes, involvement in political movements—probe the reasons for these events because they will illuminate the ties between your family and the nation's history.

When actually conducting the interview, use your prepared questions, taking care to make them as broad as possible— for example, "What was the neighborhood like when you lived there?" not simply "What was your address in 1956?" When you get an answer that seems to lead in the direction of important material, ignore your prepared questions temporarily and probe further. Don't interrupt an answer even when the point seems unimportant. Your informants are the experts on their lives, and their memories, even if not always factually correct, are essential ingredients of family history. Finally, because the intricate web of your relatives' feelings is as important as the milestones of their lives, it is best to record (audio or video) the interview if possible rather than rely on written notes. Record it all, and then collect from your tapes the information that, on the one hand, best reflects your informants' testimony about their lives and, on the other, enables you to say something of importance about those lives and the times in which they were lived. If you have the needed skills, you can turn your audio/video tapes into a document that will itself become an important part of your family's history.

If important pieces of the story are still missing—your great-grandfather's birthplace, for instance, or the age at which your grandmother married—you can supplement your own family's records and memories from official sources. Listed below are the best sources both for county and local history and for family history research. As more and more public records are placed online, the World Wide Web will become an important part of family history research.

SOURCES FOR COUNTY AND LOCAL HISTORY

American County Histories to 1900. Accessible Archives. Full text of nineteenth-century county histories. So far the database includes works on counties in New Jersey, Delaware, Pennsylvania, Maryland, and portions of New York.

A Bibliography of American County Histories. Baltimore, MD: Genealogical Publishing, 1985.

Directory of Historical Organizations in the United States and Canada. American Association for State and Local History. A large list of historical organizations in all states and provinces. Print edition, 2001. A larger list of state and regional historical offices, organizations, museums, etc., are listed on the organization's Web site: **www.aaslh.org/rlinks.htm**.

Directory of State Archives and Records Programs. Council of States Archivists. **www.statearchivists.org/statearchivists.htm**. Links to each of the state archives.

Encyclopedia of [U.S.] Local History. Walnut Creek, CA: Alta Mira Press, 2000.

Genealogical and Local History Books in Print. Comp. and ed. Marian Hoffman. 4 vols. Baltimore, MD: Genealogical Publishing, 1996–1997.

Historical Museum Guide. CensusFinder. **www.censusfinder.com/guide_to_historical _museums.htm**. Links to history museums and historical sites in all states.

National Register of Historic Places. National Park Service. **www.cr.nps.gov/nr/ shpolist.htm**. Links to state historic preservation offices throughout the United States.

State and Local History. Tennessee Technological University. **www.tntech.edu/ history/state.html**. A large collection of links.

State Censuses: An Annotated Bibliography of Censuses of Population Taken after 1790 by States and Territories of the United States. New York: Burt Franklin, 1969.

State Census Records. Ed. Ann S. Lainhart. Baltimore, MD: Genealogical Publishing, 1992.

United States Local History. Library of Congress. 5 vols. Baltimore, MD: Magna Carta, 1974.

SOURCES FOR FAMILY HISTORY AND GENEALOGICAL RESEARCH

American Families: A Research Guide and Historical Handbook. Westport, CT: Greenwood Press, 1991.

American Family Immigration History Center. **ellisisland.org/**. Much useful advice about conducting family history research. You can search ship's passenger lists beginning in 1892. Full access requires "membership."

Ancestry Library Edition. ProQuest. Genealogical information for the United States and United Kingdom taken from census, church, court, immigration, and other records. Searchable. By subscription only.

Census Finder. U.S. Census Bureau. **www.censusfinder.com/**. Some individual records are available online but most of these are at sites where a membership fee is required. The major fee-based sites are: *Cyndi's List; Genealogy Home Page; Gendex; and Ancestry Plus.*

Family Search. "Mormon" Church. **www.familysearch.org/**. A very large surname database including the 1880 U.S. Census. Access to most elements of site are free. An excellent resource.

Find Your Hispanic Roots. Baltimore, MD: Genealogical Publishing, 1997.

How to Climb Your Family Tree: Genealogy for Beginners. Baltimore, MD: Genealogical Publishing, 1997.

Immigrant Ships. Immigrant Ships Transcribers Guild. **www.immigrantships .net/index.html/**. A nonprofit group of transcribers have placed on this site passenger lists (mostly Europe to United States) from several thousand ships. The database is searchable.

NARA—Genealogists/Family Historians. U.S. National Archives. **www.archives .gov/genealogy/**. An introduction to the immense collection of NARA (National Archives and Records Administration) records of interest to family historians. The online catalogs are an important aid in family history research. But NARA records are not available onsite; you must visit one of the NARA records centers.

In Search of Your European Roots: A Complete Guide to Tracing Your Ancestors in Every European Country. Baltimore, MD: Genealogical Publishing, 1994.

U.S. Citizenship and Immigration Services. Immigration and Naturalization Service. **uscis.gov/graphics/aboutus/history/index.html/**. A very large U.S. government site that serves as an introduction to several databases. Some of these can be searched, but the data itself must be viewed at regional centers of the National Archives. Among the records indexed are "Ports of Entry and Their Records," "Naturalization Records," and "Land Border Arrival Records," "Ships Passenger Manifests."

The USGenweb Census Project. **www.us-census.org/inventory/**. One of the few nonprofit census sites. Here volunteers transcribe information from federal census data and digitize it. This is an immense task, and only a very small fraction of all census data is available here. The existing material can be searched. More extensive census information is for sale at sites such as Ancestry.com and Heritagequest.com.

Glossary

Abstract: A brief description of the contents of a short piece of writing such as a scholarly article.

Appendix: Information placed after the end or conclusion of a research paper or book. This information (for example, charts, tables, visuals) is separated because it is too long to place within the paper or book itself.

Archive: A place in which public records or historical documents are preserved. On the Web: a site where historical documents are available in digital form.

Argument: A thesis, especially the principal ideas and evidence that directly support a thesis.

Artifact: A physical object created in the past.

Atlas: A bound collection of maps, often including illustrations, informative tables, or textual matter. *See also* Historical atlas.

Bias: An attitude or prejudice that influences the way in which a subject is interpreted.

Bibliography: An alphabetical list, often with descriptive or critical notes, of works relating to a particular subject, period, or author; in student papers, a list of the works referred to or consulted.

Bookmark: A place on a Web browser (usually near the top) where you can click on any Web site that is on your screen and record the URL for future use.

Book review: An essay that comments on a particular work or a series of works on a single subject.

Browser: *See* Web browser.

Call number: A combination of characters assigned to a library book to indicate its place on a shelf.

CD-ROM: A compact disc capable of containing a large amount of data that is read by a computer. May contain text, statistics, pictures, and audio and video files.

Chart: A visual display of quantitative information. Common examples are bar charts and pie charts.

Chat room: An open forum on the Web, a place where individuals can comment on current messages. Older messages are not preserved. To take part in a more organized and recorded discussion, subscribe to a listserv. *See also* Listserv.

Cheating: *See* Plagiarism.

Chronological organization: A research paper that is organized by date.

Citation: A reference to a source of information used in preparing a written assignment; usually takes the form of a footnote or endnote. *See also* Documentation.

Conclusion: The final section of a written document in which the writer summarizes findings and interpretations.

Context: The text that surrounds a particular statement and affects the statement's meaning.

Continuity: As a component of writing, continuity is the coherent flow of an author's arguments as the author moves from one point to another.

Cookie: Information about your computer that is read by any Web site you visit. When you return to a particular site, your computer is then "recognized" by that site.

Counterevidence: Evidence that contradicts your thesis.

Cyclical school: School of historical thought that believes history repeats itself. According to this school, essential forces of nature and human nature are changeless, so past patterns of events repeat themselves endlessly.

Database: A large collection of digital data organized for rapid search and retrieval. *See also* Full-text database.

Date range: The time period covered by a large collection of books, articles, newspapers, and other documents.

Demography: The study of changes in population and the reasons for those changes.

Dissertation: An extended, usually written, treatment of a subject; specifically one submitted for a doctorate.

Documentation: The use of historical or other evidence to support a statement or argument; usually takes the form of footnotes or endnotes or material such as pictures, graphs, tables, or copies of documents.

Draft: A preliminary sketch, outline, or version of an essay or paper.

Ellipsis: The omission of words from a quotation; also, the punctuation (. . .) that indicates the omission.

Encyclopedia: A work that contains information on all branches of knowledge or that comprehensively treats a particular branch of knowledge; usually comprises articles arranged alphabetically by subject. Online encyclopedias can be searched electronically. *See also* Historical encyclopedia.

Endnote: A note of reference, explanation, or comment placed at the end of an essay or paper. *See also* Documentation.

Essay exam: A test that requires a complete, well-organized written answer on a particular topic.

Ethnohistory: The study of ethnic groups and how they evolve.

Evidence: *See* Primary document; Secondary source.

Footnote: A note of reference, explanation, or comment placed below the text on a printed page. *See also* Documentation.

Full-text database: A searchable electronic database that contains all of the text of a written source rather than merely information for finding the source.

Graph: A precise drawing, usually taking the form of a series of points and lines that make visual the numerical changes in the relationship between two or more things.

Historian: A student or writer of history, especially someone who produces a scholarly examination of a historical topic.

Historical atlas: A collection of maps that illustrate important changes over time and that provide visual descriptions of such changes.

Historical dictionary: A reference work that contains brief descriptions of historical terms.

Historical encyclopedia: Alphabetically organized short essays on historical topics.

Historical novel: A work of fiction based on actual events and people.

Historiography: The study of changes in the methods, interpretations, and conclusions of historians over time.

Home page: The first page of a Web site, with links to other parts of the site or to other sites.

Host: *See* Server

Hyperlink: A one-step connection between two different pages on the World Wide Web. Hyperlinks appear on your screen as click-on boxes or icons or as highlighted or underlined text. Usually referred to simply as a "link."

Icon: A link in the form of a graphic symbol.

Identification exam: A test that requires the brief identification of a person, place, object, or event and an explanation of its importance.

Index: An alphabetical list of persons and subjects and the page numbers where they are discussed in a book. More generally, any list by subject or by letter (alphabetical) of a specific kind of information source such as magazine articles and books.

Interlibrary loan: The lending of a book by one library to another.

Internet: A worldwide network that allows information to be transferred from one computer to another by means of servers. The World Wide Web is a network within this network. *See also* Server; World Wide Web.

Introduction: The beginning section of a book or multipage paper. It sets out the writer's thesis.

Journal: A periodical containing articles on scholarly topics. For students: a written record, created by a student, of some aspect of a course.

Keyword: A word that represents a core aspect of a topic to be researched. Keywords are used to search online catalogs, electronic databases, and sites on the World Wide Web. *See also* Subject search.

Library catalog: A catalog that organizes all the holdings of a library; most library catalogs can be searched by title, author, or keyword. *See also* Online catalog.

Library stacks: Shelves on which a library's books and journals are stored.

Link: *See* Hyperlink.

Linking paragraph: A paragraph that indicates how and why an essay is moving from one important point to another.

Linking sentence: A sentence that ties together the points made in two paragraphs. It almost always comes at the end of one paragraph or at the beginning of the very next one.

Listserv: An e-mail discussion list to which individuals who have a special interest in the topic of the list subscribe. Many listservs are moderated: someone organizes the messages by date and topic. Messages are preserved so that you can read previous exchanges between subscribers.

Microfiche: A sheet of microfilm containing pages of printed matter in reduced form.

Microfilm: A film bearing a photographic record on a reduced scale of printed or other graphic matter.

Monograph: A scholarly study of a specific topic.

Multiple-choice exam: A test consisting of questions with several possible answers, one of which is the correct or best answer.

Newsgroup: An electronic "forum" where you can read and write comments on a particular topic.

Note cards: Small cards (3-by-5 or 4-by-6) that are convenient for note taking and the indexing of notes when researching. Such "cards" can also take the form of computer "files."

Objective exam: A test consisting of factual questions for which there is only one correct answer for each question.

Online catalog: An electronic catalog that enables the user to search the holdings of a library, and possibly other libraries and databases.

Paraphrase: A restatement of a passage, idea, or work in different words. Like direct quotations, paraphrases of original work require proper documentation. *See also* Plagiarism.

Peer editing: *See* Peer reviewing.

Peer reviewing: Examining the work (usually written work) of a classmate or colleague. The purpose is to offer constructive comments so that the work can be improved.

Periodical: A publication with a fixed interval between issues.

Periodical database: A large collection of articles from journals, magazines, or newspapers in electronic, searchable form.

Plagiarism: Stealing and presenting the ideas or words of another as one's own; using material without crediting its source; presenting as new and original an idea or product derived from an existing source. Plagiarism is a serious act of academic dishonesty. *See also* Paraphrase; Quotation.

Plug-ins: Computer software that enhances the capability of a Web browser or other program.

Postmodernism: A philosophy or school of history that questions whether we can truly uncover the past.

Primary document, primary source: Firsthand evidence that records the words of someone who participated in or witnessed the events described or of someone who received his or her information from direct participants.

Progressive school: School of historical thought that believes human history illustrates neither endless cycles nor divine intervention but continual progress. According to this school, the situation of humanity is constantly improving.

Proofreading: A careful rereading of written work to correct errors of style or grammar.

Providential school: School of historical thought that believes that the course of history is determined by God and that the flow of historical events represents struggles between forces of good and evil.

Quantitative history: The use of statistics in the study of history.

Quotation: A statement that repeats exactly the words of a source. Such a statement must be enclosed in quotation marks and properly documented. *See also* Plagiarism.

Reference book: A work, such as a dictionary or encyclopedia, containing useful facts or information.

Research bibliography: A list of sources that may be needed to research a topic/theme for a formal paper; includes publication information and location of the materials.

Research outline: A list of the parts of a topic/theme to be researched and a tentative ordering of these parts.

Research paper: A formal writing assignment on a specific theme that requires the reading and synthesis of primary and secondary sources; also requires documentation such as footnotes or endnotes and a bibliography.

Research plan: When writing a research paper, an outline of the *kinds* of research you need to do, the *order* in which research tasks should be done, and an estimate of the *time* needed.

Revise: To look over again in order to correct or improve; to make a new, amended, improved, or up-to-date version of an essay or paper.

Rough draft: The first version of a written assignment; it is polished and revised in later drafts.

Search engine: Complex programs run from special Internet sites that periodically search the Web and organize information from a vast number of Web sites. When you search the Web, you actually search the information gathered and organized at these sites.

Secondary source: The findings of someone who did not observe a historical event firsthand but investigated primary evidence of it.

Server: A computer that connects Web pages to the Internet so that they can be accessed by search engines. Also known as a "host."

Short-answer exam: A test that requires brief written answers to factual questions.

Source card: The first in a series of paper cards or computer files created to hold (and later organize) the information from a particular source. Unlike the other cards in the series, the source card contains all the information you will need to cite that source in a footnote or list it in a bibliography.

Stacks: *See* Library stacks.

Statistics: A collection of quantitative data.

Subject bibliographies: Lists of books, articles, and other material organized by subject.

Subject headings: Terms used for searching catalogs and large Web sites. Each heading represents a major section of the material in the catalog or on the Web site.

Subject index: An organized list of subjects. Alphabetical listing is the most common type.

Subject search: A way of searching a catalog, database, or large Web site. A subject search brings you all of the information in the catalog, database, or Web site that relates to a specific subject.

Summary: In note taking, a brief restatement *in your own words* of facts or ideas taken from a source.

Table: A systematic arrangement of data in rows and columns.

Take-home essay exam: A test usually consisting of one or more short essays that are to be prepared outside of class.

Theme: A narrow part of a topic chosen or assigned for research. A theme sets limits on the area to be investigated and suggests the kinds of questions to be answered and the points to be made. *See also* Thesis.

Thesis: A clear statement, usually appearing at the beginning of an essay or research paper, that informs the reader of the central argument or claim the writer intends to make about the theme. The thesis results from the narrowing of your theme. *See also* Theme *and* Working thesis.

Topic: A broad subject area chosen or assigned for research.

Topical organization: A research paper that is organized by topic.

URL: Stands for "Uniform Resource Locator." A URL is the electronic address of a Web site or Web page.

Web browser: Software that allows the user to view a variety of content on World Wide Web pages.

Web site: A specific home page on the Web with links to other Web sites/pages. Each site has a unique URL.

Word processing: The creation of documents, such as notes and research papers, by computer programs that allow great flexibility in editing.

Working thesis: A tentative thesis that helps you organize your research tasks. It may need to be revised.

World Wide Web ("Web"): A part of the Internet where sites can be located by URL. These sites are connected by links to other sites.

Writing outline: Framework for a research paper that lists thoughts and ideas in an organized manner and acts as a guide for writing a rough draft.

Yearbook: A book published yearly containing a report or summary of statistics or facts.

Index

Film reviews, citations of, 139, 152
Films
    citations of, 140, 153, 184
    note taking from, 42
    Web access to, 16
First draft. *See* Draft; Rough draft
Focus. *See* Theme; Topic
Folders, in digital note taking, 112, 113
    (fig.), 114
Footnotes
    directory to documentation models
      for, 132
    essay exam with, 53
    essay with, 74
    evaluating a book for research using,
      101
    form of, 133, 161
    how many to use, 131
    placement of a number for, 133
    plagiarism and, 75, 131–32
    proofreading, 131–32
    for quotations, 128
    research paper with, 126, 130–32
    revising and rewriting and, 159
    searching for journal articles using
      citations in, 91
    secondary sources with, 11
    textbooks and, 25
    when to use, 130–32
    writing, 133–45
Foreign relations, resources on, 239–40
Format
    of bibliographic entries, 147
    of endnotes or footnotes, 133
    of quotations, 128, 176
    of a research paper, 161
    of visual materials in a paper,
      129, 130
Full-text database, 90, 143

Gender studies, 9
Genealogy. *See* Family history
Government publications
    bibliographic citations of, 152–53
    footnote citations of, 139–40
Grammar, checking for, 67, 159, 160
Graphics. *See* Graphs; Illustrations;
    Maps; Photographs; Tables
Graphs
    analyzing data on, 29–30
    citations of, 141, 154
    example of, 30 (fig.)
    incorporating into a paper, 129
Group work, 45–46
    peer reviewing and, 45, 46
    plagiarism and, 117

Guidelines
    avoiding plagiarism, 118
    clear writing, 62
    conducting Internet searches, 97
    evaluating secondary sources, 102
    evaluating Web sites, 99
    evaluating Web sources, 106
    finding an article in a periodical
      database, 90
    giving an oral presentation, 44
    incorporating visuals into a paper, 130
    peer reviewing, 46
    revising and rewriting, 159
    speaking in class, 43
    taking lecture notes, 38
    writing a book review, 71
    writing short essays, 74

Highlighting information in a text-
    book, 20, 21 (fig.)
Historians
    bias of, 14–16
    choice of subject by, 4–5
    directions of historical research and,
      8–9
    influences on, 8
    what they are trying to do, 3–4
    work of, 4–17
Historical atlases, 186–87, 190–91
Historical dictionaries, 80, 185, 186,
    187–88
Historical encyclopedias, 80, 84, 185,
    186–87, 188–90
Historical novel
    example of a passage from, 24–25
    reading, for an assignment, 22, 25
Historical research. *See* Research
Historical statistics, 199–202. *See also*
    Statistics
Historiography, 6–8
History
    career skills and research in, 17
    curiosity about the everyday world
      and, 4
    philosophies of, 5–6
    ways to use, 17
    what it can tell you, 1–3
Home pages, 100
    evaluting a site using, 98–99
    library, 84, 84 (fig.)

Identification exams, 50
Illustrations
    citations of, 140–41, 154, 184
    documenting, in captions, 130
    incorporating into a paper, 129

DIRECTORY: DOCUMENTATION MODELS